Edited by
SAMUELE SANGALLI

Ciudad de México: between Ancient Myth and Contemporary Complexity

Pontificia Università Gregoriana
Pontificio Istituto Biblico

For the Konrad-Adenauer-Stiftung the exchange of opinions and open discussions are important instruments of civic and political education. The content of this book is not reflecting the positions of the Konrad-Adenauer-Stiftung, but it is based on the exchange of young leaders, which the Foundation aims to support and promote in their development.

Cover design: Yattagraf srls

Layout: Scuola Tipografica S. Pio X - Roma

© 2022 Pontificio Istituto Biblico
Gregorian & Biblical Press
Piazza della Pilotta, 35 - 00187 Roma, Italy
www.gbpress.net - books@biblicum.com

ISBN: 978-88-7839-**483**-4

The "Alberto Hurtado" Center for Faith and Culture
Sinderesi School
Academic Year 2021-2022

Sinderesi School:
Christian Discernment
of Contemporary Social Challenges

XI Year – IV Cycle
Globalization as Urbanization?

CIUDAD DE MÉXICO: BETWEEN ANCIENT MYTH AND CONTEMPORARY COMPLEXITY

Coordinators of the School:
Msgr. Samuele Sangalli PhD, ThD – Antonella Piccinin PhD

FIRST PART – Lectures
Itineraries of Thought

Saturday 16 October 2021 (h. 16-19)
HISTORY. **The Spanish Conquest of Mexico In 1521: After 500 Years**
Dr. Pablo Vidal García LC – *Pontifical Athenaeum Regina Apostolorum* – Rome
HERMENEUTICS. **500 Years Since the Birth of Mexico**
Dr. Luis Alfonso Orozco LC – *Pontifical Athenaeum Regina Apostolorum* – Rome
SOCIOLOGY. **Impact of Globalization on Public Space: The Case of the Plaza De Las Tres Culturas in Tlatelolco, Mexico City**
Dr. Margarita Martinéz Fisher – *Sociologist* – Mexico City

Saturday 20 November 2021 (h. 16-19)
GEOPOLITICS. **Mexico in Latin America Today**
Prof. Victor Hernández Huerta – C*entro de Investigation y Docencia Economica* – Mexico City
INSTITUTIONS. **Democracy in Mexico: In the Context of Ethnic and Social Differences**
Dr. Luis Felipe Bravo Mena – *Former Ambassador of Mexico to the Holy See*- Mexico City

Saturday 18 Dicember 2021 (h. 16-19)
CITIZENSHIP. **The Problem of Migration: Separation of Families, Caravans and Remittances**
Dr. Celine de Mauleon – *Red Global Mexicanos Calificados* – Mexico City
CULTURE. **A Catholic Approach to Feminisms in Mexico City**
Prof. Julieta Becerril Romero – *Anahuac University* – Mexico City

Saturday 15 January 2022 (h. 16-19)
CHRISTIANITY. **The Miracle of Guadalupe: the Catholic Tradition and Its Influx on the Society.**
Prof. Mario Ángel Flores Ramos – *Rector Emeritus of the Pontifical University of Mexico* – Mexico City
RELIGIONS. **Popular Religiosity in Mexico: An Approximation.**
Prof. Rodrigo Guerra López – *Secretary of the Pontifical Commission for Latin America* – Vatican City

SECOND PART – Workshops
Itineraries of Research

Saturday 19 February 2022 (h.16-19)
LAW. **From Tenochtitlan to CDMX: Legal Criteria for the Administration of a City**
Gianmaria Alessandro Ruscitti
APPENDIX. **Seven Original Sins of Mexico City**
H.E. Prof. Alberto Medardo Barranco Chavarría – *Ambassador of Mexico to the Holy See* - Rome

Saturday 19 March 2022 (h.16-19)
ECONOMICS. **Sustainable Development in Mexico City**
Darius Allen Lawrence LC
Supervisor: Dr. Mylene Cano – *Coparmex* – Mexico City

Saturday 23 April 2022 (h.16-19)
SOCIETY. **Santa Fe: From a Garbage Dump to a Qualified City Neighborhood**
Balam Quitzé Loza Ramos LC
Supervisor: Dr. Rodrigo Iván Cortés Jimenez - *Red Familias* – Mexico City

THIRD PART – Forum

Memories and Experiences

Saturday 21 May 2022 (h.14-19)
CINEFORUM. **The "Roma" Neighborhood of Mexico City**.
Speaker: Dr. Santiago García LC – *Pontifical Athenaeum Regina Apostolorum* – Rome
FOLKLORE. **Mexican Cuisine: Tradition and Culture**.
(in collaboration with the Pontifical Mexican College)
Final dinner with typical Mexican cuisine.

Table of contents

Foreword   9

Sinderesi Lecture – *The Many Méxicos and Their Capital City.*   13

Part One: *Lectures.*

HISTORY – *The Spanish Conquest of Mexico in 1521: After 500 Years.*   35

HERMENEUTICS – *500 Years Since the Birth of Mexico.*   61

SOCIOLOGY – *Impact of Globalization on Public Space: The Case of the Plaza De Las Tres Culturas in Tlatelolco, Mexico City.*   73

GEOPOLITICS – *Mexico in Latin America Today.*   103

INSTITUTIONS – *Democracy in Mexico: In the Context of Ethnic and Social Differences.*   127

CITIZENSHIP – *The Problem of Migration: Separation of Families, Caravans and Remittances.*   163

CULTURE – *A Catholic Approach to Feminisms in Mexico City.*   185

CHRISTIANITY – *The Miracle of Guadalupe: the Catholic Tradition and its Influx on the Society.*   197

RELIGIONS – *Popular Religiosity in Mexico: An Approximation.*   213

Part Two: *Workshops.*

LAW – *From Tenochtitlan to CDMX: Legal Criteria for the Administration of a City*   227

Appendix – *Seven Original Sins of Mexico City*   265

ECONOMICS – *Sustainable Development in Mexico City*   277

SOCIETY – *Santa Fe: From a Garbage Dump to a Qualified City Neighborhood.*   313

Afterword   337

Foreword

Never have I found myself in front of a study so rich and well articulated about my hometown. Mexico City is, without any doubt, a fascinating, hard and contradictory town. Actually, I think it would be more correct to say that Mexico City is a combination of various cities, of various souls, that is impossible to understand if you don't examine in depth Mexican history. Mexico being a country itself very complex, with an extraordinary history that makes it an emblematic case for understanding the challenges between the past heritage and the actual globalization that must be faced all over the world. From the scholars, experts, historians, sociologists, economists, professors, come to life, as in a puzzle, the different souls, lights and shadows of this town that you can love for its historic center, for its marvelous residential areas, its parks, its buildings and its museums, or hate for its contradictions, its inequality in the income of his inhabitants, its slums, its inequality in access to green public spaces and basic services, its uncontrolled growth, its pollution and its traffic. However, I'm sure that this town won't ever leave you indifferent. Mexico City is a real example of syncretism with the case of the Plaza de las tres Culturas that we find in this book is a perfect example of the coexistence between the past, with the archeological zone, religion and churches, and modernity with modern buildings and the headquarters of the ministry of foreign affairs. This plaza is, as Pierre Nora says, a place of the Mexican collective memory and represents a unique example for the understanding of what Mexico City was in the past and is in actuality. For the comprehension of the various souls of Mexico and Mexico City I think it is also fundamental to note, as we see in this book, the presence of the shrine of the Virgin of Guadalupe. Guadalupe is not only the

Mother for all Mexicans, even if they aren't Catholics, she is also a magnificent example of true inculturation and a message that can help Mexico face the challenges and heal the wounds of inequality and racism that still exist in Mexican society. In his recent trip to Canada, Pope Francis says: Guadalupe, "the America's mother, during the drama of the Conquista, was the one who transmitted the true faith to indigenous people, speaking their language and wearing their own garments, without any violence or imposition". I hope this book will help readers to understand the amazing challenges of this town and to find the ways to overcome them.

Dr. Valentina Alazraki
Journalist – Vatican Correspondent

Part One

Lectures

Sinderesi Lecture

The Many Méxicos and Their Capital City

Now in its eleventh year at the Pontifical Gregorian University's "Alberto Hurtado" Centre, the Sinderesis School has moved onto its fourth triennial cycle, on urbanisation as the foreseeable future for an ever more globalised world. With the goal of understanding how 21st century cities are being configured, the focus has shifted, after last year's detailed analysis of Rome (Sangalli 2021), to Mexico City, one of the most interesting megalopolises in the planet's history.
Seven hundred years since Tenochtitlán was founded (1325), five hundred since Hernán Cortés' conquest (1521) and two hundred since national independence (1821), Mexico's capital represents the ideal setting to try and understand how contemporary Latin American models for development are taking shape, combining the legacy of the past with the challenges of the present.
Over the first part of the year, sessions from scholars in history, religion, politics, economics, law and social science enabled students to undertake their own research in the fields of law, economics and sociology and to focus on specific case studies. Each represented a different expression of the "Latin-American way" of planning modern, people-friendly cities in the wake of the huge challenge presented by the pandemic. Today this has been exacerbated by the conflict in Ukraine, which has shaken the template for social organisation and development to its core.
What do we mean, though, by Latin America – and Mexico as part

of it? As the historians De Giuseppe and La Bella write: "Contemporary Latin America has come to be identified in Western culture with a certain set of defining features, often resulting in schematic stereotypes. Accordingly, it is the land of *caudillos*, dictators and revolutionaries, of populism and military bases, dependency and exploitation, *peones, bandoleros, cangaçeiros* and *gauchos*, street children and shamans, *narcos* and dancers, able to shift between the bolero of the early 20th century and the *reggaetón* of the early 21st" (De Giuseppe – La Bella 2019:7). Sinderesi School was set up precisely to educate people out of such stereotypes.

What characterises a people? What defines it? Its history, certainly, i.e. the human journey that has given birth to its culture, worldview and formation as a society. For this reason, the present work contains a number of history-focused presentations, though all the submissions actually draw on historical considerations. However, as we have already observed (Sangalli 2018: 59-86), identity, in both its personal and community dimensions, is in constant flux. Thus, we use the plural "Mexicos", to indicate the different facets of the country; and the survey here demonstrates yet again that is the case too with *Ciudad de México*. In a way, one might even say that this vast megalopolis of twenty-one million people seems to reflect precisely what is going on within the wider human family, whose population, according to recent estimates (Roser 2019), will exceed the ten billion mark by the end of the century. An acceleration that we are already well aware of thanks to our previous inquiries into the pace of change over recent decades (Sangalli 2016:28); but something that, up until the beginning of the last century, would have been pretty unthinkable.

Significantly, the curtain came down on this year's journey of discovery by watching then discussing "*Roma*", a film by Mexican director Alfonso Cuarón, which was released in 2018 and won the Venice Film Festival's Golden Lion for Best Picture. In this story of a typical middle-class family, the level of violence is noteworthy, as is the fight for survival, the comfort that religion seems to provide, the tenderness of the bond between women and their exploitation by the *macho mexicano*. The long opening sequence of a floor being washed without ever becoming clean appears metaphorical, the symbol of a history that is still struggling to find harmony and peace. Mexico, which did not properly exist prior to Cortés' conquest and the creation of *Nueva España* in 1521, emerged from the 'integration' of indigenous populations [of whom there are around sixty-eight even today, each with their own language! (Atlas:2020)], *criollos*, African Americans and those of mixed-race. Such a unifying feat has still not succeeded in substance, although at the same time it is a constantly recurring theme, a dream to be turned into reality by the event of Guadalupe. It is important to realise that Guadalupe goes well beyond merely religious symbolism, since all Mexicans, Catholics and non-, see themselves as 'Guadalupans'. Throughout its independent history, 'Guadalupanism' has, in fact, evolved into a number of contradictory forms in Mexico. Positively, the face of the *Morenita* of the *Tepeyac* has meant refuge and consolation for millions of its citizens and served to rouse the masses to seek independence; equally, it has been manipulated for nationalist-patriotic aims and used to mask over vast social inequality. Today it is a symbol of resistance for migrants to the US and beyond (Gomez Izquierdo-Sanchez 2011). Certainly, for a "Guadalupan" Mexican, the ideal citizen is someone with a kind-heart, who is in solidarity with everyone, rich or poor, from outlying areas or the city, and is able to make him/herself useful, while harbouring a great desire for justice and the firm hope of a better future. Therefore, along with violent and discriminatory attitudes, which seem contradictory and in opposition to the ideals of Guadalupe, it must be recognised that positive aspirations too are well-established traits of the Mexican people.

Our voyage of exploration to *Ciudad de Mexico* begins with the two historical sketches from Fr Luis Alfonso Orozco and Br Pablo Vidal Garcia, both Mexican members of the Legionaries of Christ who trained at the *Regina Apostolorum* Athenaeum in Rome.

The first conference, with more of a chronological emphasis, helps to retrace the key points of Mexican history, starting with the foundation of Tenochtitlán by the Aztecs in 1376. This was a well-structured and complex city, built around its temple and a lake. By the time the Spanish arrived in 1492, Tenochtitlán's population was already estimated to be around eighty thousand, comparable to the major European cities of the time. As the positive message of the miracle of Guadalupe spread, the colonial period of *la Nueva España*, between 1521 and 1750, envisaged the creation of a new society, bringing together the various ethnic groups and cultural communities. However, what in the end came to dominate relations between the social classes was inequality. Indeed, it was there from the very beginning and, rather than being healed during the time of "Enlightenment" that foreshadowed independence, this wound had, paradoxically, already begun to cause even more pain. The whole of Mexican history is, in fact, pervaded by the theme of inequality and today in Mexico it is as prominent as ever.

Another Mexican 'staple' is revolutionary tension and institutional instability. Between 1821 and 1850 alone, thanks largely to military coups, there were fifty different governments. One concomitant factor in this instability, from the time of the Benito Juarez-led *Leyes de Reforma* in 1859, which authorised a complete separation from the State, has been Mexico's tortuous relationship with the Church. The failure to reinstate the monarchy of Maximilian of Hapsburg in 1867 heralded another turbulent time of republicanism, remembered especially in the end for the forty-year presidency of Porfirio Diáz, the so-called 'Porfirian period'. While these events helped to modernise the country both economically and culturally, rather than ridding Mexico of the inequalities between the small élite of super-rich families, its miniscule middle class and an immense multitude of poor, they instead made it worse, with the number of impoverished ever increasing. Then came the time (1910) of the revolts of Emiliano Zapata and Pancho Villa, before the Constitution was formulated in 1917. This, however, failed to prevent new insurrections and the anti-religious persecution by Plutarco Elias Calles during the *Guerra Cristera* (1926-1929). The establishment of the *Partido Revoluzionario Institucionale* (PRI), which remained in charge uninterruptedly until the millennium, and the political antagonism of the *Partido Acción Nacional* (PAN), helped to consolidate the nation, through their burgeoning democratic dialectic. They also markedly improved the economy, the social and cultural level of the country and, despite the occasional explosions of revolt in the name of greater social justice (famously, that of 1968) and the problem of widespread corruption, through them Mexico was introduced to the principles of the market. The new millennium has seen Mexico aligning itself to the American economic model, with political polarisation pervasive in society. Notwithstanding the numerous attempts at reform, undertaken most recently also by Andrés Manuel Lopez Obrador, President since 2018, the inequalities are, sadly, only being perpetuated.

The contribution of Fr Orozco is, by contrast, more thematic. Its intention is to look closely at a number of Mexico's historical 'acquisitions' as a way to understanding the national identity. Essentially, this takes the form of making us aware that Mexico only becomes a nation, a heterogenous unity, with the arrival of the Spanish and their conquest of the Aztecs in 1521, having been a generically Mesoamerican terrain previously. Since the Conquistadors' act of violence created an unassailable barrier with the indigenous peoples, the unification of the country can only logically be attributed (by delving into the historical truth) to missionary endeavour *in primis*, and above all to the twelve first Franciscan 'apostles' who, regardless of whether they were respected or merely tolerated by the Spanish, gained for themselves the esteem and trust of the natives through the authentic humility of their life and the defence of indigenous rights. It is these who opened the path to the religious, social, linguistic and cultural unity that gave an identity to this nation. Despite the difficulties involved, which we are well aware of, that Mexico felt itself to be a real, separate entity from this point onwards is beyond dispute. Unity is to be recognised as fruit of the humble work of these apostles of the Gospel and of the many, largely anonymous, people who followed in their footsteps over the course of Mexican history. These were the 'Good Samaritans' who tended the sundry wounds inflicted on the poorest that grew deeper over the centuries of struggle and opposition. How much of their work of integration was lost, for example, with the suppression of the Society of Jesus, when more than 2,200 religious throughout Latin America had to abandon their myriad mission stations, parishes, social works, schools, centres of support and literacy for the indigenous and rural world

(Dussel 2021). The official *damnatio memoriae* of these noble figures – laments Orozco – in favour of other protagonists of Mexican history, who were not, like them, creators of communion and peaceful cohabitation, makes it difficult to rediscover the real roots and motives for unity. And yet, after a number of troublesome years, this is precisely what is needed today to ensure lasting peace and development in Mexican society.

After carrying out research projects on the subject of urbanisation at the *Universitad Autónoma Metropolitana* of Azcapotzalco, the sociologist Margarita Fisher in her paper lays bare, for the first time, the effect globalisation has had on the Mexican people, 81% of whom now live in urban areas. Focusing on *Ciudad de México*, the complexity of trying to configure public spaces for human cohabitation, with all that that involves, is clearly revealed. Her choice to present us with the case of the urban *Plaza de las Tres Culturas* complex, built in the Seventies by the architect Mario Pani, shows us how Mexico has tried to come up with a modern structure for a (post-) industrial – today globalised – city. At stake is the entire philosophy of human shared living, to try to improve on the current way of ordering urban environments, which, thanks to liberal neocapitalism, are made up of self-contained agglomerations that are unable to communicate with one another. Instead, a number of alternatives paradigms, which prioritise spaces for encounter and exchange and, therefore, favour the construction of an inclusive society, need to be promoted.

Can the ambitious dream of urban regeneration in Mexico City be judged a failure? Or might it be understood as a perfect example of that romantic Latin-American mentality that is low on practicality and high on ideology, incapable of facing up to reality and thus constantly unable to finish what it started, therefore – paradoxically – making the problems worse by adding the disappointment of unfulfilled dreams to them? Perhaps it is just a case of misfortune, since who could have predicted the earthquake and the ensuing economic crisis? Certainly, the challenge of being stewards of the public spaces of cities is a key factor in determining the quality of life there and will serve to shape the way humans co-exist in the urbanised global world in the future. Fisher correctly observes that it is not simply a question of organising spaces, but the adoption of a certain social model and the promotion of a culture where education in citizenship and respect for shared norms forms part of a people's *paideia*. Only thus can the scandal be stopped from becoming entrenched of how rich residential districts, as fortified spaces that are off-limits to non-residents, co-exist alongside the degradation of the *barrios,* populous areas often lacking the most basic urban services. *Plaza de las Tres Culturas* is, therefore, famous for being a place of collective Mexican memory and for the events that have already happened there. A symbol against every form of social injustice, to stand for all time as an exemplar for the global city, and to foster the processes needed for genuine humanisation. From this vantage point, our research then felt the need to look deeper into Latin-American context of Mexico's current geopolitical situation. May one speak of a healthy democracy that is able to respond to the key anthropological-social question posed above? Prof Víctor Hernández-Huerta, from the *Centro de Investigación y Docencia Económicas* (CIDE) in Mexico City, helped us elaborate an answer. As it stands, President López Obrador's pragmatic approach means that Mexico swings between the Pan-Americanism of the Organisation of American States (OAS), headed by the US, and the Latin-American Sovereignty project, ideated by the Venezuelan Government, which has already formed supranational organisations such as the Bolivarian Alliance for the Americas (ALBA) and the Community of Latin-American and Caribbean States (CELAC). Hernández-Huerta denounces contemporary Mexican foreign policy, which supports various kinds of authoritarian regime in the region, such as those hybrid forms, somewhere between totalitarianism and democracy, that are commonplace today and are characterised by a lack of pluralism. This represents a worrying decline in the liberal-democratic standard in Latin America. But is it an inexorable process that should cause us concern, an example of how totalitarianism and democracy are being pitted against each other in the wider world? The danger of a return to authoritarianism in Mexico or to an illiberal democracy, induced by an unbridled resurgence in populism, is also warned of in the recent evaluation undertaken by another Mexican political scientist: Alejandro Landero Gutiérrez of the University of Anáuac (Gutiérrez 2021: 35-48). He reaches the same conclusion in his dissection of President López Obrador's style of internal politics. Bearing all of this in mind, the first-hand testimony given by Dr Luis Felipe Bravo Mena, a well-known Mexican politician, parliamentarian, former President of the *Partido Acción Nacional*e and latterly plenipotentiary Ambassador to the Holy See, on the state of health of Mexican democracy, proved even more enlightening. His condemnation of polarisation within the media, palpable in public discourse within Mexico, leads us to reflect seriously on how difficult it is for Mexico today to tackle the issues that will determine its destiny, while also trying to maintain the necessary equanimity. Bravo Mena's paper on the state of democracy in Mexico, inspired by Avishai Margalit's notion of *Decent Society* (Margalit 1996), aims at promoting respect for democratic freedoms, which he sees as integral to the notion of human dignity, and the surmounting of all the inequalities that have tainted Mexico's history since the birth of the nation. The consequence of such prolonged disparity has been that the ethno-cultural mix that makes up Mexican society, which should be treasured as something beautiful, has been disfigured and allowed to become an economic and human tragedy. Breaching this divide was the motive behind Bravo Mena's involvement in political life, his commitment to the party, and the reason he attempted to set up, in this land marked by manifold differences, a large-scale network of centres and opportunities for culture, so as to create inclusion-minded and responsible citizens: What Fisher hopes will be the cornerstone of sustainable urbanisation. Still today in Mexico, for indigenous and Afro-Americans, it is extremely difficult to elude a life of poverty and far easier to fall into one, even when hailing from a comfortably-off social background. In his survey of the different phases of post-independence Mexican history, Bravo Mena points the finger at secularism, which had already become a destabilising factor during the pre-constitutional (1821-1867) period. For decades, public and institutional space in Mexico was denied to the Church, with no recognition of the real contribution it was making. Despite it being a majority-Catholic country, diplomatic relations with the Holy See were only established in 1992 and, even today, much still remains to be clarified about how the Church fits in to Mexican civil society. The practice of ostracising the Church has been a calamitous error, analogous to the destruction of the agrarian society of the *indios*, which was carried out by tearing up the existing legislation, created by the Spanish viceroys to safeguard them, and replacing it with the capitalist exploitation of their lands. Even after all those decades in power, the *Partido Revoluzionario Institucionale* did nothing to reform the dictatorial, oligarchic system that encouraged social inequality. Unfortunately, complains Bravo Mena, even subsequent periods, including the time of constitutional democracy that began around the millennium – and despite the good intentions of the latest Constitutional Charter of 2016 – have failed to provide full recognition of the rights of indigenous peoples. The history of Mexico is one of lights and shadows – gains in the face of severe resistance, and regression, at other times, in terms of the universal recognition of human dignity, especially for the weakest. The presidency of López Obrador seeks, as already noted, to concentrate power in the ruling party and the Head of Government, though, paradoxically, the effect is to aid and abet organised crime. Over recent months and years the number of unlawful killings in Mexico has been scarcely believable, especially those of journalists, human rights activists and priests, all murdered without any observable legal consequences. Evidently, according to Bravo Mena, despite the Constitution of 2016 appearing ultra-modern, the Mexican State is in need of wholesale decentralisation, to encourage a strengthening of participation and an active and responsible civil society, which is a truly essential condition if inequalities are to be overcome. Thus, the centrality of the principle of subsidiarity (Sangalli 2014) comes back into focus, of education towards active citizenship within a civil society, something which has already been a central plank of the formational offering of the *Scuola Sinderesi* (Sangalli 2015).

This focus on civil society, particularly regarding the fight against inequality, was developed in the formational offerings of January 2022. The well-established problem of migration and its impact on Mexican families was looked into by Dr Celine de Mauleon and an analysis of feminism in Mexican society presented by Prof Julieta Beceril Romero.

For her conference, the President of the Italian Branch of the Global Network of Qualified Mexicans (*RedGlobalMX*), Dr De Mauleon, a legal scholar with vast experience in international cooperation and multilateral diplomacy, began by recapitulating the general picture with regard to international migration, which the Synderesis School spent a whole year on (Sangalli 2018). She then devoted specific attention to the Mexican situation, highlighting the great difference, in terms of a nation's development, between the migration of the unskilled and skilled. The first, mass form of migration, is caused by poverty, instability, lack of access to education and other basic services. It is a plague to be fought against, since its principal cause is social injustice and afflicts Mexico's southern states and rural indigenous communities much more severely. The discourses of Pope Francis on this matter, especially at Ciudad Juárez on 17th February 2016, during his Apostolic Visit to Mexico (2016), speak precisely of this. By contrast, the second form of migration, whose impact on civil society has been largely ignored by experts in the field, recognises migrants as true agents of cooperation and development. In Mexico, which is the 11th most populous state in the world yet and the first exporter in Latin America, the capital, which contributes 17.7% of GDP and offers more opportunities than other parts of the country, could be the driving force for the rest of the nation, if they only knew how to get the most out of the human capital present by providing a decent standard of formation. For something that is ordinarily – same again! – more the object of censure than scientific analysis, Celine de Mauleon highlights the ways in which migration can be turned into a positive opportunity for Mexico to improve the situation of its people. Since it is top of the Latin American league in terms of exporting skilled workers and sixth worldwide among OECD countries, the *RedGlobalMX* network represents such an occasion for Mexico. This body works by bringing together national governments, the private sector, academia and civil society, with the aim of transforming what is commonly designated as a 'brain drain' into a 'circle of knowledge, development and integration'. The aim of *RedGlobalMX* members is to make a positive impact in the host countries by their presence there, to stimulate development and for Mexico to participate in the global economy in specific sectors such as entrepreneurship, creative industry, social research, technological and industrial development and academic cooperation, as well as promoting Mexican culture. A look at the organisation's activities, and the likely positive repercussions for the mother country, allows us to welcome them as one of the many signs of hope for the development of Mexican society.

The contribution of Prof Becerril Romero, Dean of the Law Faculty at the University of *Anáhuac* in Mexico, is in the same vein. For years she has been involved in the struggle for equality of the sexes and against violence on women, which is primarily a cultural problem in Latin America. We know, in fact, that, that femicide remains a severe problem within Mexican society, where statistics show that an average of ten women are murdered every day. Mexico City, in particular, has the highest rate of this type of violence, that targets women, but is against all human dignity. To understand the subject correctly, so that it is not simply a matter of trying to stop such discrimination through censure, which does not get very far, the author invites us to put it in the context of efforts towards building a comprehensively peaceful society, that is only made possible when there is real justice. In Mexico, gender inequality is endemic, depriving women of their rights and feeding the culture that leads to repeated episodes of violence, be they physical, sexual or psychological, which without a widespread policy of cultural struggle against inequality and every type of discrimination will not be rooted out. This starts with equal pay between the sexes, and leads to equal opportunities where merit, whatever the setting, determines the value of the work. Fortunately, for a number of years now, the silence has begun to break. There is a powerful feminist movement in Mexico, but it will not succeed – warns Becerril – unless it immerses itself in wider efforts to bring peace to a society that has many contradictions and is a seedbed of continual conflicts. As part of such a *peace-building process* a series of legal measures against gender-based violence and in favour of equal opportunities need to be introduced at the international, national and local level. Actions that will result in the creation of a new social model. The fact that Mexico has entered the *Global Network of Women Peacebuilders*, recently promoted by the United Nations, is a concrete step on the way to a change that is above all cultural. Another seed of hope, which will take considerable time before we see any effective and lasting fruit.

At this point of our investigation into the social changes afoot in Mexico, with the capital as the main focus, questions concerning the effect of religion there could not be ignored, specifically how national identity has been contributed to and shaped by it. Rev Prof Mario Angel Flores Ramos, emeritus Rector of the Pontifical University of Mexico, Director of the National Observatory of the Mexican Episcopal Conference and member of the International Theological Commission, takes the miracle of Guadalupe as the starting point for his paper, and helps us to reflect on how much of an impact Catholic tradition has had on Mexican society. Beyond simply recounting the tale of Tepeyac hill in 1531, and the long *Wirkungsgeschichte* of its reception, the theoretical model that emerges from the story is these days 'taken as Gospel', so to speak, as part of the self-understanding of the whole Mexican community, as Pope Francis also recalled recently in his Letter to the Mexican bishops for the bicentenary of independence. Specifically, it represents a style of inculturation of the Good News that sets complete store by the context in which it occurs, proffering a paradigm of the fundamental tenets of Christianity worthy of exhibition and transmission. Guadalupe, today a sanctuary within *Ciudad de México*, is a perennial warning against any form of cultural colonisation; the dismantling of every supposed superiority of one civilisation over another. By the same token, however, the image imprinted on the *tilma* of the Indian Juan Diego and the events which surround its appearance do not lead to a neutral or purely formal anthropological model. Through this "divine intervention", the seed of another way of understanding human co-existence has been powerfully sown, based on mutual respect, care for the weakest and, thus, the celebration of a shared human dignity. Guadalupe is a categorical imperative against the scourge of inequality, which challenges the Church and Mexican society unremittingly, becoming a criterion for every social action, not just religious questions, which, in any case, are no longer the exclusive preserve of the Catholic Church.

À propos of this latter point, the paper of Prof. Rodrigo Guerra López, a social philosopher and current Secretary of the Pontifical Commission for Latin America, seeks to amplify the purview of Mexico's complex, popular religiosity, especially with regard to the capital. Our author spells out immediately, with reference to recent statistical data (De La Torre – Gutierrez 2021), that in the last few decades, in an increasingly secularised society, there has been a steady decline in the number of Catholics, while the opposite has been true both for Christian evangelicals, mainly Pentecostalists, who do not see themselves having any official religious affiliation, and adherents of other religions, traditional or not. This abandonment of Catholicism has undoubtedly been fuelled by the appalling scourge of clerical abuse as well as the rigid hierarchical structure which limits the level of active participation in the life of the Church. And yet, scholars of the phenomenon identify in popular piety a 'hard core' of resistance to this trend. Catholic popular religiosity, the true heir of the Guadalupan *Weltanschauung*, has been the subject of a serious rethink by the Latin American episcopacy since the Medellin Conference in 1968, especially in the documents of the Aparecida Conference (2007), identifying in it all that is needed for a true journey of faith that encompasses all aspects of human life, thus enabling the culture to be authentically evangelised. We know how, from the time of the Apostolic Exhortation *Evangelii Gaudium*, the Pontificate of Pope Francis has entrusted the Church with the task of re-evaluating the whole theological enterprise of popular piety, its anthropological worth and significance, in order that the Gospel can itself become the culture that challenges all aspects of the breakdown in hope, implied by the processes of secularisation. There is, thus, a real task ahead to try and understand evangelisation anew. This duty has been commended to the Mexican Church as it works towards the jubilee celebrations for Guadalupe in 2031. Such a hermeneutic process, if it is to set in motion the practical changes necessary for social regeneration, cannot but involve those people, from both rural and urban backgrounds, who feel most keenly the need for healing from the inequalities we have reproved, so that their surroundings are reached.

In response to this information, our Centre set up research laboratories to look more closely at the things - legal system, model of development and management of social dynamics - that shape people's daily lives in a megalopolis like *Ciudad de México*.

Thanks to the invaluable assistance of the Mexican Embassy to the Holy See, the lawyer Gianmaria Ruscitti introduced us to the legal criteria with which the thirty-one United Mexican States, while placing great value on the aforementioned historical steps to hybridisation, today oversee the living arrangements in their administratively independent capital, Mexico City, one of the largest metropolitan areas in the world. The injustices of the past take the form of criminal cartels responsible for drug-trafficking, which have now gone global, endemic corruption, which places Mexico in an unfavourable position internationally, and persistent problems surrounding racial integration, which threaten the peaceful future of this coexistence. For this reason, in close imitation of the Berlin and Vienna models, Article 40 of the modern Constitutional Charter of 2016, seeking to bridge the gap between Federal District and autonomous City State, strove to provide direct rule by the Federal Government in the city and, at the same time, to ensure democratic representation for its people. The clear prioritisation of the safeguarding of human rights, which is fundamental in this Constitution, would want, first of all, to guarantee the beginning of a process of democratic development, able to stand up to criminality and corruption. This ought equally to point the way in terms of urban development, through careful planning and regulation to ensure minimum standards for all, services to residents and, contemporaneously, tutelage of the historical, artistic and cultural heritage of the various ethnic groups and unique features of some districts.

How can this be considered an effective legal model and potentially one to be recommended for comparable megalopolises? In his own contribution, also forming part of this collection of writings, the current Mexican Ambassador to the Holy See, Dr

Alberto Barranco Chavarría, sought to draw attention to what he terms the 'Seven original sins of Mexico City', i.e. the historical challenges that make civil cohabitation in Mexico City abidingly problematic. These could be transformed into 'conditions of possibility' if properly managed, and are perfect examples of areas requiring intervention: Pollution level, instability of the water table, flooding, overcrowding, water network, racial conflicts and degree of lawlessness.

Such a *cahiers de doléances* led onto Br Darius Allen Lawrence LC's reflection, in conjunction with Dr Mylene Cano from Coparmex, regarding the development model for Mexico City. It was undertaken to examine how sustainable development might be achieved using the eleven objectives prescribed by the United Nations, which, as well illustrated by Dr Anna Luisa Lippold of the Adenauer Foundation (Sangalli 2021: 30-42), are criteria designed to determine how successfully a city is organised, which we too adopted last year in our analysis of Rome. There are two relevant pieces of information to bear in mind here: Firstly, *Ciudad de México* has transformed, in the space of a few centuries, from a place whose economy was principally dependent on agriculture, to an industrial hub and, latterly, seat of the service economy, where the majority of the whole country's development is concentrated. Consequently, it is here that population growth has been the greatest, in an uncontrolled way. Secondly, the key verification criteria currently considered indispensable for assessing a city's liveability are the following: Housing and basic services available to all; a system of sustainable transport; urban settlements which promote participation and integration; the conservation of world-renowned cultural sites; a reduction in the mortality rate; a reduction in practices harmful to the environment, particularly with regard to waste disposal; safe and universally accessible green spaces. Assessing each of these criteria, Allen Lawrence's analysis of the *Ciudad de México*, confirms the gains, affords harsh criticism of delays and points to future prospects. Above all, he identifies, as others have previously, the main problem which marks the real difference between Latin American megalopolises and European cities of a type similar to Rome (Sangalli 2021: 99-158): The vast discrepancy in living standards between rich and poor. For instance, 3% of the metropolitan area of Mexico City, which equates to around 650,000 people, does not enjoy ordinary access to water!

The thoroughgoing account of Allen Lawrence and the complex debate it provoked among affiliates of the Synderesis School, reminded us again of how new global cities are exercising an increasingly central role on the world stage. They are places where momentous changes are taking place, with polarising effects, as Romano Guardini warned (Guardini 2007) and as we mentioned last year in our synthesis on Rome (Sangalli 2021: 13-28). Megalopolises are simultaneously havens of opportunity and breeding grounds of insecurity, loneliness and indefensible disparity. They are cities that, as they grow to mammoth proportions, risk losing their local identity. Often, there are no spaces where everyone can meet, that might foster a sense of collective identity, inevitably making life more individualistic. In the end, this only leads to social breakdown and conflict. Interconnection, especially among developing countries, can reduce the sense of isolation but, then again, the economic advantages arising only seem to benefit one class, further broadening the gap between rich and poor and making "watertight compartments" out of the shared living spaces. This latter aspect came out especially in the last of the presentations published here: The description, by Br Balam Quitzé Loza Ramos LC assisted by Dr. Rodrigo Iván Cortés Jimenez, of *Red Familias*, recounting the transformation of the *Santa Fe* area of *Ciudad de México* from dumping ground to professional-class ambient. In this district, which is a well-off financial area housing many major international companies as well as a national centre for economic and financial development, what remains of Don Vasco de Quiroga's (known as Tata Vasco) inclusive *hospital* project begun in 1532 and lasting until the XVIII century, before it became one of the city's most depressed areas? Ultimately, what model of society, inspired by individualist neocapitalism, is suited to managing public space? These are questions which challenge the current media practice of reducing the fate of humanity to a global-scale conflict between 'democracies' and 'totalitarian

regimes'. As Loza Ramos suggests in his reflection on the social phenomenon of *Santa Fe,* the reality is far more complex. Along with Cortés Jimenez, he aroused lively debate within the School concerning the criteria to be used for organising social policies and urban planning and even more so on what role the Church, especially lay Christians, might play in the process of re-semanticisation, whereby the old concepts of freedom and equality, the core principles of democracy, undergo the radical recalibration they need in favour of the common good.
At the end of our Mexican itinerary, it was obvious to all how the unbridled ingress of neoliberal ideology had, on the whole, made things worse for a society already deeply scarred by inequality, something that can be traced back to the origins of this country. There is no doubting that the colonial period was characterised more by mass killings, injustice and discrimination than by the events of Guadalupe, the first twelve, the humble missionary fathers who succeeded them or by the work of *Tato Vasco.* However, in the consumer society that Mexico has now become, thanks to its assumption of a neo-capitalist development model, there is a charge even to gain access to public spaces and, because of the way urban areas are laid out, wealth-based discrimination is only accentuated. The city thus ceases to be a place of free encounter and exchange between persons and becomes, as we see especially in megalopolises, a series of attached yet 'diversely accessible spaces' segregated through inequality. In Mexico City, which falls within the ambit of American economic imperialism, this inequality-rich society is concomitantly plagued by contradictions. For example, on the one hand, there is an extremely modern legal system committed to human rights, on the other, an equally pervasive practice of violating these rights. They are the 'many faces of Mexico' which co-exist side by side and risk continuing the history of discrimination. In *Ciudad de México* we see how neocapitalism has made the problems inherent in the modern construction of the 'people's city' worse. Inequality here is, in fact, much more of a factor than comparable European cities, still 'places' – as the economist Silvia Bruzzi (Bruzzi 2018) wrote – 'saved' from the social economy of the market, a specific inheritance from the production model

legislated for by the European Union. The paradigm of the market social economy, combining economic freedom and social justice, has helped create a sizeable middle class in Europe, which unfortunately today is imperilled. So, what about Latin America?

The invitation made by Pope Francis to *Ciudad de México,* before an audience of the country's leading institutions, remains remarkably pertinent. He reminds us how the energies of a people, especially when it is made up mainly of the young, need to be utilised in the construction of the common good: "Experience shows us that whenever we seek the path of privilege or the benefit of a few to the detriment of the common good, sooner or later life in society becomes a fertile ground for corruption, drug trafficking, exclusion of different cultures, violence and even human trafficking, kidnapping and death, causing suffering and hampering development" (Pope Francis 2016). In this call for justice and responsibility, made by the Pontiff, we remember the link between faith and justice established at the XXXII General Congregation of the Society of Jesus. We also are reminded of the teachings of one of the martyrs of justice in Latin America, P. Ignacio Ellacuría, among the greatest minds in terms of the ideation of a different kind of society in Latin America, one not based on inequality. Formed in the school of Xavier Zubiri, with whom he later closely collaborated, Ellacuría underlines that "it is duty of those of us who enjoy a wider exercise of freedom to dedicate our talents and efforts towards the construction of such a society ... in which more people (ultimately, all people) are freed from basic wants (inflicted on them by poverty) so that they can exercise their praxis. In other words, the full self-realization of the privileged lies in their enlisting themselves in the struggles of the oppressed. ... The struggles of the oppressed represent the leading edge of reality's further development" (Gandolfo ISSN 2161-0002). As the Mexican jurist José Antonio Lozano Díez affirms in a recent Adenauer Foundation-sponsored publication (Lozano Díez 2020: 34-49), concerted effort to this end would help to overcome serious limitations, present in the liberal model, that arise as a result of reducing the human to the individual (most Western constitutional and contemporary international law is, in fact, based on this conceptualisation) and ignoring his true nature as a social animal. Unfortunately, a liberal democracy of a relativist and individualist persuasion prospers in a post-truth culture and leads, ultimately, to a neglect of the common good and the birth of new forms of authoritarianism. The alternative, a legal re-appraisal of the dignity of every person, within – and not separate from – his/her social sphere, would not only allow there to be a fresh insight into how the 'public space' is also the place of the "common good", but would also allow a re-evaluation of how religious communities have contributed and been involved in this redefinition and future enactment. It is a discussion which, obviously, goes well beyond the analysis of *Ciudad de México*, but one which the Synderesis School promises to return to in a future edition.

For now, for what has been accomplished thus far, it only remains to offer my sincere thanks, firstly to Fr Jorge Mora LC, who, along with Br. Pablo Vidal Garcia and Mons. Luis Tun Tun, helped me to structure the programme analysing *Ciudad de Mexico* and involve our various illustrious contributors, among whom Mexico's Ambassador to the Holy See and the Embassy staff, the Rector and Superiors of the Pontifical Mexican Seminary in Rome, to whom sincere thanks must also go for their hospitality. Finally, particular thanks go to our friends at the Rome branch of the Adenauer Foundation, without whose support this edition would not have been published, and all the people involved at the Pontifical Gregorian University, who are very much of its formational offering and, as was the case with the present volume, acquire a taste for research there. A final word of personal thanks to Dr Antonella Piccinin, for all the support provided this year too, and Rev Laurence Gambella, always well-disposed to render my words in readable English.

Msgr. Samuele Sangalli

References

Bruzzi S., "Democrazia, sviluppo economico e solidarietà. Il contributo dell'Economia sociale di mercato ad un nuovo ordine economico mondiale", Sangalli S. (ed.), *Solidarietà e democrazia. Mediazione e dialogo tra ideali e realtà concrete*, GBP, 2014: 55-87.

De Giuseppe M. – La Bella G., *Storia dell'America Latina contemporanea*, Il Mulino, 2019.

De La Torre R. – Gutiérrez C., "México: menos católico, más diverso y menos religioso que hace una década", *Nexos*, March, 29th, 2021. (https://www.nexos.com.mx. Accessed 23/07/2022)

Dussel E., *Historia de la Iglesia en America Latina*, Ariel Publisher, 2021.

Ferraris M., *Documanità. Filosofia del mondo nuovo*, Laterza, 2021.

Gandolfo D.I., "Ignacio Ellacuría", *Internet Enciclopedia of Philosophy* (ISSN 2161-0002 https://iep.utm.edu/ignacio-ellacuria/. Accessed 24/07/2022.

Gomez Isquierdo Joge – Sanchez Maria Eugenia, *La ideologia mestizante, el guadalupanismo y sus repercusiones sociales*, Ed. Lupus Inquisitor, 2011.

Guardini R., *Der Gegensatz. Verzücke zu einer Philosophie des Lebendig-Konkreten*, Grünewal-Schöningh, 2007.

Instituto Nacional de los pueblos indígenas, *Atlas de los pueblos indígenas de México*, (altas.inpi.gob.mx. Accessed 18/07/2022).

Konrad Adenauer Stiftung, *Agenda 2030. Basic Law of sustainability*, KAS, 2019.

Landero Gutiérrez A., "La democracia en México: transición sin Renovación", *El futuro de la democracia en América Latina, Pensiamento Social*, 8, 2021: 35-48.

Lozano Díez J.A., "Los desafíos a la libertad religiosa en el actual context social y politico global", Valvo P. (ed.), *La libertà religiosa in Messico*, Studium, 2020.

Margalit A., *The Decent Society*, Harvard University Press, 1996.

Mazzinghi L., *Abitare la città*, Qiqajon, 2015.
Messner D., "Il secolo delle città. Percorsi di sostenibilità", *Concilium*, 2019, 1: 25-37.
Papa Francesco, *Discorsi del Santo Padre nel Viaggio Apostolico in Messico 12-18 febbraio 2016*, (https://www.vatican.va/content/francesco/it/travels/2016/outside/documents/papa-francesco-messico-2016.html. Accessed 23/07/2022).
——, *Fratelli Tutti. Lettera Enciclica sulla fraternità e l'amicizia sociale*, LEV, 2020.
Prosperi A., *Un tempo senza storia. La distruzione del passato*, Einaudi, 2021.
Roser M., *Future population Growth* (https://ourworldindata.org/future-population-growth#global-population-growth. Accessed 17/07/2021).
Rosito V., *Dio delle città. Cristianesimo e vita urbana*, EDB, 2018.
Rosito V., *Metamorfosi del Centro. Cultura, fede e urbanizzazione*, Edizioni Messaggero Padova, 2019.
Sangalli S. (ed.), *A Changing Humanity. Fast-paced living as a new model of being*, GBP, 2016.
——, *Africa: The Unknown. Resources and Gains*, GBP, 2021.
——, *Beyond the Limits. Consequences of Technological Revolution in Society*, GBP, 2017.
——, *Europe as a project. Being protagonist of our future*, Rubbettino, 2019.
——, *Immigration. Understanding and Proposals*, GBP, 2018.
——, *La sussidiarietà. Mappe e rotte di esplorazione*, GBP, 2014.
——, *Religion and Politics. Religious Liberty and confronting new ethical challenges: What is the public role of faith in today's globalized world?* GBP, 2016.
——, *Rome: Three Millennia as Capital. What's next?* GBP, 2021.
——, *Sinderesi: fondamenti di etica pubblica*, GBP, 2012.
——, *Solidarietà e democrazia. Mediazione e dialogo tra ideali e realtà concrete*, GBP, 2014.

Lecture n. 1

HISTORY
The Spanish Conquest of Mexico in 1521: After 500 Years

Pablo Vidal Garcia LC – Pontifical Athenaeum
Regina Apostolorum – Rome

The historical reality that today we call Mexico was shaped as a result of the territorial and human organization and integration that Spain brought to the Mesoamerican space, based on the indigenous realities that had been constituted in it and the response given by the indigenous peoples to Spanish action. As a result of this process, the geographic and human space of the future Mexico acquired a unity -and with it a personality, a specificity, a meaning of its own- that came to be recognized both from within and from outside. Under the name of Nueva España, Mexico would become a human community, the subject of history and endowed with a characteristic culture. [...]
In an assessment of Mexican nationality from its history, we would need to recognize the central role played by the Valley of Mexico [the region where Mexico City is] as a true capital in the genesis and sustainability of nationality, without forgetting the regionalities that enrich, prolong and project this nationality. (Martínez Albesa, 2007)

This document is a brief outline of Mexico's history, from the Spanish conquest until the recent years. With it we try to introduce this year's itinerary in *Scuola Sinderesi*, and more specifically to the lecture The Spanish conquest of Mexico in 1521: after 500 years. that has shaped the development of Mexico as a country and of its capital: Even though its content is not the same one we will listen at the lecture, we hope that it serves as a good preparation to set the basis for the discovery of the rich history and culture Mexico City. We follow the division of historical periods provided by Cosío Villegas in his famous *Historia Mínima de México* (1974) and *Historia General de México* (2000), while enriching it with the remarks of Martínez Albesa, which we find very adequate for the reflection we are looking to bring forward.

Tenochtitlán and the Spanish conquest (Prehispanic period-1521)

In order to understand Mexico, we need to start by giving a glimpse to the pre-Hispanic culture that was settled in the Valley of Mexico. After the fall of the ancient empire of the *toltecas*, a series of small states began to be stablished across the central part of Mesoamerica, which matches with the region of the Valley of Mexico. Around the 15th century, there lived the Mexica, a people considered as insignificant by the neighbors, so much that they had to live in an abandoned island in the middle of the lake of Texcoco. In 1376, the Mexica's emperors began to rise, and the City of Tenochtitlán (that little city in the abandoned island on the lake) began expanding. As a result of 2000, years of life in Mesoamerica, during the reigns of Montezuma I and Montezuma II, and thanks to their great skills as military and social leaders, the Mexica (also known as Aztec) empire grew so much as to arrive to the lands that today constitute Guatemala. They had conquered al the neighboring peoples and in less than a hundred years they built an enormous empire. The main source that we have of the Aztec's way of living are the writings of the Spanish conquistadores. A very rich description of what the Spanish found upon their arrival is offered by Bernal Diaz in his *Historia de la Conquista de la Nueva España*[1], of which we present some lines:

> During the morning, we arrived at a broad causeway and continued our march towards Iztapalapa, and when we saw so many cities and villages built in the water and other great towns on dry land and that straight and level Causeway going towards Mexico, we were amazed and said that it was like the enchantments they tell of in the legend of Amadis, on account of the great towers and cues and buildings rising

---

[1] A full version of the text, which is worth reading in order to undesrtand how the conquistadores intially saw the Aztecs, can be found in https://my.tlu.edu/ICS/icsfs/BernalDiazConquest8pg.pdf?target=a35ae5d9-0a08-459f-b693-6f4c5b1e2850

from the water, and all built of masonry. And some of our soldiers even asked whether the things that we saw were not a dream. It is not to be wondered at that I here write it down in this manner, for there is so much to think over that I do not know how to describe it, seeing things as we did that had never been heard of or seen before, not even dreamed about. [...] Our Captain and all of those who had horses went to Tlaltelolco on horseback, and nearly all of us soldiers were fully equipped, and many Caciques whom Montezuma had sent for that purpose went in our company. When we arrived at the great marketplace, called Tlaltelolco, we were astounded at the number of people and the quantity of merchandise that it contained, and at the good order and control that was maintained, for we had never seen such a thing before. The chieftains who accompanied us acted as guides. Each kind of merchandise was kept by itself and had its fixed place marked out. Let us begin with the dealers in gold, silver, and precious stones, feathers, mantles and embroidered goods. [...] Some of the soldiers among us who had been in many parts of the world, in Constantinople, and all over Italy, and in Rome, said that so large a marketplace and so full of people, and so well regulated and arranged, they had never beheld before. (Bernal Diaz, 2008)

The amusement of the conquistadores regarding the Aztecs was well founded, as the estimated population of the City of Tenochtitlán (which would later become Mexico City) upon their arrival in 1592 was of about 80,000 people. At this historical moment, only four European cities had more than 100,000 habitants: Paris, Naples, Venice and Milan (Moreno Toscano, 1974). We also have to take into consideration that the City was extremely well organized. Standing in the middle of a lake, it was divided into four neighborhoods, had four bridges in order to access it and right in the middle of it stood the huge *Templo Mayor*, the main temple of the empire.
It was in this temple that the majority of human sacrifices were made. The polytheist Aztec religion focused mainly in the figure of Huitzilopochtli, god of the sun. The Aztecs believed that every day, at sundown, Huitzilopochtli had to fight against other deities,

and in order to give him strength so that he could defeat them and rise again the next morning, they provided him with the blood of human sacrifices. For this purpose, mainly captured enemies were used, and in order to have captive enemies, the Aztecs had to constantly go to war. This was one of the principal reasons of their huge expansion, but it was also one of the reasons why the subjugated peoples around them hated them so much.

Before the time of the conquest, the small Spanish army leaded by Hernán Cortés was first well received at Tenochtitlán by Montezuma II, but eventually they captured the Aztec emperor. This event, followed by a massacre of Indians assisting to a religious ceremony was the spark that light the fight between Spanish and Aztecs. The Spanish, however, were not fighting all by themselves with their small army.

> As regions were conquered by Cortés, more Native people joined the anti-Aztec army, which gradually decreased the Spanish element until they were by far the minority. […] these so-called 'allies' referred to themselves as conquerors and letters from different Indigenous groups (Xochimilca, Tlacopaneca, Tenocha, Azcapotzalca) affirm their active participation in the Conquest. (Fuller, 2021)

Thanks to these allies, the advantage of horses, gunpowder and the fear that some of the Natives had for them, in 1521 the Spanich managed to site and conquer the City of Tenochtitlán. With fall of this stronghold, the conquest of the New Spain had begun.

However, even when the year of the conquest is certain, "we cannot point to a date for the birth of a national community. There are no birth certificates for nations, documents that establish a certain political-legal personality to a natural community do not create that community" (Martínez Albesa, 2007). Even before the date of the conquest, the Spanish and the Mesoamerican Indians were already mixing, giving birth to a whole new and different society that, in some way, combined both cultures.

> Obviously, the non-Aztec indigenous peoples did not become 'Mexicans' -novohispanos first- through their integration into the historical

community born of the conquering experience of the Aztec people in the 15th century; rather, the diverse non-Aztec indigenous historical traditions were added to the community that today we can call Mexico through their integration into New Spain or independent Mexico. New Spain received the historical inheritance of the Aztec Empire; but it was neither territorially, socially, humanly nor culturally speaking, its evolution. (Martínez Albesa, 2007)

The colonial period of La Nueva España (1521-1750)

As we've just mentioned, "a double starting point is imposed on us: the Mesoamerican indigenous world and the Spanish enterprise. Both are conditioning factors in the constitution of the Mexican community experience. The structure of the indigenous reality defines the conditions for the Spanish enterprise and will thus endow the results of Spanish action with its own peculiarity" (Martínez Albesa, 2007).

After the conquest of Tenochtitlán, the colonial period, which lasted around 200 years, began. During this time "the legal-social organization within New Spain, as in the rest of the Indian kingdoms, was articulated according to the dual model of the 'republic of Spaniards' and the 'republic of Indians'" (Martínez Albesa, 2007). This model didn't intend to isolate the two different populations, instead it was an attempt to give a social and legal structure to the recently conquered lands, trying to promote coexistence and social harmony between the two peoples. Through this organization model, submitted to the monarchy, and trough the arrival of Catholicism, a melting pot of uniting elements began to take place, allowing us to speak about the formation of a community.

During this period, the consideration that the Spanish had about the Indians constantly changed, some looked at them as slaves, some even didn't consider them as human beings and some, on the other hand, tried to defend their condition and to avoid hard labor for them:

> The Indian is considered by Spain as a recipient of evangelization and as a subject at the same time. To the Indian the Christian faith

is preached and, from this point of view, as a recipient of salvation, he is equal to the European; however, while it is enough to preach to the Spaniard, before the Indian it is necessary to start an active transculturation, in which different appreciations towards the indigenous cultures will intervene. There is no doubt that the conquest meant, for the contemporary and immediately subsequent indigenous generation, a profound cultural trauma. On the other hand, the indigenous people are integrated as subjects of the Hispanic Monarchy and, in the new State, the indigenous people will conserve their ancient rights in several aspects and will obtain legal recognition for their own communities. (Martínez Albesa, 2007)

It seems as though many Indigenous groups actively embraced their new status as citizens of the Spanish crown in order to emphasize the king's responsibility to them, using their status as Spanish subjects to their advantage. [...] In order to support their cause, they would highlight their participation in the Conquest, their role in the pacification and settling of New Spain and their status as Christians who facilitated the spread of the true faith. (Fuller, 2021)

At the same time that the military conquest took place, the evangelization process began. Friars had already arrived with the first ships coming from Europe and they tried very hard to understand the native culture in order to bring the Gospel to the Indians. However, these saw them with diffidence, as the friars were part of the Spanish people that had conquered them. A real miracle was needed in order for the Indians to start converting in great scale. The apparitions of Our Lady of Guadalupe to San Juan Diego in 1531 were the turning point for evangelization in the New Spain. The Indians saw in her image a lot of their own religious symbols, which helped them recognize her as the mother of the God that was above all the other gods.

On the economic issue, the main structure that appeared in the New Spain was the *hacienda*. These consisted on great extensions of land owned mainly by Spaniards, which employed natives for agriculture. In the haciendas, the employees were usually poorly treated, but after the great population decrease suffered during the conquest (which was also accentuated by the new diseases brought by the Europeans) this was the best way the natives could find labor opportunities and survive while keeping their families together with somewhat of a stable way of living. On the other hand, mines also existed, which acted as one of the main economic incentives for Europeans to arrive to this new lands. Contrary to what happened in the *haciendas*, the natives that worked in the mines usually had more liberty, although the labor was very risky and required abandoning the countryside and moving to the cities.

The commerce between the New Spain and Europe was characterized by the high prices of the imported products, which the people living in the colony repaid with precious metals. Thanks to its geographic position as well as to the role that it had played in the Aztec empire, the Valley of Mexico became the most important commercial center and when ships arrived to the ports, almost all their merchandise was taken to Mexico City. This commercial monopoly helped centralization and the importance of the City began to rise, making it become the center of the colony.

Regarding culture, the "Hispano-American societies will present a common cultural tradition – the Hispanic culture – and diverse indigenous cultural traditions. This is an adaptation of the peninsular Spanish to the American, the root of a new culture that Mario Hernández characterizes as 'American identification and Hispanic identity': the way of thinking, of expressing oneself, of seeing, is Hispanic, but it appears oriented or referred to the American reality". (Martínez Albesa, 2007)

This period was a key one in the formation of what would become Mexico, especially in the initial consolidation of its cities, commercial centers, mixture of cultures and mechanisms of an independent economy. (Moreno Toscano, 1974)

The formative period, from the Independence to the Republic (1750-1867)

The arrival of the Enlightenment to the New Spain traced a new direction for its development. During this years, the nation that would later emerge began to take a solid shape. The territory grew with new conquests in the Nord and the South, the politic system began to change, new social groups arise and the path for independence was slowly being paved. The most important of these new groups were the *criollos*, Spanish descents born in the colonies, which gained a big place in the society, but still were usually not allowed to hold important economic or political charges.

> In the eighteenth century, the cultural movement of the Enlightenment encouraged state reformism, but also critical attitudes towards this reformism on the part of the criollos. The Enlightenment, in fact, meant the awakening of a high critical sense supported by a reason conceived as the only instrument of knowledge, disregarding supernatural Revelation. Everything is open to criticism and questionable for enlightened reason. Rational criticism should lead, according to the new faith in progress, to man's happiness. From this cultural movement, the criollos criticized tradition, the state of the Hispanic Monarchy, etc., and, above all, polarized their antagonism with the European Spaniards in the Indies. Criollismo is becoming imbued with the same vindictive positions as those of the European bourgeoisie. (Martínez Albesa, 2007)

As Martínez Albesa puts it: "the historical reality that we have seen originate in the XVI century and today we call Mexico appears at the beginning of the XIX century with its own personality, it is endowed with nationality" (Martínez Albesa, 2007). If we wish to discover the features that make up the Mexican nation, we need to look at its cultural mix of Spanish-Indian features, since both animate the Mexican national culture. We can get a glimpse of this arising culture by taking a glimpse into the Baroque period. In the colonies, it permeated all of the arts, from literature to architecture. Most of the spectacular Mexican cathedrals come from this period. This Baroque period was so important in the New Spain, that a Latin-American version of it was born: the colonial stile. With the Baroque, we find a sensibility characterized by the intellectualization of reality, the exaltation of the search for personal fulfillment and a crisis in religious conscience that leads to a dialogue between religion and science. "Carlos de Sigüenza y Góngora and Sor Juana Inés de la Cruz, will be high representatives of the novo-Hispanic baroque. This baroque would become an expression of Creole intellectual nonconformism, which discovers the Hispano-American as a reality that exists with its own meaning and will be devoted to participate as a protagonist in the transformation of reality" (Martínez Albesa, 2007). A very good glimpse at what this cultural shift meant for the society and for the formation of an independent spirit can be found precisely in the works of Sor Juana. According to Muriel, she would be a "nationalist because of the love with which she mentions what belongs to these lands, because of the eagerness to show its value in front of the European. What she imposes [...] is the strengthening of values, of what was born here, but cemented and sustained by Spanish culture, without which her world would not be understood" (Muriel, 1982).

> The concept of homeland will little by little distance the criollos from the peninsular Spaniards and will make them feel solidarity with the past of the American land, which is their own. Enrique Florescano develops this idea, explaining how in New Spain there was no precise conception of Mexican nation but the idea of homeland was developed. The first emancipating nationalism would therefore be a patriotic sentiment basically reduced to the identity with the soil where one was born and supported by a set of shared religious values. (Martínez Albesa, 2007)

However, as the *criollos* grew and the colony seemed to advance in economic and cultural power (it had become the biggest mining center in the world, exporting huge quantities of gold and silver to Europe), the inequality between social classes also increased. At the beginning of the 19th century, there were five million *indios*, *mestizos* and *mulatos* and one million white people. The first group was, in practice, mainly treated as slaves. The second group was divided between peninsular Spaniards and Europeans, which had the political and economic power) and *criollos*. The difference between the different groups was so big that, when in

1803 Alexander von Humboldt returned to Europe after visiting the New Spain, he used to say that "it is the country of inequality, there is a tremendous inequality in the distribution of richness and culture". While the upper classes, concentrated in the cities, adopted the French style that was permeating Europe, the lower classes lived in poverty in the countryside. Sadly, as we will later see, this inequality has always been present during the history and is, still today, a common and very present thing in Mexico.

The contrasting situation in the colony arrived to its highest point at the dawn of the 19th century. For the *criollos*, the concept of homeland was only true if it enjoyed freedom and, the concept of the new homeland began to born. It was not only the idea of a simple inheritance, but also a union of wills that, insofar as they were committed to achieving freedom were, in some way, giving it life. It was the awakening of the independence movement (Martínez Albesa, 2007). The present that the *criollos* faced was one of extreme social inequality, political despotism from the viceroys and full dependence from the Spanish crown. Instead, they proposed equality achieved through the recognition of every man's rights, commercial and economic equality and democracy against the viceroyalty system. These ideas gave birth to the fight for independence.

Although the independence war and its process are very complex and still today are seen under different perspectives, we can identify some essential events on its developing. From the begging of the 19th century, different independence projects were being born. The first serious steps were given taking advantage from Napoleon's occupation of Spain in 1808. But it wasn't until 1810 that the first armed group arise, leaded by Miguel Hidalgo. Hidalgo was the priest and teacher of the little town of Dolores, he had an elevated intellectual reputation and a lot of political contacts (Brom, 2007). In the morning of Sunday September, the 16th, he rang the bells of his church and gave his famous speech known as *grito de independencia* or *grito de Dolores*, calling the people to stand against the government. Initially, his group consisted of around 600 people very poorly armed, but as they marched through different town, the army grew. The movement became so important that they even arrived to Mexico City and Hidalgo was able to make a request in order to speak with the viceroy. However, the request was denied and his army suffered several defeats, having to make different retreats until when, in 1811, Hidalgo was captured and sentenced to death.

After these events, the next famous general that took the lead for the independence fight was José María Morelos y Pavón, achieving very important military victories in the years 1812 and 1813. In this last year, after taking the city of Acapulco, he arranged the gathering of an independent Congress and gave his famous speech that he entitled *Sentimientos de la Nación* (the feelings of the nation), where he called for three things: the independence from Spain, the proclaiming of Catholicism as the only true religion, and the sovereignty of the people. During this period the Congress wrote the so called Constitution of 1814, but it never was actually applied in the country, as the military independent movement began to lose force and finally, in 1815, with the execution of Morelos, everything seemed like it was coming to an end.

During the next five years, there wasn't a big independent movement. Only small gatherings were organized and some small military groups attempted to stand against the viceroy. In 1820, the generals Agustín Iturbide and Vicente Guerrero, which at first were fighting against each other, came to an agreement to defy the viceroy and try to put forward a big movement for achieving the independence. While Guerrero was in some way the successor of Hidalgo and Morelos, Iturbide aimed for a more diplomatic solution, favoring the search for independence without such profound social changes. With their alliance, they proclaimed the Treaty of Iguala, in which the ideas of Iturbide had the best part. They stated that there was only one religion, that there should be equality among every social group, that Mexico was independent from any other country and that it would have a constitutional monarchy. This time, the movement focused more on the diplomatic end and the military fight was very reduced. In 1821, the viceroy agreed to sign the Treaty, on September the 27th Iturbide's army made its triumphal entrance into Mexico City and on the 28th the first independent government was established, with Iturbide leading it.

With these facts, the new nation was being born, although we have to take into consideration that a lot of optimism was arising and almost no one was taking into consideration the profound damage that the ten years of fighting had inflicted in the country. There was scarcity of natural resources and of population, as well as a very disorganized economy (Brom, 2007). Many tried to establish Mexico as a completely new entity, but in the end, the people and the culture that made up the country were the same than before the independence war. As Martínez Albesa puts it:

> A nation is continually being made in time, constantly redefining itself, permanently being born. Thus, it can and should be said that the Mexico of the 19th century is no longer the New Spain, but a new historical reality. At the same time, however, we cannot fail to recognize that, being distinct realities, there is a historical continuity between them, that they are distinct stages in the history of a historical community which, as such, is subject to permanent change. (Martínez Albesa, 2007)

The instability of the country was evident, and almost immediately after the institution of the monarchy, in 1822, the general Antonio López de Santa Anna initiated an armed revolt and proclaimed the Republic, forcing Iturbide to settle down the crown. A year later, finally a new Congress established the Constitution of 1824, which affirmed the republic and divided Mexico intro 19 states and five territories, applying the classical three government powers to the federal government. Guadalupe Victoria was appointed president and he ordered Iturbide's execution, fact which reflects the complete chaos that was going on during the years of the independence. The next years were characterized by an ever increasing social disorganization. Between 1821 and 1850, there were fifty different governments, produced almost always by military revolts. From these, eleven were leaded by Santa Anna, who gained importance by helping in the defense against a French army that tried to conquer Mexico. But, almost immediately after that, the United States organized an invasion in order to take the lands of Texas, New Mexico and New California, which were claiming independence from Mexico and trying to add themselves to the United States. The American army took Mexico City on 1847 and Santa Anna was forced to yield a huge amount of territory to the U.S.

During these years, the economy of the country was not flourishing either. Each region had to become auto sustainable and produce what they needed to survive. The cultural and intellectual fields, however, did show an important growth. Many journalists, historians and artists came forth and sustained the intellectual side of Mexico. After some time, this intellectual class was eventually divided into two groups, the conservatives and the liberals. In the end, both wanted more or less the same thing for Mexico: that it would recover from the crisis, have a stable government and achieve the long-desired peace. Nevertheless, their methods and programs for getting there were extremely different. The conservatives tried to keep the things more or less in the same way they were before, they tried to go back to the old European monarchical order. On the other hand, the liberals were against any form of bonding with the Hispanic, Indian and Catholic tradition. (González, 1974)

After different successions of governments, Santa Anna regained political power and auto proclaimed himself as Serene Highness. This fact, in addition to the different reforms he did (like, for example, adding taxes to horses, cats and windows) and the complete chaos of his government, arouse discontent in the country, even within the conservative side that initially supported him. In 1854, Santa Anna, criticized by everyone, turns his back against the conservatives and, taking advantage of this, the liberals overthrow him. Three years later they write a new Constitution, but the internal fights kept going and, with the absence of a stable president of the executive power, Benito Juárez, liberal minister of the court of law, takes its place and declares the constitutional order as reestablished. During his government, he tried to bring back stability to the country while pushing forward the liberal ideas. He proclaimed the *Leyes de Reforma* in 1859, a set of laws that established the complete separation between the State and the Church, the expropriation of the ecclesiastic goods, closing of convents, secularization of cemeteries, abolishment of national religious holidays and the beginning of a civil registry for births and marriages. These laws represented a defeat for the conservatives, who tried to fight back, propitiating more instability, which resulted in the government of Juárez travelling to different cities by evading the military conflict.

Due to the poor economic situation, the president decided to stop paying the huge external debt to England, France and Spain. The three countries came together to intervene by the force in Mexican ground and demand the payment of the debt. The liberals managed to arrange a solution with England and Spain, which retired the troops that had been sent to Mexico. Nevertheless, the French, under the ruling of Napoleon III, saw a big opportunity of allying with the conservatives and trying to impose a monarchy in Mexico. Between 1862 and 1864 they managed to expel Juárez from the center of the country and he had to find shelter in the border with the U.S. With this, the French army offered the crown to Maximilian von Habsburg, who made a compromise with Napoleon III and committed the country to repay the complete external debt. However, after some months, it was seen that Maximilian actually had more liberal ideas than conservative ones. With his imperial laws he sustained the liberty of religious cult, supported the expropriation of the ecclesiastic goods, the creation of the civil registry and the imposition of some restrictions to bishops; these laws, however, were never proclaimed. This completely unexpected outcome represented yet another opportunity for a new change of government. At this time, Napoleon III had to retreat his troops from Mexico to defend France from Prussia, and the opportunity was taken by the liberals to violently overthrow the government and finally, in 1867, Maximilian was taken before a firing squad and. (González, 1974)

Modern era and the Revolution (1867-1920)

The Mexican modern era starts with a failure and ends with another failure. It starts in July 1867, with the fall of Maximilian's empire, and ends in May 1911, with the fall of the government of Porfirio Díaz. This era, then, takes up forty-four years, that are usually divided into two periods. The first one, made up of only ten years, goes from 1867 to 1876 and is called the Restored Republic. The second one, of thirty-four years, is called Porfiriato. (Cosío Villegas, 1974)

After the overthrowing of Maximilian's empire, Mexico entered the period of the Restored Republic, called like that because mainly the same characters were the ones who came back to the government, guided, once again, by Benito Juárez. This liberal victory over the conservatives seemed to open the door for the so longed desired stability, progress, internal peace and separation from the European countries as well as from the U.S. However, this period wasn't an easy one either. The economic situation of the country was very bad after the continuous revolts and wars and Mexico had no relations with countries that could lend it money. On the social field, there was an immense generational division occasioned by the war and its outcome; young people had matured very quickly and now wanted to occupy the leading roles in the society. As a consequence, new revolts spontaneously took place and didn't allow the country to remain in peace and growing.

During the Restored Republic, Juárez had twice the same political contestant running for president: Porfirio Díaz. Díaz had been one of the most important generals supporting Juárez in the overthrowing of the Empire, but now he wanted to get the highest political position in the country. The first time, Juárez won the election by far. The second one, there were three contestants, the result was very tight and the Congress appointed Juárez as president. When the next election was arriving, Díaz rose up in arms against Juárez, but unexpectedly in 1872 Juárez died from angina and Sebastián Lerdo de Tejada became president. The military movement of Díaz was defeated, but he didn't give up. Three years later, he foresaw that Lerdo de Tejada was going to reelect himself and rose up in arms again. This time his military campaign was successful and he entered triumphal in the capital city on 1876. The next year elections were called and Díaz won them legally. His first period as president wasn't an easy one, still discontent was around and the economic situation was as bad as before. After his first presidential period, Manuel González was elected president from 1880 to 1884. González was a supporter of Díaz and, in fact, in 1884 Díaz became president again, constantly reelecting himself until 1911.

Seeing the political, economic and social situation in the country, Díaz adopted a policy of little politics and a lot of administration. His government, even when it remains a controversial one, is usually recognized for being eminently practical and for pushing forward the Mexican economy and culture. This formula worked very well for long years, because the country was in deep need of stability, peace and growth, and the society was tired of military conflicts. So, the constant creation of labor and the introduction of technological advances seemed as a very good idea to most of the population. For example, Mexico passed from having one single railroad line with 460 kilometers in 1877 to having a railroad network of 19,000 kilometers at the end of the Porfiriato. Postal, telegraph and telephone systems were developed and the agriculture, mining, commerce and industry also grew. (Cosío Villegas, 1974)

This time, the problem was that, with all of these advances, social inequality was quickly spread. There were very few rich families, an almost inexistent middle class and a lot of poor people. It was extremely difficult for someone appertaining the low class to get out of it. However, some young people managed to study and get university degrees as doctors, engineers or lawyers, and they began to feel uncomfortable with the government of Porfirio Díaz which seemed to be closing in itself and not letting them participate in the political life of the nation (Cosío Villegas, 1974). In 1910, after thirty-four years of what seemed a prosper and peaceful period, serious political problems arouse again. Different political parties were created to contend for seats in the Congress, even though they didn't win even one single post. With respect to the presidency, they were willing to let the octogenarian Díaz reelect himself as long as he allowed the vice-president to be changed. The main opponent of Díaz, Francisco Madero, had the very clear idea that the Mexican society was ready for a real democracy, that the people had to be able to elect their government freely. In fact, in 1908, Díaz himself had stated the same idea in an interview with an American journalist, even when he would later demonstrate the opposite by reelecting himself and his vice-president. This fact, led, inevitably, to an armed revolt that Madero began on November the 20th of 1910, giving start to the Revolution war.

In the beginning, the armed movement seemed to be composed only of local riots and the government thought they could be easily controlled. However, a national scale movement arouse, not only with Madero, but with generals such as Emiliano Zapata. The armed fight lasted only six months and leaded to the defeat of Díaz and the appointing of Madero as president. But, after two years he had not still been able to solve one of the main problems of the country, social inequality and the exploitation of peasants. Once again, Madero's government lasted very little. A new armed revolt was guided by Victoriano Huerta in 1913, resulting, in just a few days, in the assassination of Madero and the naming of Huerta as president. As it could be expected, such a sudden and violent movement didn't win the approval of the people and new revolts took place, mainly leaded by Zapata and Pancho Villa. From this new conflict, Venustiano Carranza arose as leader and new president. He tried to lead Mexico to a new period of peace and called for a Congress that would elaborate a new Constitution, which was completed in 1917. Elections were called and again Carranza was elected as president.

> An examination of the events conforming the armed movement of 1910 to 1917 allows us to affirm that, in the midst of multiple contradictions and confusions, many outdated social structures were broken down and new ways of development were opened for the country, with a strong popular participation. Nevertheless, the economic and social inequality persisted, leading to the development of new struggles and problems. (Brom, 2007)

Late XX century and present day (1920-2021)

In 1920, the relative peace in the country allowed new presidential elections to take place, which seemed to close the historical period of the Revolution and give place to the new Mexican development. The elected president was Álvaro Obregón, who was recognized as an outstanding military man during the revolts of the Revolution and who represented the middle class, that appeared to be the one that could best bring together the different social classes. In contraposition with his predecessors, he understood that the guidance of the country could not only be concentrated in himself, but needed to be sustained by the Constitution. (Blanquel, 1974) He actually did support a law to bring more equality for peasants and tried to reorganize the political power according to the new laws of 1917. After him came Plutarco Elías Calles, who began his presidency in 1924. He tried to keep the same governing strategies as Obregón and gave an impulse to agriculture, public services, healthcare and education.

His time as president was, however, deeply marked by the so-called *Guerra Cristera* or *Cristiada*, a period of religious persecution, mainly against the Catholic church, in the center and west areas of the country, which lasted from 1926 to 1929. By this time, Catholic leaders were involved in politics and also the vast majority of the people living in the countryside, whose inequality problems were still not completely solved by the Revolution, was catholic. In 1926, Calles dictated a law that limited the number of priests, dissolved the monastic orders, abolished the religious education and prohibited public acts of cult. This decision provoked general discontent among the Catholic people. Violent persecutions began, and the killing of priests and lay people who were opposing Calles' laws took place. Amongst the Catholics, there wasn't certainty about what to do. Most bishops called the people not to fight back, but many raised up in arms with the ideal of justly defending their right for religious belief. The government's repression and violence only enkindled the Catholics' ideals and they kept fighting back, some with arms, some through politics and some only by praying and sustaining their fellow believers. In the end, neither army was able to win the conflict and a pacific arrangement was settled on 1929. However, after this, most of the *Cristero* leaders were killed or disappeared.

Meanwhile, Mexican politics were changing again and the political power began to be institutionalized instead of being carried only by the figure of a president (Blanquel, 1974). In 1929, the first big political party was established, the Revolutionary National Party, that would later become the Institutional Revolutionary Party (*Partido Revolucionario Institucional* in spanish, known as PRI). From this moment, until the year 2000, this political party would always win the presidential elections, and the control of the party usually was claimed by the president in turn and the persons close to him. It was no more only the president who held the power, but a complete political party, although it was always run by small groups of people.

Between 1934 and 1940 big changes took place in Mexico. The president during this period was Lázaro Cárdenas, who tried to support the growth of the national economy. He gave the control of the agricultural lands to the peasants and tried to improve their way of living, giving them legal, economic and technical assistance. He also proclaimed the nationalization of the petrol companies that were not willing to change their way of treating their workers, and so, the petrol industry fell under the control of the government. Finally, he tried to give an impulse to education and to the development of arts. During these years, in 1939, the National Action Party (*Partido Acción Nacional* or PAN) was born, regrouping many of the middle and high class leaders that somehow opposed the PRI's way of governing and representing its biggest political opposition. (Brom, 2007). Altogether, this period helped consolidate the nation, improving the economic, social and cultural sectors.

> During the four decades that followed the agitated presidential process of general Cárdenas, the government affirmed to keep sustaining the process of the Revolution of 1910, but stopped insisting in the defense of the working and peasant classes to give preference, instead, to national unity. In the intense debates and political fights for the direction of the country and about the most adequate ways of incrementing and distributing the richness, not only different national groups showed their own diverse preferences, but, in a way, they reflected the confronting forces at a global level. The relative

> calm of the first thirty years was interrupted by the workers' strikes of 1958 and the students' movement of 1968. During the next period, [...] the general crisis that arouse led to a new change in the life of the nation. (Brom, 2007)

This change of governing towards national unity first began with president Ávila Camacho in 1940. The successive governments kept more or less the same lines and favored the private initiative and foreign investment. In 1958, different important workers' movements began, demanding better wages and ending in the achievement of syndical representation and better working conditions. The global revolution of 1968 also arrived to Mexico and in October of that year, during a gathering of mainly middle-class students that were in discontent with the government, a massacre took place and many of them were killed or disappeared. However, the period that goes all the way to 1982 is usually considered as a peaceful and somehow prosperous one, due to the centralization of politics in Mexico City, the development of industries (mainly the petrochemical one), the opening of banks and, in general to the more capitalistic way of government.

> [From 1982 until the year 2000] Mexico entered in a new rapid succession of deep changes. [...] The role of the State in the national economy was reduced and it was opened to the international market. The political life suffered important alterations that culminated, in the year 2000, with the PRI's loss of the presidency. Social, economic and political differences in part remained the same and in part grew between the different parts of the country, some of which advanced rapidly, while others stayed behind. (Brom, 2007)

It was during these years that Mexico acquired most of the shape that it has nowadays. The free market economic system prevailed and made the government take a step back in the control of the economy. In this period, Mexico entered different international economic and political treaties that helped the country. Nevertheless, there were some profound economic crisis during the 90's. Political discontent regarding the governing party, PRI, also appeared, and while PAN still represented the opposition, a more liberal party, the Democratic Revolution Party (*Partido de la Revolución Democrática*, PRD), was formed in 1989. The Mexican people felt a deep corruption problem in the governing party and in the official institutions and finally, in the elections of the year 2000, a new change seemed to begin with the victory of PAN's candidate Vicente Fox.

In the end, we can address the actual period of Mexican history, although, as it is so recent, it is very difficult to have a full picture of it and to draw conclusions on how the events are affecting Mexican history, so we will talk about it in very general lines. The period going from 2000 to 2012 was characterized by the two successive presidencies of PAN's candidates. The first period, from 2000 to 2006 was a difficult one, because Fox had a strong opposition in the Congress. Mexico's economy had become very close to the one from the U.S. and so, it suffered in these years, without much growth. Unemployment grew a little and informal work, with people working without being registered as tax contributors, became very present. From 2006 to 2012 the economic issue was improved by president Felipe Calderón, but peace and social issues began to suffer. The president decided to fight the illegal drug industry which had become immensely big, but the drug cartels fought back and insecurity took over many cities. However, the political and economic issues improved. From 2012 to 2018, the president was PRI's candidate Enrique Peña Nieto. He tried to impulse new reforms that would improve Mexican economy and technological advancement. Regarding the social issue of insecurity, he diminished the fight against drug cartels, but still violence kept going, with daily homicides still taking place. From 2018 to the present day, the Mexican presidency is held by Andrés Manuel López Obrador, who had previously lost two presidential elections, but taking advantage of the deep division between social classes, won the most recent election. His campaign ideal was to fight against corruption and to give the people the control of the nation. However, his decisions have been very controversial, as apparently insecurity continues, there is no economic growth and politics are being retained by his political party. Social inequality and political polarization have grown and there is a big division regarding how the country is being leaded.

Conclusion

As we can see throughout this brief history of Mexico, the nation has continually suffered deep changes in many levels and the conformation of its identity has been modeled by them. From the time of the Spanish conquest, to the present days, Mexican history presents itself to us as an intricate series of events, as a mixing of cultures and ideas that has given birth to what we now know as Mexico. We hope that this historical outline helps us start an enriching dialogue about this beautiful nation and about its capital city: Mexico City.

References

Blanquel E., *Historia Mínima de México*, ed. Cosío Villegas D., Mexico 2007: 135-156.
Brom J., *Esbozo de historia de México*, Mexico, 2007.
Cosío Villegas D., *Historia General de México*, Mexico 2000.
Cosío Villegas D., in *Historia Mínima de México*, ed. Cosío Villegas D., Mexico 2007; 117-134; 157-164.
Diaz del Castillo B., *History of the Conquest of New Spain*, translation Carrasco D., United States 2008: 156-179.
Fuller A., The Fall of Tenochtitlan, *History Today*, United States, August 2021.
González L., in *Historia Mínima de México*, ed. Cosío Villegas D., Mexico 2007: 73-116.
Martínez Albesa E., *La Constitución de 1857. Catolicismo y liberalismo en México*, Mexico 2007.
Moreno Toscano A., in *Historia Mínima de México*, ed. Cosío Villegas D., 2007: 47-72.
Muriel J., *Cultura femenina novohispana*, Mexico 1982.

Lecture n. 2

HERMENEUTICS
500 Years since the Birth of Mexico

Dr. Luis Alfonso Orozco LC – Pontifical Athenaeum Regina Apostolorum – Rome

Mexico today is a nation with nearly 130 million inhabitants in a territory that is around two million square kilometers. It is the first in the world in number of Spanish-speakers and has the second most Catholics, behind Brazil. In America, it ranks fifth in territorial extent but its biodiversity places it among the top eight in the world.
Modern Mexico is half the size it was when it achieved its independence from Spain in 1821, which was even smaller than before the conquest by Hernán Cortés in 1521. Before this event there was a huge territory known as Mesoamerica, in which hundreds of native ethnic groups swarmed with their different languages, customs and governments; they were often enemies among themselves to the point of death. There was not the remotest idea of unity or nationhood among them before 1521.
There was no trade or cultural contact among those primitives. They were already divided by the abyss of the diversity of languages-Tarasca, Cuitlateca, Maya, Mixteca, Zapoteca, Totonaca, Zoque, Otomi, Nahua, etc. (Schlarman 1993: 37).
Two prominent Mexican historians, José Vasconcelos and Eugenio del Hoyo, solidly affirm the thesis of the birth of Mexico as a nation from the arrival of the Spanish and the conquest of the Aztec empire in 1521.

> The history of Mexico begins as an episode in the great odyssey of the discovery and occupation of the New World. Before the arrival of the Spaniards, Mexico did not exist as a nation; a multitude of tribes separated by rivers and mountains and, the deepest abyss, of their three hundred dialects, inhabited the regions that now form the homeland. The Aztecs ruled only an area of the plateau, in constant

rivalry with the *Tlaxcaltecas*, and to the west the *Taraschi* exercised independent sovereignty, as did the *Zapotecas* to the south. No national ideas related to castes; on the contrary, the fiercest enmity fueled perpetual warfare, which only the Spanish conquest ended. (Vasconcelos 1998: 35)

Mexico became that magnificent *mestizo* fruit of the conjunction of two opposite worlds: the Renaissance Spain and the indigenous Mexico, which clashed violently in the Conquest and from whose violent clash was born our *mestizo* nationality: I argue that before the Conquest there was no Mexican nation, no Mexican state: there was not! Indigenous Mexico is presented to us as a complex, rich mosaic of peoples, cultures, languages, beliefs, customs (...) neighboring peoples who could not understood each other due to the diversity of languages, more than half the territory in the north inhabited by primitive nomads. This was pre-Cortesian Mexico (Del Hoyo 1997: 2).

Joseph Schlarman, the author of the great book *Mexico: Land of Volcanoes*, which is a classic on the history of this North American nation, points out the nonexistence of Mexico as a nation or as a unified empire before the Spanish conquest:

It is, therefore, inexcusable anachronism to imagine the Castilian conquistadores as invaders of Mexico. Neither as a political, nor social, nor religious, nor ethnic unit did Mexico exist. It was an immense mosaic of peoples of widely varied cultural levels that ranged from savages lost in the rain forests and nomads of the arid steppes of the North to the slightly more civilized peoples of the temperate lands of Mesoamerica. The so-called Aztec empire was nothing more than a heterogeneous collection of peoples and regions, subjugated by the strength of the bold tribe that had replaced the Toltecs in the Valley of Mexico: the Mexicas (Schlarman 1993: 45).

The name of Mexico

It is a compound word from the Nahua or Mexica language: "Mexico, a word derived from Mexitl, seems to come from the word *Metztli* – the Moon – and *xictli* – center or bellybutton –, so that Mexico was figuratively 'the city that lies in the middle of the Moon (or lake)'." (Alvear Acevedo 1964: 92)

The lake in question refers to the ancient lake of Texcoco where the Aztecs founded their capital city *Tenochtitlán* around the year 1325. The Aztecs thought they installed the city at the center or navel of the moon, and its name became the name of the whole country after the Spanish conquest. Today there is the triple coincidence of the name because the national capital is named Mexico, one of the country's 32 federated territories is named the State of Mexico, and the official name of the country is the United Mexican States.

2021: an important year for Mexico

In 2021, Mexico's history sees important anniversaries: 500 years have passed since the painful birth of the new nation, the result of the union of Spanish and indigenous blood. The conquest of the Aztec capital by Hernán Cortés in 1521, gave rise to the new country now inhabited by nearly one hundred and thirty million people. 2021 also marks 490 years since the apparitions of Our Lady of Guadalupe on the *Tepeyac* hill; thus it begins a decade of preparation to celebrate 500 years since Mexico's baptism.

The year 2021 also marks the 200th anniversary of national independence by the hero Agustín de Iturbide. It was 1821 when New Spain came of age and gained its independence from the Spanish motherland; then began its historical journey as independent Mexico, which later experienced struggles and other painful fragmentations of territory. By 1810 the struggle for its independence had begun, but only in 1821 was it truly reached.

This means that during those **three centuries,** from 1521 to 1821, Mexico already existed but as a child under a parent, under the rule of Spain. Hence the name New Spain. Those three centuries are known as the colonial era. Cultural and national identity were forged there, under one common language, Spanish, with one religion, Catholicism and one Western culture. The thousands of missionaries who came from Europe to transplant the faith of Christ were the ones who civilized and evangelized Mexico, beginning in 1524.

The first group of Franciscan missionaries to arrive were known as the *Twelve Apostles* of Mexico. The subject of Catholic missionaries in Mexico deserves a separate study, so I will only mention them here because of their basic importance in shaping the Mexican nation. Twelve were the first Franciscan missionaries to arrive in Mexico in 1524, three years after the Spanish conquest of the Aztec empire. They arrived to begin the evangelization of the huge territories of the new country that grew out of that painful birth. Twelve like the first apostles whom Jesus chose personally to constitute His Church and sent to evangelize the whole world.

These missionaries who civilized carved the 'statue' of the homeland by fusing in the crucible of their immense love the various metals of the peoples: the native languages, customs, religions. In their wake, cities flourished, wars ended, cannibalism, witchcraft, and drunkenness ceased. They raised the cross on mountain peaks and brought to the wandering and miserable peoples peace, abundance, light ... Of these giant civilizers, even their names are unknown ... and since they are unknown and it is right that they should be known, we have decided to popularize the story of their wonderful deeds (Trueba 1961: 3-4).

The Twelve Apostles of Mexico[1]

Once embarked on their evangelizing mission, these missionaries left the Andalusian port of Sanlúcar de Barrameda on January 25, 1524. On February 4 they arrived at *La Gomera*, one of the Canary Islands; then on March 5 to Puerto Rico; on March 13 at the island of Hispaniola or Santo Domingo; and on April 30 at Villa de la Trinidad. They finally arrived at the port of San Juan de Ulúa, in Veracruz, on May 13, 1524. On that date, the group of Franciscan missionaries, known lateras the Twelve Apostles of Mexico, arrived, sent by Pope Adrian VI and King Charles I of Spain.

---

[1] See Iraburu 2003: 100-112.

These were to be the first group of missionaries in charge of converting the Indians of New Spain to Catholicism. At the head of this mission was Fray Martín de Valencia, superior of the Spanish Franciscan province of St. Gabriel and who, at the request of Francisco Quiñones, the Minister General of the Franciscan order, chose with extraordinary care the twelve missionaries for the expedition.

The names of the twelve Franciscans were: Martín de Valencia, Francisco de Soto, Martín de Jesús (or de la Coruña), Juan Suárez, Antonio de Ciudad Rodrigo, Toribio de Benavente (Motolinía), García de Cisneros, Luis de Fuensalida, Juan de Ribas, Francisco Jiménez, and the lay brothers Andrés de Córdoba and Juan de Palos.

Hernán Cortés learned of the arrival of these missionaries when he was in Mexico City, and immediately went to receive them, accompanied by many Indians and *caciques,* chiefs, including Cuauhtémoc (the last Aztec emperor). The poor clothing of these friars shocked the Indians, seeing that they were dressed differently, since they were used to seeing the soldiers of the conquest well dressed and protected. Cortés bowed to these Franciscans by kissing their clothing, thus the Indians did the same. But most of all, they saw the respect and obedience the missionaries received. Since their arrival, these Franciscan friars won the affection and trust of the natives because of their humble lifestyle.

They walked half barefoot and in poor clothing, slept on mats and were very frugal in their food. The Indians appreciated their industriousness, their effort to teach them, the loving treatment they gave them, and their interest in defending the Indians from those Spaniards who mistreated them. Indian rights were an achievement of the Catholic missionaries. (see the work of Brother Francisco de Vitoria, Bishop Brother Juan de Zumárraga, etc.). The Indians were amazed to see that group of poor friars so affable and humble. Speaking of it, they used the word *Motolinia*, until Father Toribio de Benavente asked what it meant. They told him it means 'poor'. And from then on, Fray Toribio took the long-lasting nickname *Motolinia* (*Ibid*: 102). The missionaries were, ever since their arrival, the protectors, fathers and civilizers of the natives, integrating them little by little and with enormous efforts into the new country that emerged after the conquest.

What elements make the emergence of a nation possible?

We stated that the birth of Mexico as a nation occurred in 1521, and from then on its historical journey began. There are three basic elements in forging national unity. The first is political unity, which includes territorial unity under an organized government. Every nation has experienced large or small changes in the process of its social and political unity for decades or centuries, and Mexico has been no exception.

The second element is social unity, which is achieved by adopting a common language as a bond of unity among the various groups and ethnicities living in the national territory. The Spanish language is the official language of Mexico.

Thirdly, is cultural unity, which brings together the various traditions that are recognized as the nation's heritage and have forged its identity. To speak of Mexico today as the 'Aztec country' or the 'Aztec team' (in the World Cup), is just poor reductionism, since the Aztec element represents only part of the social and cultural whole that constitutes modern Mexico.

Not forgetting at all the vast cultural tradition of its various indigenous people, Mexico grew from 1521 under the tutelage of Western civilization brought by Spain, which gave it language, religion and culture. The predominant Catholic religion has been the soul of the Mexican nation, under the protection of the Blessed Virgin of Guadalupe, a symbol of its *mestizo* identity, for in her sweet face are reflected the various ethnic groups that make up this diverse nation. The Guadalupan event, since 1531, is of fundamental importance in understanding Mexico's cultural and religious identity.

These three elements mixed together forged the Mexican nation that emerged in 1521 and during the three centuries that followed, when it bore the name of Viceroyalty of New Spain. In 1821, its political independence was achieved, but it did not break its cultural or religious ties with its 'mother country'. These three centuries as a colony are absolutely essential to understanding Mexico's historical development, because in them its social, religious and cultural unity were forged, even if not so much its political unity. To claim that Mexico was born only in 1821, with independence from Spain, is incorrect because neither history nor the facts support that statement. There is a whole ideological line that has insisted on teaching that the year 1821 was a 'recovery' of Mexican nationality. This line claims that the three centuries as a viceroyalty or colony were something akin to an oppression, a painful parenthesis to Mexican-ness imposed by the Spanish empire.

Behind this ideological and historical reductionism, is the intent to deny with one stroke of the pen all the civilizing and evangelizing work of the Catholic Church from Spain, despite the fact that this was the essential element in the formation of the Mexican nation. It has been proven that before 1521 there was no Mexican nation, not even a remote idea of national identity or Mexican-ness, because the very different tribes and ethnic groups in the pre-Cortesian territorial space each had their own language, religiosity, and customs, all of which usually made them mortal enemies of each other. By 1821, Mexico existed with its own cultural and religious identity, and the next step was to achieve its political independence from Spain.

2021: an important date between Mexico and its history

History is *magistra vitae*, with the lessons of its irrefutable facts. We hope the year 2021 helps to clear up many misunderstandings about Mexico's birth as a nation. It did not exist before the pre-Hispanic period, nor did it begin its historical journey in 1821 – the year of its independence – as some claim. Mexico was born five centuries ago; it grew up for three more centuries as New Spain until it came of age and became independent two centuries ago, when it took its name according to its *Nahua* roots and adopting the tricolor flag with the shield of the eagle devouring the snake (an Aztec symbol).

Its culture bears the Western imprint, and its predominant religion is Catholicism, which has forged the soul of the Mexican people. The true fathers of the Mexican homeland and civilizers of the Indians were the heroic Catholic missionaries, who on many occasions shed their blood in martyrdom to bring the most primitive indigenous groups out of barbarism.

Few historians have given due place to the centuries of enormous work of missionaries the Americas, and Mexico is a case in point. One of these authors affirms in vehement words:

> That is why we must say that all these regions are currently Mexico, thanks to the Jesuit missionaries who enlarged the Mexican homeland with their great evangelizing efforts. And of Franciscans, Dominicans, Augustinians and other religious, the same must be said: the missionaries were the main creators of today's Mexico. However, today we see in the cities of this nation heavy statues, in the purest style of Soviet realism, dedicated to Juárez, Obregón, or Carranza, but we are unlikely to find any memory of these holy fathers of the Mexican homeland (…). (Ibid: 237)

This is the historical truth; to pretend to deny it or adjust it would be demagoguery and ideology, which deny the facts. That is why it is so important for a people to know their history well, so that they do not repeat the mistakes of the past but learn from the accomplishments of their ancestors and continue them. Building a democratic, more just and honest Mexico is the task of all citizens, under the protection and loving gaze of the Blessed Virgin Mary of Guadalupe, mother of the nation and authentic symbol of its national unity.

References

ALVEAR ACEVEDO C., *Historia de México*, Jus 1964.
DEL HOYO E. et al., *Historia de México: Conversaciones con Don Eugenio del Hoyo*, México 1997.
IRABURU J. M., *Hechos de los Apóstoles de América*, Gratis Date 2003.
SCHLARMAN J., *México tierra de Volcanes*, Porrua 1993.
TRUEBA A., *Cabalgata Heroica. Misioneros Jesuitas en el Noroeste*, Jus 1961.
VASCONCELOS J., *Breve Historia de México*, México 1998.

Lecture n. 3

SOCIOLOGY
Impact of Globalization on Public Space: The Case of the Plaza de Las Tres Culturas in Tlatelolco, Mexico City

Dr. Margarita Martinéz Fisher – Sociologist – Mexico City

Globalization is a far-reaching process that generates diverse impacts on people's lives. One way to understand its effects is to analyze its consequences on the configuration and dynamics of our cities. And we care about cities because by the year 2020, according to the United Nations, 56.15% of the world's population was urban. In Mexico, according to 2020 data from the World Bank, 81% of the population lives in cities.
The globalization process accelerated the urbanization; however, its impacts are different depending on each region and respond differently to the multiple and complex historical, cultural, demographic, economic and other contextual variables of each society.
While globalization has consequences on different scales and spheres of city life, such as migration, land and housing supply, the way of occupying the territory, the configuration of public services, the transformation of economic activities, environmental impacts, quality of life, among others, in this paper, I propose to look at the evolution and configuration of public space.
The city is the space that concentrates the social heterogeneity of a large and dense population group. To exist, it requires meeting and contact spaces, tangible (squares) or intangible (imaginary), that allow the diverse to rebuild unity in diversity (the city) and define citizenship (democracy). (Carrión 2020).
To reflect on the impact of globalization in Mexico City, I will present the case of the Plaza de las Tres Culturas, an emblematic site located in the Conjunto Habitacional Nonoalco Tlatelolco, built in the 1960s by architect Mario Pani, one of the main representatives of the Mexican modernist movement.
Tlatelolco refers to two issues. On the one hand, it is a neighborhood of pre-Hispanic origin; on the other, it is the Non-

oalco-Tlatelolco-Tlatelolco Housing Complex. The Plaza de las Tres Culturas is the central space of the latter: there coexist the Santiago Tlatelololco Church to the south, the Chihuahua Building to the east, the 15 de Septiembre Building to the north, the archaeological zone to the west and, behind the Church, the former headquarters of the Ministry of Foreign Affairs, today the Tlatelolco University Cultural Center (Allier 2018).

In the light of Urban Sociology, I will discuss the implications of globalization in the specific case of the Plaza de las Tres Culturas from four dimensions:

First, I present a brief historical and geographical context of the great Nonoalco-Tlatelolco housing complex as a project of the modern Mexican nation.

Next, I will discuss, based on the research and theoretical approach of Emilio Duahu and Angela Giglia, the transformation of modern public space, starting from its configuration in the industrial city and how it has been transformed in the global city.

After several field tours in the Plaza, I will present some representative cases of this space as a territory of citizen memory and some new daily practices in the current public space, in particular I am interested in reflecting on these activities in the post pandemic COVID-19.

To conclude this paper, I propose to promote a public space of encounter and inclusion as opposed to the insular city of today's global mercantilism.

1. Historical and geographical context of the great Nonoalco-Tlatelolco housing complex as a project of the modern Mexican nation.

Pre-Hispanic Period

Teotihuacan groups were present in the region since the 7th century. From the 14th century it was inhabited by dissident Nahua groups, who separated from Tenochtitlan and migrated to an islet in the western part of Lake Texcoco called Xaltelolco – which means "place of the mound surrounded by sand" –, where a settlement grew, which came to be among the most important in the region for its commercial dominance, in fact, in Tlatelolco was the largest market in the region.

Tlatelolco is considered the twin city of Tenochtitlan. Its design is similar, it had a Templo Mayor from which the profane and sacred space was organized. The temple marked a vortex where all the divine essences of the thirteen heavens and the nine underworlds of the vertical plane and the four corners and the sacred vertex in the horizontal plane converged; founded according to its cosmovision divided into four large neighborhoods, surrounding its ceremonial precinct (Toscana & Aparicio, 2018).

Although the political and religious hegemony corresponded to Tenochtitlan, the importance of the tianguis was significant, hence there was a Tecpan – 'place of the stone house' which translates as 'palace' – where a group of judges lived who were dedicated to resolve conflicts that arose from the exchange of goods and which was the seat of commercial control, there taxes were collected. In this way, commercial activity governed the life of the city.

In 1475 the cities of Tlatelolco and Tenochtitlan clashed in a war that Tenochtitlan won and from then on a political, economic and military unit known as the great city of Mexico Tenochtitlan-Tlatelolco was formed (Flores, 1968 cited in Toscana & Aparicio, 2018). After this war, in which Tenochtitlan reaffirmed its religious and political hegemony, and Tlatelolco its commercial hegemony, the Tecpan of Tlatelolco also began to be used as the seat of military governors until the Conquest.

Colonial Period

At the beginning of the Conquest in 1521, a battle took place that led to the slaughter of thousands of indigenous people and the defeat of Cuauhtémoc (last Mexica tlatoani of Mexico-Tenochtitlan), a moment that is considered the origin of the Mexican nation. From this period some constructions survive in what is currently a small archaeological zone (Toscana & Aparicio 2018). In the 16th century in Tlatelolco, a temple dedicated to Santiago Apostle was built over the commercial city and its constructions, thus inserting Catholic architecture into the landscape. The temple of Santiago reordered the pre-Hispanic city of Tlatelolco, introducing western culture and imposing it over the indigenous culture. The construction of the temple was done in the medieval style: seen from the heights it has the shape of a cross. It was inaugurated in 1609 by Fray Juan de Torquemada and thus reaffirmed the Spanish dominion over the Aztecs. (Toscana & Aparicio 2018).

As part of the process of territorial reorganization and evangelization, the Colegio de la Santa Cruz was built by the Franciscans and it educated young indigenous sons of nobles, so that they could learn Latin and Spanish. At the end of the 16th century this College became a school of first letters for indigenous children (Toscana & Aparicio 2018).

In the area of Tlatelolco, the surviving indigenous people were accommodated and thus a neighborhood of indigenous people was formed, known as Barrio de Santiago. Tlatelolco retained certain privileges within the viceregal regime, so its nobility were recognized rights and prerogatives. Cuauhtémoc continued to be "king of Mexico and lord of Tlatelolco" and claimed territorial rights and fishing jurisdiction. The Tecpan was rebuilt and was Cuauhtémoc's house and seat of civil power (Toscana & Aparicio 2018) until it was suppressed in the early 19th century, when an "Independent Asylum for the Corrected" was established there and the "Correctional College of San Antonio" was formed in 1853 to confine young delinquents there.

The Tecpan had that use until 1909 when it began to be used as a school: first it was the "Manuel Eduardo Gorostiza" school, then the "Escuela Vocacional de la Beneficencia Pública" and then the 'Pedro Díaz' school, until 1962 when it was closed due to the construction of the Unidad Habitacional Nonoalco-Tlatelolco and to convert the school into a "precinct of homage to Cuauhtémoc" (Toscana & Aparicio 2018). The original construction was preserved until 1962 when it was stripped of the gate which was moved to the Colegio de la Santa Cruz. The Tecpan is now a museum that exhibits murals by David Alfaro Siqueiros. The Tecpan, because of its indigenous name and the style of its construction, is probably the first mestizo work to be built in Mexico City.

XIX Century

The gardens and orchards of Tecpan and the Colegio de la Santa Cruz were converted into an urban garden at the end of the colonial era: the Santiago Tlatelolco garden, which years later was incorporated into the design of the Nonoalco-Tlatelolco Urban Complex.
In the 19th century, the Tlatelolco area was home to families living in extreme poverty.
Between 1855 and the middle of the 20th century, the Santiago Tlatelolco prison was established in the Colegio de la Santa Cruz, which had 322 inmates. A military barracks was also installed. During this period, the neighborhood was crossed by the railroad and the Buenavista station and the customs house were built there. The church was used as a warehouse for the National Railroads until 1948 when it reopened its doors as a Catholic compound. Although some institutions closed during the Revolution (1910-1920), the prison endured and even housed notable people, among them Pancho Villa (Alfaro and García 1987, cited in Toscana & Aparicio 2018).

Modern Mexico

Mexico's modern era, located between 1920 and the mid-1980s, is manifested in the Adolfo López Mateos Nonoalco-Tlatelolco Urban Complex (known as Tlatelolco), built during the six-year term of President Adolfo López Mateos (1958 and 1964), framed in the social housing policy developed since the 1930s, which sought to solve the problem of lack of low-income housing and the growth of irregular settlements, already registered since then. It is one of the urban complexes (housing units) of the architect Mario Pani that sought, through its design, to modernize the city, under the inspiration of the French architect Le Corbusier and the principles of the Athens Charter (Toscana & Aparicio 2018).

Ciudad de México

In Latin America it was the largest housing project of the time, almost an autonomous city within Mexico City, of 76.86 ha, a functionalist mega construction of 12,004 apartments contained in 102 buildings of 4, 7, 8, 14, and 22 floors, to house approximately 78 thousand people; the project included green areas and walkways, 600 stores (currently grocery stores, chicken shops, locksmiths, beauticians, laundries, dental clinics, veterinary clinics, restaurants, among other businesses), 21 schools, six health units and hospitals, three sports centers, three theaters, a movie theater and six parking lots; all this arranged in three sections: La Independencia, La Reforma and La República, surrounded by important avenues that guarantee its connectivity: to the north by Eje 2 Norte, to the south by Av. Ricardo Flores Magón; to the east by Paseo de la Reforma; and to the west by Insurgentes. It also housed the Foreign Relations tower, now occupied by the Tlatelolco University Cultural Center, and the Banobras Tower, flagship of the complex, almost 130 meters high, which housed the offices of the Banco Hipotecario Nacional and Public Works, a building very different from the others due to its peculiar triangular shape, distinctive of Nonoalco-Tlatelolco (Toscana & Aparicio 2018).
Designed to contribute to the abatement of the housing and overcrowding problem that had already existed in the City since then, due to the population growth both natural and by migration from the countryside as a result of the industrialization policy of the City, the apartments were intended for professionals and state workers, an 'enlightened' middle class composed of engineers, lawyers, teachers, doctors, artists, secretaries, journalists and federal employees (Toscana & Aparicio 2018). But in addition, it sought to improve the quality of life of the population, so the Conjunto had a wide diversity of services, and represented a renewed urban culture that would remain in force in the country for several more years (Toscana & Aparicio 2018).
In the architectural discussion of the time, in more developed countries, these urban complexes or large-scale housing units were spoken of as the solution to various problems; Mexico then, copied the model and implemented it in the central area of the capital. What was new in this complex was the "different man-

agement of the modular blocks that recomposed the architectural image" (Toscana & Aparicio 2018), which would be built on inhospitable land populated by tenements and slums and other constructions that evidenced the poverty and misery of the city's population, population that was relocated to make way for families of the country's working middle class and thus achieve 'urban regeneration' (although some small buildings were destined for families of minimum wage workers and others for workers with a higher socioeconomic level, these were located on the Paseo de la Reforma, the most elegant avenue in the city). Of the 50 thousand people who inhabited these lands, the 'horseshoe of slums', who were supposed to occupy the new apartments, only a few did so, since they did not have sufficient economic income, which is why they were displaced to Iztapalapa, one of the cheap, distant and inhospitable peripheries of that time.

The 'horseshoe of slums', according to Pani, prevented the healthy growth of the city, the miserable and overcrowded living conditions, would give way to a modern urban macro complex with green areas and services for the population, and with a higher housing density that would allow to accommodate many more families that at the same time would enjoy urban services, green areas and recreation.

In this Urban Complex, Mario Pani managed to rescue and integrate pre-existing elements into the landscape and in combination with the modernity of the residential buildings, gave rise to the unique Plaza de las Tres Culturas, the most distinctive feature of Tlatelolco's landscape and one of Mexico City's tourist attractions. As in models of housing units proposed by Le Corbusier, the idea was to articulate the area so that it would function as an independent organism of the city based on the possibility of uses offered by the buildings:

> 102 buildings to house 11,916 apartments for 70,000 inhabitants.
> More than 600 commercial premises.
> A supermarket and a shopping plaza (the mercantile center).
> 19 schools and 13 kindergartens.
> A technical secondary school and a high school.

An archaeological zone.
A church.
Three social clubs, one per housing unit.
Three medical clinics.
A movie theater.
And the subway station built in 1970.

The urban complex has been the protagonist of relevant events both for the country and for the City, which are considered fundamental for the emergence of civil society in Mexico and for the transition from a single-party political system to a multi-party system committed to democracy: the student movement of '68, as the Plaza de las Tres Culturas was the scene of the massacre of civilians at the hands of the police and the army, which ended the movement; and the 1985 earthquakes, as Tlatelolco was one of the most devastated places, the Nuevo León building, collapsed, and with it one of the symbols of modernity, development and prosperity of Mexico City was cracking (Toscana & Aparicio 2018).

During the reconstruction, this urban group was also important, since before the earthquakes there were neighborhood organizations that gave rise to the Coordinadora Única de Damnificados (CUD), an organization that achieved the reconstruction of more than 80 thousand collapsed or damaged houses in situ, This organization avoided massive relocations to the peripheries of the city, as usually happens in cases of disaster, and later to the Asamblea de Barrios (AB), an organization that inherited the political and social capital of the CUD and continued the struggle for housing in Mexico City for several more years, becoming until today a political-electoral force of the left with considerable weight.

In spite of the neighborhood strength in this reconstruction process, many families abandoned Tlatelolco after the earthquake, the price of the apartments depreciated, although the buildings were repaired, a wave of fear surrounded Tlatelolco and families with lower incomes and other socioeconomic profiles joined the unit, attracted by the offer and the magnificent location of the complex.

Urban complexes of this type stopped being built. In addition, the economic crisis and the change in the economic development model of the 1980s also contributed to the end of this social housing model.

Contemporary Mexico

Currently the landscape of Tlatelolco shows signs of deterioration, for example, the movie theater, which once transmitted high quality films, closed its doors more than 15 years ago, when it went bankrupt, and now a group of homeless people live in it.
The economic crisis, social breakdown and delinquency have left their mark on the bars that can be seen in all the windows of the first floor apartments. The expression of the youth gangs can be seen in the graffiti on the walls of the buildings. Street hawkers and beggars are colonizing the exit of the Tlatelolco subway station. However, in an attempt to reverse the deterioration, a cultural center has been installed in the former Foreign Relations building in an attempt, since 2007, to revitalize the area and give options to young people to keep them away from vices: Centro Cultural Universitario Tlatelolco is a multidisciplinary complex dedicated to research, study, analysis and dissemination of topics related to art, history and resistance processes. It promotes the cultural formation of the immediate community, university students and the general public, conceived as agents of participatory interaction with the National Autonomous University of Mexico. There are neighborhood projects that also promote community life, for example a herbal garden in the third section and a composting workshop in the second section.
The area is currently undergoing a revitalization process as part of the renewal process of the city center; it is no longer the northern edge of the city nor the limit that housed the poorest and most marginalized sectors, now its position is central and very advantageous: two of the city's main avenues surround it, Insurgentes and Reforma, it has a subway station and three Metrobus stations, which guarantee its connectivity and all kinds of services.

2. The transformation of modern public space, from the industrial city to the global city.

For Duahu and Giglia, one of the main themes of the current debate on the contemporary city – also known as the global city, megalopolis or megacity – is the evolution experienced by urban public spaces during the last decades of the 20th century and so far in the present.

We speak of the crisis of public space, a topic that various scholars have raised from the perspective of a clear decline in the quality of urban life.

When speaking of the crisis of public space, Duahu and Giglia warn that it evokes the ghost of urban disintegration, the impossibility of 'living together' in large cities and the dissolution of the urban as a place for meeting and exchange.

The authors suggest that there is a model or ideal type of modern public space that operates as an explicit or implicit reference point for the contemporary debate on the so-called 'crisis of public space'.

Public space as a social fact and as an ideal type

In order to speak of an ideal type of public space, the authors propose the existence of a set of attributes characteristic of public spaces in the modern city, which are listed below:

1. Spaces assigned to the use of all, i.e., not reserved for anyone in particular, whether specific individuals or belonging to a certain category, social status or class.
2. Of free access – unrestricted, as in the case of parks and public streets, or subject to the satisfaction of certain conditions, such as the payment of an entrance fee (stadiums, theaters, cinemas),
3. Where the co-presence of strangers is admitted and, consequently, each and every one of the co-presenters legitimately enjoys anonymity, that is, the fact of being one more among a conglomerate of individuals who remain together in a place or pass through it at the same time for circumstantial reasons, reasons that only concern each one of them;

4. Where the condition of equality prevails in the sense that everyone has the right to be present and to be respected in their integrity, intimacy and anonymity, regardless of their individual characteristics, including age, sex, ethnicity, appearance, etc., and that,
5. They function as places where the city-dweller realizes the experience of coexisting peacefully and equally with the different others and is in the predisposition to enjoy the eventual encounter with a stranger or the occurrence of the unexpected (Duahu and Giglia).

In order to make the existence of public spaces with these characteristics possible, a series of conditions characteristic of modern society and the modern city were required:

1. Equality of basic civil rights, guaranteed by a public power that holds the monopoly of physical violence on behalf of all;
2. The elimination of rights attributed exclusively to certain groups (e.g., statal rights);
3. The constitution of a set of urban goods and spaces legally assigned to the use of all (urban furniture, streets, parks, squares, promenades, means of transport) (Sabatier, 2002), and
4. The diffusion of establishments and premises intended to serve an anonymous public (stores, restaurants, coffees, movie theaters, stadiums, etc.).

From my point of view, the Nonoalco Tlatelolco urban complex was built considering the ideal modern vision of public space previously stated.
The housing unit was built and administered at the time by Mexican state institutions. It was presented as an integrating and organizing project of urban social relations with the purpose of providing basic and equal civil rights to a determined group of citizens.
In its ideal conception, there is no intention of attributing certain rights exclusively to certain groups, not even to its inhabitants, since the spaces of the Unit can be accessed by any person.
In the Unit there are urban goods and spaces legally assigned to the use of all and establishments and premises intended to serve

an anonymous public: schools, stores, clinics, theaters, gardens, squares, museums, restaurants, Metro station, urban furniture, etc.

Regarding the proposed characteristics of the ideal modern public space proposed by Duahu and Giglia, I identify the following in a general way and from the perspective of the original design:

> 1. The spaces of the Housing Unit were intended for the use of all its inhabitants and any person who is not an inhabitant of the same.
> 2. The housing unit was built in a manner open to the public, without doors or customs that would impede free transit in the area.
> 3. In its gardens, corridors and diverse spaces, as well as in the Plaza de las Tres Culturas, the residents of the Unit meet on a daily basis, but also people who do not live there: tourists, diverse visitors, cyclists, sports groups, service providers, public servants, etc. In addition, due to its historical character, the Plaza is a meeting point for members of various collectives and social movements that participate in protests and political commemorations.
> 4. Although the inhabitants of the Unidad are not strangers to each other, it is possible to affirm that for those of us who are not residents, it is possible to go to its spaces and meet strangers while legitimately enjoying anonymity.
> 5. All people have the right to access the gardens, facilities and the Plaza. In these spaces we are respected regardless of our individual characteristics.
> 6. In the public spaces of Tlatelolco in general and in a suitable way, it is possible to coexist peacefully and equally with others and it is possible to meet strangers.

Now, for Duauh and Giglia, the question of the legal status of public space is fundamental:

We refer to the gradual constitution of a sphere or domain of the urban public as a set of legally public spaces, that is, freely accessible, under the jurisdiction of the public power and consecrated to the use of all (Sabatier, 2002) and, along with it, the conformation of what we can call an urban regulatory order (Duhau and Giglia, 2004), as a set of formal regulations for that domain, which involved codifying and regulating the legitimate uses of public spaces, which implied establishing schedules, separating functions and, in many cases, simply prohibiting certain uses or activities in certain places, either by confining them to other spaces or simply eliminating them.

Public space, although we like to think of it as an open and free space, is marked in its essence not only by the question of the coexistence of heterogeneous subjects but also by the question of common rules and the common acceptance of rules, whether explicit or implicit, formal or informal, rigid or flexible.

In this sense, one of the most important contributions of Duahu and Giglia (2004) to sociological studies of Mexico City is the perspective of urban order:

The argumentation and illustration of the conflicts that arise around space and that are characteristic of different urban contexts are supported by the concept of urban order, understanding it as the set of norms and rules both formal (belonging to some hierarchy of the legal order) and conventional to which the inhabitants of the city explicitly or tacitly resort in the development of practices related to the uses and forms of appropriation of public or collective use spaces and goods that, beyond housing, are the constituent elements of the city.

According to the authors' research, in Mexico City we find a set of historical forms of production that have coexisted and combined in the urban space and currently give rise to four 'cities', that is, as many urban contexts that, among other factors, are differentiated from each other by the type of conflict that appears as dominant in each of them with respect to space.

The urban spaces from which the growth of Mexico City was structured and the processes of conurbation took place correspond to different urban models, that is to say, to various ways of designing and organizing urbanized space, among which the following stand out:

(i) Iberian urban planning, which was formalized in the Laws of the Indies and defined an urban fabric organized by means of a checkerboard layout and a centrality defined by the seat of political and religious power. The Historic Center of Mexico City and the original layout of colonial towns such as Coyoacán, Tlalpan and Azcapotzalco, among others, correspond to it.

(ii) Modern urbanism, whose paradigmatic examples in the world include the Haussmannian reconstruction of Paris and the expansion of Barcelona. This is an urbanism that produced the city from public space and organized the urban fabric through the hierarchization of public roads, the relationship between their width, the characteristics and height of buildings, and the centralities defined by commercial corridors, parks and squares. This form corresponds in the case of the ZMCM to a significant part of the neighborhoods currently located in the four central delegations of the Federal District.

These first two forms of urbanism converge today in the conformation of the same type of urban context that the authors define as the 'city of contested space', taking into account the type of conflicts that predominate there.

(iii) The third urban model corresponds to that of the rural settlement and to those nuclei that in Mexico City have preserved the denomination of 'barrios' or 'pueblos' and that originated in the colonial traces of the old villas (for example, the neighborhood of La Conchita, the Quadrant of San Francisco and Los Reyes, in Coyoacán). These are settlements in which the relevant public spaces are usually limited to the church and its atrium and the street where the market is located. Originating as housing groups and not having been destined to the performance of urban functions or to the representation of an idea of the urban but of a community organized around worship, they present an irregular layout, and their circulation spaces are generally reduced to narrow alleys.

On the other hand, with the exception of the incorporation of old nuclei that were conurbations and that present the structure of the traditional rural town or of the villa or autonomous urban unit, since the fifties the growth of Mexico City has adopted three major modalities:

I. Suburban developments or subdivisions, which respond to what we could call the 'classic' model of the residential suburb in that they are functionally dependent on the central city;
II. The social interest housing developments; and
III. Popular neighborhoods.

Suburban developments intended primarily for the middle classes and sometimes for the upper class can be defined as 'classic' because they are developments that are presented as an alternative for access to home ownership in a context that is positively qualified precisely because it is suburban and residential. The paradigmatic case, for being the first in time, is surely Ciudad Satélite in the municipality of Naucalpan.

Suburban urbanism breaks with modern urbanism by producing the city from a residential fabric where public space is defined fundamentally as the setting for housing to the extent that its functions are reduced to circulation and its surroundings are not expected to be disturbed by other non-residential urban functions and activities, which, when permitted, are concentrated in areas designated for this purpose.

The second modality, the housing complex, whose diffusion responds to the constitution of the housing solidarity funds in the seventies, although not its first examples, presents a logic of peripheral location that responds to the lowering of costs through the acquisition of cheap land and the exploitation of economies of scale. In general, such complexes were designed as self-contained spaces, clearly separated and differentiated from the adjacent urban fabric, existing or future. In this modality we find the Unidad Habitacional Nonoalco-Tlaltelolco, which was built with public funds in the 1960s, as we have seen, in a peripheral area of that time – today it is a central area of the city – with an open perspective and integrated to the surroundings. Tlatelolco was understood at the time as a city within the city.

The third modality, that of popular urbanism, corresponds to the city produced from housing and basic services by means of what we usually call 'popular urbanization', based on the production of cheap lots for self-built single-family housing and, in most cases, in conditions of legal irregularity. These are urban spaces whose structure responds to the search for a maximum use of land for the production of housing lots.

It is obvious that as time goes by, other uses are incorporated, which tends to transform these spaces to some extent into areas where residential uses coexist with commercial and service uses.

In order to understand the current problems of the Unidad Habitacional Nonoalco-Tlaltelolco, I take Duahu and Giglia's description of what they consider to be the city of collectivized space.

This urban order corresponds to the housing developments that are predominantly, although not exclusively, of social interest. The character of these depends on their scale and not only on the fact that they are organized in condominium form. In other words, the morphology and urban insertion of an apartment building in an urban context where different urban activities and various housing typologies coexist is totally different from the characteristics and problems of housing complexes. The latter result from the agglomeration of a significant number of multi-story buildings or duplex houses that repeat a single housing type or a very limited number of them and whose spatial and architectural configuration – in most cases framed by a perimeter wall – ostensibly breaks the continuity of the surrounding urban fabric.

This 'city of collectivized space', projected according to the perspective of a naïve functionalism, has been imagined as a self-managed urban space of communal appropriation of the goods and spaces shared by a collective made up of a supposed community of residents. It is an urban context in which the relationship between the private and the public is marked by the difficulties to identify and establish a differentiated management for private family goods, private collective goods (collective property of the residents) and public goods (belonging to the domain of the city).

It can be considered as a sui generis urbanity that we can call 'induced collectivization'.

The authors refer to some of the problems associated with neighborhood management and collective goods in these spaces:

a. The social interest housing complexes and units built between the 1970s and the mid-1990s, and the 'urban complexes' that have come to replace them in recent years, have been conceived, when their scale permits, to function as independent and self-contained urban units, and therefore imply a frank rupture with the surrounding urban fabric, current or future.
b. The considerable number of dwellings goes hand in hand with public spaces, facilities and infrastructures whose amount is more or less proportional, together with the fact that these are not traditional urban spaces where the distinction between private and public domain, and between private and public space is generally unambiguous, fundamentally determines the resulting problems.
c. In the context defined by the housing complex, its inhabitants are faced with the need to make decisions, contribute resources and agree on the management of spaces, goods and services that, except in gated communities under condominium regime for high-income population, usually belong to the public domain or are part of the obligations and costs of condominium housing. Hence, they tend to become the object of endemic disputes, from the use and maintenance of green areas and recreational spaces, to the question of surveillance, security and the places where the presence of the preventive police will be accepted, to the supply of basic services such as water and gas, and give rise to a multiplicity of perverse effects.

In the case of Tlatelolco, the administration of shared spaces was initially carried out by state institutions and was modified over the years. A direct impact of the establishment of state reform in Mexico since the 1990s is that the government initiated a very important privatization process. In the case of In Tlatelolco, the inhabitants took over the administration of the spaces, which has generated several conflicts typical of the management of collective goods.

In these cases, as the complex is a privately owned space, the delegations and nowadays the mayor's offices cannot intervene in the maintenance and surveillance of these spaces. It is possible to observe that over the years there has been an important process of deterioration in the Unit.

Notwithstanding the above, it is possible today to observe diverse efforts of organized inhabitants of the Unit to rescue and maintain the collective spaces where we observe new uses and daily practices that we will see below.

For Duauh and Giglia, the issue of 'large complexes' is not exclusive to Mexico or Mexico City. In France they have been and are the object of specific programs, they are a priority on the urban agenda and have given rise to the production of a vast literature, both academic and journalistic, and in some cases to solutions as definitive as demolition. But in any case it is important to emphasize that unlike in Mexico, where social housing developments are owned by the agencies that manage them as rental housing stock, social housing in Mexico is acquired, in principle, as property, and for that very reason the management of the developments as urban spaces is not, despite what many of their inhabitants assume to the contrary, the responsibility of the agencies and companies that finance, promote and build them.

3. Places of civic memory and new daily practices in the public space after the COVID-19 pandemic.

Architectural memory

In 1924 Mexican architects began to study the possibilities of serial construction. The functionalist theories proclaimed by the modern movement in architecture in France and Germany sustained as a fundamental principle of the creative process the idea of form derived from function [...] that is, from human behavior within the space, determines the form of the architectural structure (Graciela de Garay, Modernidad habitada: multifamiliar Miguel Alemán. Mexico City, 1949-1999, Instituto Mora, 2004: 15.).

During the early 1930s, Le Corbusier presented a new version of his ideal city in his plan for the Ville Radieuse (radiant city):

> [...] it was a centralized and densely populated proposal, although most of its surface area was granted to areas for leisure and relaxation:

parks, playgrounds, sports, entertainment. Based on his early theories, Le Corbusier also included wide roads to facilitate traffic circulation, whether between the countryside and the city or between different parts of the city, although he reserved for pedestrians roads separated from automobiles; in this way, the traditional street disappeared. Likewise, as in the utopian Renaissance plans, social order was expressed through symmetry and symbolic geometry. Even an anthropomorphic image, composed of thorn, arms, heart and head, implicitly organized the whole complex.

The Nonoalco Tlatelolco Urban Complex, inaugurated on November 21, 1964 by President Adolfo López Mateos, was the most ambitious work ever built by the Mexican government; for its design, unique in Latin America, the architect Mario Pani Darqui was commissioned, under the influence of utopian ideas and views of European architectural modernity that envisioned new types of habitat. This implied introducing verticality as a symbol of modernity, together with the creation of urban centers of great demographic density, in order to solve the important challenges implied by the accelerated development and expansion of large urban concentrations.

Thus, the Nonoalco-Tlatelolco space was destined to the 'general regeneration process' unleashed during the six-year term of López Mateos.

The Unidad Habitacional was conceived as a 'pilot' project; it was the starting point for a more ambitious plan aimed at the total regeneration of Mexico City. In the words of President Adolfo López Mateos, the complex represented 'a peaceful revolution', as it avoided a violent revolution. The design of the unit was influenced by the political project of the Mexican State at the time and it was decided to divide the housing unit into three sections, as a symbol of three transcendental stages in national history, thus identifying the historical project of the present with the past: Independence, Reform and Revolution.

In the inaugural speech of the housing unit, Guillermo H. Viramontes, general director of the Banco Nacional Hipotecario

Urbano y de Obras Públicas (Banobras) said: "443 years later, you (President López Mateos) give new life to Tlatelolco by putting into service this imposing city erected within the great capital, next to the same venerable stones of our ancestors, exalting the dignity and heroism of our race".[2]

The design of Tlatelolco found the legitimate expression of a way of living and seeing the world in the 1970s, taking shape in both material life and ideas. The central area of Mexico City, considered by the government as a place of 'slums', deteriorated and unhealthy, was transformed into green spaces that constituted the backbone of the new complex, in order to lead a hygienic life in a more pleasant environment. The modern discourse involved in the construction of Tlatelolco maintained a complex coexistence with the cultural heritage of the archaeological zone and historic buildings.

The Plaza of the Three Cultures, resistance, tragedy and protest

Pierre Nora defines the place of memory as that where 'memory crystallizes and takes refuge'; they are those places where the exhausted capital of collective memory is anchored, condensed and expressed (Nora 1989).

The Plaza de las 3 Culturas is to be considered as a place of the Mexican collective memory. De Alba considers that the initial message with which it was built -tradition and modernity- has been practically forgotten and it is currently a symbolic space that recalls the struggle for the democratization of the country.

The historical events that give new meaning to this space are the massacre of students on October 2, 1968 and the earthquake of September 19, 1985. Both events, tragic situations that precede the loss of strength of the then PRI as the country's hegemonic party.

In 1968 an enormous student protest arose in Mexico City against the government of Gustavo Díaz Ordaz (of the Institutional Revolutionary Party, PRI) whose main axis was anti-authoritar-

---

[2] See: *El Nacional*, November 22, 1964: 8.

ianism and whose central demands were the fulfillment of the Constitution, the end of government repression, the punishment of those responsible, compensation for the families of the dead and wounded, freedom for political prisoners and the demand for dialogue. Marches, rallies and meetings were at the center of the movement and the government's response was repression. Although not all scholars agree, many consider that, although the movement continued until December 6, 1968, its splendor was experienced between August and September. And almost all agree with the idea that October 2 would have meant its end, due to the notable decrease in popular participation (Aguayo 1998; Montemayor 2000). The movement is given a relevant weight in the process of democratization of society and the Mexican State.

At the end of the 1960s, the Unidad Habitacional was one of the most important bastions of the student movement, after the universities and educational centers (Álvarez 1998; Monsiváis 1999; Rodríguez, 2003); in addition, the Plaza de las Tres Culturas was also the scene of the greatest military repression against the peaceful demonstration organized by the students on October 2.

When talking about Tlatelolco, invariably comes to mind the Student Movement of 1968, an event whose memory permeates the Plaza de las Tres Culturas. This movement is one of the most recounted episodes in the recent history of the country and especially of Mexico City. The most visible moment within the movement is October 2, 1968, precisely in the Plaza de las Tres Culturas, where a crossfire killed many demonstrators and the movement was repressed.

The 1968 movement has been described as a turning point between the miracle of the mid-twentieth century and a period of generalized crisis in the last decades of the twentieth century and the first decades of the twenty-first; it has also been interpreted as the beginning of the end of PRI hegemony, the heroic birth of a new left, and the beginning of a prolonged transition to electoral democracy, it has also been interpreted as an instance of anagnorisis, when those who witnessed the repressive events that October 2 in the Plaza de las Tres Culturas, "realized the extensive magnitude of the dark side of the Mexican miracle" (Walker 2014: 71). But the fruits of the movement can only be appreciated as the years go by, as well as the official recognition of the victims of the massacre and the repression, which are reflected in the landscape in the 68 memorial in the Plaza (1993) and the Cultural Center (open to the public since 2007). The movement has been the subject of study and debate and artistic works, and thanks to this it has been possible to keep it in memory and easily link it to the landscape through photographs and films of the October 2 rally in the Plaza de las Tres Culturas that have circulated in various spheres over the last decades.

Years later, Tlatelolco would again gain visibility due to another tragedy. The 1985 earthquake, which is the largest disaster associated with a natural phenomenon in the city. Several buildings were damaged and subsequently had to be demolished. But the greatest damage was the collapse of the Nuevo Leon building, which was attributed to the lack of maintenance to be provided by the State, in its place there is today a small square with a sundial that marks the time when the earthquake happened (7:19 AM). Nearly 500 corpses were recovered from the rubble of the building, of which only 189 were identified; no one claimed the rest, since entire families perished. Next to the clock there is a memorial to the victims and a bust in honor of the participation of the tenor Placido Domingo in the search and rescue efforts.

The unveiling of the Stela was impressive: "on October 2 [1993] thousands of comrades attended the march and rally; a huge piece of construction paper with the V for victory and the slogan 'October 2 is not forgotten' covered the Stela and was torn by the girls of '68 [...]. Dozens of comrades witnessed the act. The people who arrived at the Stela formed a cordon and made sure that no one climbed onto the platform of the stele. The night appeared and a white light emerged from the ground floor to illuminate the Stela and ascend to the sky; a feeling of respect and admiration flooded the atmosphere; while the insufferable speeches went on, the stairs of the base platform were filled with flowers and the Stela became an altar" (Aquino 1998: 305-306).

From that day on, the Estela became part of the landscape of Tlatelolco and the neighbors adopted it. In addition, it became a refuge for those who had participated in the movement and for the members of the 686 Committee (Allier Montaño 2015). Since the beginning of the 21st century, the Estela de Tlatelolco became a space where former leaders of the student movement regularly went to talk about their experiences.

De Alba discovers in an investigation that the emotions expressed in front of a photo of the Plaza are sadness, indignation and anger against an authoritarian and rigid government, which preferred repression to dialogue. He emphatically assures that the rest of the meanings given to that site occupy a minor place compared to those two recent events. Classifying the events of 1968 and 1985 under the heading 'history', 85% of those interviewed have such a relationship with the Plaza de las Tres Culturas (39% affective; 22% a personal relationship; 15% political; 4% national identity). In synthesis, Tlatelolco signifies two historical dates: October 2, 1968 and September 19, 1985, two tragedies, two wounds in Mexico City society. It should be noted that the memories of 1985 have now been linked to those of the 2017 earthquake that, by a tragic coincidence, also occurred on September 19 (Allier Montaño 2018).

Starting in the 21st Century, Tlatelolco has also become a third space of protest. On the one hand, traditionally leftist movements have protested and become visible in Mexico's main square, the Zócalo. And movements identified with the right, the National Action Party and the higher income sectors meet to protest or commemorate at the Angel of Independence.

In recent years, a third place has become a space of memory and denunciation: the Plaza de las Tres Culturas. It is impossible to say when it happened, but what is certain is that this Plaza, in Tlatelolco, has been transformed into a place that appeals to denunciation. After the massacre of October 2, 1968, the memory linked to Tlatelolco is a memory of denunciation. It is a memory that evidences the wound left by an excessive state violence, which is linked to the demands for justice and clarification (Allier Montaño 2015). And so, the Plaza de las Tres Culturas no longer serves only to denounce the repression committed in 1968 against students and citizens, but also provides a space for the imputation of any injustice, this without referring directly to October 2. Three examples.

a) In 1987, during the mobilizations of the University Student Council (CEU) against the increase of fees at the University.
b) In 2012, in the midst of the #Yosoy132 mobilization, students held a demonstration starting from Tlatelolco. Let's remember that the student movement of 2012 had as its origin a protest against the then presidential candidate, Enrique Peña Nieto, at the Universidad Iberoamericana, for his action and omission in the case of police violence against the people of Atenco, in 2006. On June 30, 2012, the students organized the march 'En Vela por la Democracia' (*In Candle for Democracy*) to continue with their demand for democracy and national reconstruction. The students had called for a meeting at 6 p.m., a symbolic moment close to the beginning of the shooting in 1968. The contingent left Tla- telolco towards Televisa, and then concluded their march in the Zócalo.
c) In 2016, a protest was also held in the Plaza by people attacked in the events of Nochixtlán, Oaxaca.

4. Public space of encounter and inclusion versus the insular city of today's global mercantilism.

Contemporary concerns about the privatization, segregation, deterioration and even disappearance of public spaces are undoubtedly marked by the contrast between the ideal public space of the modern city and the way in which these spaces have evolved in reality.

Until the mid-twentieth century, legally public space was practically all urban space, with the exception of housing and other private premises. Since then, and with the changes in production and commercial processes that gave rise to the globalization process, we find various impacts on it.

A fundamental phenomenon described by Duahu and Giglia in their research is that there is a dissociation between the legally public space and the practices of daily life, in the sense that the latter, in metropolises such as Mexico City and, above all, for the middle and upper classes, have less and less to do with the legally public space...that is to say that the current experience of a good part of the inhabitants of the metropolis is not carried out in public spaces of this nature.

To explain this phenomenon, the authors state that the ideal modern public space implied that people came and went to a great extent on foot between private premises and public spaces, a fundamental change is that today the coming and going is done using the automobile.

Jane Jacobs (1992) taught us that the use of public spaces depends to a large extent on the presence and mix of premises surrounding them and the corresponding activities associated with such premises: residence, offices, stores, workshops, restaurants, bars, public offices, markets, etc. To the extent that a good part of these premises and activities make up spaces of private domain but of public use, and that the very use of legally public spaces depends then in varying degrees on premises that are private but of public use, the animation and variety of the uses of public spaces has always depended to a large extent on the activities to which the adjoining private premises and spaces are destined. The uses of private spaces and their accessibility constitute an important element in understanding the nature of public space.

The analysis of the transformations in the forms of linkage between public and private spaces makes it possible to account for the so-called crisis of public space today.

A first meaning of the process of privatization of public spaces refers to the proliferation of facilities intended for public use but statutorily privately owned and, therefore, subject in principle to purposes, uses and rules of behavior defined and assigned by their owners. The clearest example of this type of facilities are shopping malls and the so-called 'recreational' or 'theme parks'. The idea of privatization in these cases refers to the fact that they concentrate in an area under private control activities – shopping, strolling, having a coffee, attending a show, going to the movies, eating in a restaurant – that traditionally – or rather, in the modern city- are linked to the use of legally public spaces.

With globalization, the city has evolved and what was once public space as the organizer of the city is now a set of spaces for automobile circulation between two points, from the home to the workplace or from the home to the shopping center. In this case, the researchers provide important evidence of how the city's inhabitants are increasingly turning to private spaces for public use, specifically shopping malls.

The shopping mall is a place to go to, to enter and to leave, and where the entrances and exits are conceived as barriers where, at least potentially, a control of the public-clientele takes place.

A second meaning of the idea of privatization of public spaces is that of closure, closure, surveillance and private control of legally public spaces. In many Latin American cities (Cabrales Barajas 2002), including of course Mexico City, it has become very common for neighborhood organizations to close and control access to streets in areas where residential use dominates and where, therefore, vehicular traffic is diverted to a main road. In these cases, the argument commonly put forward is 'safety'.

A third meaning refers to the appropriation or control exercised by specific groups over places in which, although they remain physically open and formally continue to be public, the degrees of openness, freedom of circulation, congregation of a socially heterogeneous public and diversity of uses are limited as they are appropriated for different forms of private use (Da Costa Gomes 2001). This occurs in some main modalities. One of them consists in the appropriation of public spaces for the development of the informal economy: street vendors, car caretakers, service providers, etc.

The fourth meaning corresponds to the production and organization of proximity or local space, at different scales, as a private habitat, whose use is restricted to residents. Large sectors of the middle and upper classes self-segregate through closed residential enclaves, incorporating consumer and recreational equipment for the exclusive use of the residents of these enclaves.

The first and most evident effect of the closed habitat consists in the elimination of the space of proximity as public space and of the set of goods for collective use as public goods. This fundamental fact is related to a set of effects in each case.

First, the larger the scale, the more the enclosed habitat, given its introspective character, separates itself from the surrounding environment.

Secondly, this separation implies that connectivity and accessibility become central issues that displace interest in what is found in the immediate vicinity; to the extent that the condominium, complex or gated development self-produces its own environment, it can dispense with the immediate exterior.

Thirdly, the management of the habitat becomes independent of local and urban management, except for the link with the general infrastructure.

Finally, the closed habitat by definition breaks the continuity of the urban fabric and, consequently, of the circulation routes, or simply lacks spatial links with the urban fabric.

It is worth remembering at this point that the ideal type of public space in the modern city is based on a set of urban spaces and artifacts under the domain of public power and assigned for the use of all. Spaces that developed in association with the economic and social functions of the state.

References

Aguayo S., *Myths and (mis)perceptions: Changing U.S. Elite Visions of Mexico*, Lynne Rienner, 2000.

Allier-Montaño E. – Crenzel E. (eds.), *The Struggle for Memory in Latin America. Recent History and Political Violence*, Palgrave Macmillan, 2015.

Cabrales Barajas L. F., *Latinoamérica. Países abiertos, ciudades cerradas*, Universidad de Guadalajara : Organización de las Naciones Unidas para la Educación, Ciencia y Cultura (UNESCO), 2002.

Duhau E. – Giglia Á., "Espacio público y nuevas centralidades. Dimensión local y urbanidad en lascolonias populares de laCiudad de México", *Papeles de Población*, 10/41, 2004: 167-194.

Jacobs J., *The Death and Life of Great American Cities*, Reissue, 1992.

Nora P., "Between Memory and History: Les Lieux de Mémoire", *Representations* 26, 1989: 7–24.

Toscana Aparicio A., et al., *Estudios de la Ciudad de México y su Constitución*, Universidad Autónoma de México 2018.

Walker L. E., *Waking from the Dream. Mexico's Middle Classes after 1968*, Stanford University Press, 2014.

Lecture n. 4

GEOPOLITICS
Mexico in Latin America Today
The Principle of Non-intervention Meets Democratic Backsliding

Prof. Víctor Hernández-Huerta –
Centro de Investigación
y Docencia Económicas (CIDE), Mexico City

At the closure of a unipolar order of world power, characterized by the near hegemony of the United States, we witness the rising of a multipolar world. In the Americas, there are two competing projects of regional integration: Pan-Americanism, led by the United States (U.S.), with the Organization of American States (OAS) as its core institution; and an opposing project of Latin Americanism with a strong emphasis on the sovereignty of Latin American countries, which has recently been supported by the Venezuelan government with the creation of new supranational organizations such as the Bolivarian Alliance for the Americas (ALBA, by its Spanish acronym) and the Community of Latin American and Caribbean States (CELAC, by its Spanish acronym).

In this period of realignment, the government of López Obrador has pushed, at least in its discourse, for the strengthening of Latin Americanism, and particularly of the CELAC, and has also called to put an end to U.S. interventionism. However, López Obrador is a pragmatist who knows that the anti-imperialist discourse has its limits and that the U.S. is not only Mexico's neighbor but also its main trading partner. In practice, López Obrador has been a close collaborator of the U.S., particularly during the Trump era. López Obrador bowed to Trump's demands to contain the mass movement of migrants traveling through the country toward the U.S. border and has *de facto* converted Mexico into "Trump's wall" by using Mexico's National Guard military police to violently repress and contain Central American immigrants. Another example of how López Obrador became Trump's close ally is how in the aftermath of the latter's defeat in the 2020 presidential election, López Obrador condemned Twitter and Facebook for blocking Trump's account when he was falsely claiming election fraud. Later on, López Obrador refused to condemn the assault by Trump supporters on the U.S. Capitol, citing his policy of not interfering in other countries' affairs. López Obrador, together with Vladimir Putin, was one of the last world leaders to acknowledge Biden's victory.

This paradoxical behavior of denouncing U.S. interventionism and supporting the CELAC, on the one hand, but simultaneously becoming Trump's close ally, on the other, can be better understood if we think of López Obrador's foreign policy as an attempt to support fellow authoritarian governments by making selective use of the principle of non-intervention. López Obrador's efforts to replace the OAS, based in Washington D.C., with the CELAC, a regional organization that excludes Canada and the U.S., can be read in the context of the OAS's policy of condemning authoritarian governments, denouncing fraudulent elections in the region, and several failed attempts to apply the Inter-American Democratic Charter against Venezuela – measures that the Mexican administration has opposed. The Mexican government has had clear disagreements with the OAS, and its Secretary-General Luis Almagro, as in the case of the Bolivian crisis of 2020. Mexico frequently cites its policy of not interfering in other countries' affairs when it comes to taking a stand against authoritarian governments, but openly supports fully authoritarian leaders. On the same weekend, Mexico received Nicolás Maduro as a speaker at the CELAC regional summit, causing a clash with Uruguay, Paraguay, and Colombia. Two days earlier, López Obrador made Cuban President Miguel Díaz-Canel a key-note speaker at Mexico's bicentennial independence celebration; never before had a foreign leader been invited as a speaker to an independence celebration. Díaz-Canel had recently received international media attention for harshly repressing protests in Cuba and jailing the movement's leaders. These and other examples show a systematic tendency to support authoritarian leaders, in the north and the south, under the administration of López Obrador.

A Brief History of Opposing Projects of Integration

Historically, Latin America has been immersed in two opposing projects of regional integration: one led by the U.S., identified with the label of *Pan-Americanism*, and another with its origins in the region, identified as *Latin Americanism*.

According to Anderson (2014), *Pan-Americanism* had its origins in 1823 with the birth of the Monroe Doctrine, which proclaimed "America for the Americans", an ideological attempt to develop a geopolitical strategy that could exclude the United Kingdom and Spain from regional affairs. The territorial expansion of the U.S. in North America was partially based on this doctrine. James Blaine, U.S. Secretary of State, convened the Pan-American Conference of 1889 with the goal of creating a U.S.-led customs union, with a permanent court of arbitration in Washington and a common currency. However, this attempt failed, partially in response to Cuban Consul José Martí's suspicion of an ever-expanding U.S. imperialism. Martí was able to gain the support of other Latin American delegates in rejecting Blaine's proposition. But even if this U.S. attempt at regional integration failed, a new Pan-American organization was finally created when the U.S. emerged as a major economic and political power after World War II. In 1948, the Charter of the Organization of American States was adopted at the Bogotá Conference with the goal of "consolidating the many Inter-American agreements and practices" that have had an amorphous existence for almost 50 years (Davis 1948, 439).

On the opposite side of the spectrum, there is *Latin Americanism*, an alternative approach to regional integration thought of as counter-hegemonic, nourished by the history of anti-colonialism and anti-imperialism in Latin America (Anderson 2014). This alternative to integration has its origins in Bolivar's dream of creating a confederation of Hispano-American nations. Even before Bolivar had obtained a decisive military victory in Peru, he had already sent ministers to negotiate the celebration of a regional Congress to discuss his ideas of political unity. In Mexico, his ideas were well received by the Minister of Foreign Affairs, Lucas Alemán (Liévano-Aguirre 1968). In 1846, the Congress of Panama took place, with the goal of creating a confederation "in order for it to allow the dynamic coexistence of the political sovereignty of its member states with the strengthening of their supranational unity", all cemented in the foundation of a common cultural heritage, and therefore excluding the United States (Liévano-Aguirre 1968, 203). However, due to differences regarding the terms of the union, internal political differences in the newly established independent states, and intrigues involving the U.S. government, the Congress failed.

These dreams of Latin American integration were vigorously boosted once more by Hugo Chávez almost 200 years after Bolivar. Chávez also believed in the need for Latin American unity as a geopolitical strategy to put a stop to U.S. interventionism in the region. This idea was further reinforced after the attempted coup against Chávez in 2002, when Venezuela's economic elite set in motion a series of protests and strikes, supported by workers and businessmen, which culminated in the remotion of Chávez from power with the support of some military actors. The international community condemned the coup, particularly members of the Rio Group, but the U.S. government swiftly expressed its support for the interim president, Pedro Carmona, head of the Venezuelan Federation of Chambers of Commerce and Associations of Commerce and Production. This event "heightened to Chávez the importance of establishing greater autonomy from the United States for both Venezuela and the Region" (McCarthy-Jones 2014: 52). Therefore, Chávez strongly supported alternative mechanisms of regional integration to those commanded by the U.S.; instead, he engineered the creation of ALBA and was a committed supporter of the CELAC, a regional organization that includes all of Latin America and excludes the U.S. and Canada, and whose constitutive declaration explicitly links its rationale to fulfilling Bolivar's dream of regional unity and anti-imperial fraternity (Anderson 2014).

A Paradoxical Foreign Policy: Supporting Latin Americanism but Bowing to Trump

A country's foreign policy can be understood as a set of actions taken by organs of the State regarding its external environment with two subjacent logics: 1) attempts of the State to exert influence on international processes, and 2) how to deal with international influences on the country's internal processes (Anaya 2019). Historically, Mexican foreign policy has been used "to promote Mexico's top domestic policy priorities, defined by its successive presidents," usually to preserve national security and sovereignty, and to enhance economic, cultural, and social wellbeing (Schiavon 2022: 6). What are the goals of Mexico's foreign policy under President López Obrador?

On July 24th, 2021, during a ceremony commemorating the 238th anniversary of Simon Bolivar's birth, López Obrador stated: "The slogan of 'America for the Americans' ended up disintegrating the peoples of our continent and destroying what was built, […] by Bolívar. […] Since that time, Washington has never stopped conducting overt or covert operations against independent countries south of the Rio Grande."[1] In this speech, López Obrador aligned himself with the Latin American project of integration, with a strong emphasis on defending the sovereignty of Latin American countries and clear opposition to U.S. intervention in regional affairs. In the same speech, López Obrador attacked one of the symbolic institutions of *Pan-Americanism*, saying: "The proposal is […] to build something like the European Union, but attached to our history, our reality and our identities. In this spirit, the replacement of the OAS by a truly autonomous body, not a lackey of anyone, […] should not be ruled out," calling for a new scheme of regional integration in which the CELAC could take preeminence. Based on this, we could argue that López Obrador is trying to position himself as a Latin American leader of a group of nations that opposes U.S. interventionism in the region; however, it could also be plain rhetoric and show complacent behavior towards the U.S. in practice.

Along the same line of argumentation, Marcelo Ebrard, Mexico's Minister of Foreign Affairs, has made negative assessments of the

---

[1] López Obrador, Andrés, "Discurso del presidente Andrés Manuel López Obrador en el 238 Aniversario del Natalicio de Simón Bolívar, desde el Castillo de Chapultepec." July 24th, 2021, https://lopezobrador.org.mx/2021/07/24/discurso-del-presidente-andres-manuel-lopez-obrador-en-el-238-aniversario-del-natalicio-de-simon-bolivar-desde-el-castillo-de-chapultepec/ (accessed on November 9th, 2021).

OAS's work and openly accused the organization of causing the fall of Evo Morales's government in 2020. In an interview with *La Jornada*, Ebrard said: "The OAS undoubtedly participated in the 'coup' in Bolivia. Everything is documented. The current shape of the OAS reflects a geopolitical design that was infused in that organization".[2] In the same interview, he later suggested that the 2021 CELAC summit in Mexico could serve as an arena to discuss replacing the OAS with the CELAC.

In this context, the Mexico City CELAC summit took place on September 18th, 2021. In the opening address, López Obrador stated that "the CELAC can become the main instrument to consolidate relations between our Latin American and Caribbean countries and to achieve the ideal of economic integration with the United States and Canada within a framework of respect for our sovereignties",[3] emphasizing the principles of non-intervention and self-determination. It is important to highlight that he added a point in relation to his conception of how the international community should act towards violations of human rights or threats to the stability of democracy in the region: "The controversies about democracy and human rights should be settled at the request of the parties and resolved by truly neutral instances created by the countries of the Americas".

However, despite López Obrador's discourse expressing his desire to strengthen Latin American integration as an instrument to limit 'U.S. imperialism', he has also displayed complacent behavior towards the U.S., and in particular towards Donald Trump. Notwithstanding the many insults Trump made towards Mexicans during his 2016 presidential campaign, including that Mex-

---

[2] Velázquez, Miguel Ángel, "Un signo de que el modelo de la OEA está agotado es el embargo a Cuba." *La Jornada*, September 18th, 2021, https://www.jornada.com.mx/notas/2021/09/18/politica/un-signo-de-que-el-modelo-de-la-oea-esta-agotado-es-el-embargo-a-cuba/ (accessed on September 18th, 2021).

[3] López Obrador, Andrés Manuel, "Discurso del presidente Andrés Manuel López Obrador durante la VI Cumbre de la Comunidad de Estados Latinoamericanos y Caribeños." September 18th, 2021, https://lopezobrador.org.mx/2021/09/18/discurso-del-presidente-andres-manuel-lopez-obrador-durante-la-vi-cumbre-de-la-celac/ (accessed on November 10th, 2021).

icans are drug dealers, criminals and rapists[4], López Obrador has cooperated on issues that are key to the U.S. agenda. One clear example is how López Obrador turned Mexico into the U.S.'s new border patrol. As president-elect, López Obrador promised that his government would give Mexican visas and job opportunities to the Central American immigrants requiring them[5]; instead, his government has used Mexico's National Guard military police to violently repress and contain Central American immigrants, which has *de facto* turned Mexico into Trump's Wall.[6] The NGO *Human Rights Watch* has denounced the excessive use of force by Mexican immigration police and the National Guard: "The recent violence is an extreme consequence of the disastrous heavy-handed immigration strategy Mexico is implementing at the behest of the United States."[7] In the face of these cases of human rights violations, it is hard to sustain a discourse of Latin American fraternity and unity.

Additionally, López Obrador has proved to be a close ally of Trump, with attitudes that go beyond diplomatic courtesy towards Mexico's neighbor. In the aftermath of the 2020 U.S. presidential election, when Trump was crying out fraud without any evidence, López Obrador condemned Twitter and Facebook for blocking Trump's account and criticized it as an act of censorship against

---

[4] Scott, Eugene, "Trump's most insulting — and violent — language is often reserved for immigrants." *Washington Post*, October 2nd, 2019, https://www.washingtonpost.com/politics/2019/10/02/trumps-most-insulting-violent-language-is-often-reserved-immigrants/ (accessed on November 10th, 2021).

[5] Nejar, Alberto, "Caravana de migrantes: AMLO anuncia un inédito programa de visas de trabajo en México para tratar de contener la migración centroamericana a EE.UU." *BBC Mundo*, October 18th, 2018, https://www.bbc.com/mundo/noticias-america-latina-45898633 (accessed on November 10th, 2021).

[6] Agren, Davis, "'Mexico has become Trump's wall': how AMLO became an immigration enforcer." *The Guardian*, January 26th, 2020, https://www.theguardian.com/world/2020/jan/26/mexico-immigration-amlo-enforcement-trump (accessed on November 10th, 2021).

[7] Vivanco, José Manuel, "Mexican Soldiers and Immigration Agents Violently Detain Asylum Seekers." *Human Rights Watch*, October 8th, 2021, https://www.hrw.org/news/2021/09/08/mexican-soldiers-and-immigration-agents-violently-detain-asylum-seekers# (accessed on November 10th, 2021).

the U.S. president.[8] López Obrador also refused to condemn the attack on the U.S. Capitol by Trump supporters, instigated by Trump himself, and in that case he selectively made use of the principle of not interfering in other countries' affairs: "We do not take a position. We wish that there is always peace, that democracy prevails."[9] Needless to say, López Obrador refused to acknowledge Joe Biden's victory until the very last minute, trying to give his political support to Donald Trump. Along with Vladimir Putin, López Obrador was one of the last world leaders to recognize Biden's triumph.[10]

The Rise of Authoritarianism in Latin America and Mexican Support for It

Perhaps the sympathy that López Obrador has shown to Donald Trump and his support for other authoritarian leaders in the region, such as Evo Morales, Díaz-Canel, and Nicolás Maduro, is no coincidence. Adding up the cases in which López Obrador has refused to take a position and the other cases in which he has expressed and given material support, it seems that he is selectively using the principle of non-intervention to support the continent's authoritarian leaders.

Like the Spanish political scientist Juan Linz, I conceptualize authoritarian governments as those intermediate regimes be-

---

[8] The Associated Press, "Mexico leader condemns Twitter, Facebook for blocking Trump." *ABC News,* January 7th, 2021, https://abcnews.go.com/International/wireStory/mexico-leader-condemns-twitter-facebook-blocking-trump-75123130 (accessed on November 10th, 2021).

[9] Tourliere, Mathieu, "AMLO sobre asalto al Capitolio: no intervención, lamentamos las muertes, que prevalezca la democracia." *Proceso,* January 7th, 2021, https://www.proceso.com.mx/nacional/2021/1/7/amlo-sobre-asalto-al-capitolio-no-intervencion-lamentamos-las-muertes-que-prevalezca-la-democracia-255784.html (accessed on November 10th, 2021).

[10] Khurshudyan, Isabelle and Kevin Sieff, "Russia's Putin, Mexico's López Obrador recognize Biden's win, more than a month after the election." *Washington Post,* https://www.washingtonpost.com/world/europe/putin-congratulates-biden-election/2020/12/15/bd8c3444-3ea8-11eb-b58b-1623f6267960_story.html (accessed on November 10th, 2021).

tween totalitarianism and democracy, characterized by a limited pluralism (Linz 1975). Similarly, Levitsky and Way (2002, 53) conceptualize competitive authoritarianism as an intermediate form of regime, between democracy and full authoritarianism, in which there are systematic violations of the criteria for being considered democratic[11] that "create an uneven playing field between government and opposition". Therefore, when I speak of authoritarianism, I am referring to governments that impose limits on free political competition and expression of ideas, that harass and intimidate the media and the opposition, and so on.

It could be argued that instead of supporting authoritarian leaders, López Obrador is in fact supporting populist leaders, since Donald Trump, Nicolás Maduro, Evo Morales, and Nayib Bukele also fit into that category. However, populism is more a communication strategy in which leaders divide the political spectrum between the good people versus the corrupt elite, and this division is not built upon sociological characteristics but rather discursively built in the people's imaginary (Casullo 2019: 49). Of course, it is possible that authoritarian values are disguised by populist rhetoric and that these two phenomena can be confounded (Norris and Inglehart 2019); however, populism is not a fully articulated ideology, and the division between the good people and the evil elite can be built upon any problem that the leader chooses. Authoritarian leaders can instead be identified by clear behavioral warning signs such as the rejection, in voice or actions, of the democratic rules of the game, denial of the legitimacy of political opponents, toleration or encouragement of violence, and willingness to curtail the civil liberties of opponents, including the media (Levitsky and Ziblatt 2018, 21-24). Leaders like Donald Trump clearly fit these criteria (Levitsky and Ziblatt 2018, 61-67) and other Latin American leaders such as Díaz-Canel (Cuba), Nicolás Maduro (Venezuela), Daniel Ortega (Nicaragua), and Nayib Bukele (El Salvador) have also displayed these behavioral warnings. In

---

[11] For example, free and fair elections, the universal right to vote, and respect and protection for political rights and civil liberties.

fact, the first three are clearly conceived as fully authoritarian regimes (Economist Intelligence Unit 2022).

In recent years, Latin America has experienced a slight decline in the levels of liberal democracy[12] (green line in Figure 1) that stands in crisp contrast with the wave of democratization that the region experienced between 1978 and 1992 (Mainwaring and Pérez-Liñán 2005). Indeed, it has become common worldwide to speak of a process of democratic backsliding, characterized by the "the incremental erosion of democratic institutions, rules and norms that results from the actions of duly elected governments, typically driven by an autocratic leader" (Haggard and Kaufman 2021, 1). This process of democratic backsliding has been more pronounced in countries such as Bolivia (blue line) and Venezuela (purple line).

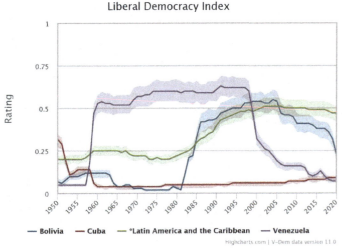

Figure 1. Liberal Democracy Index for Latin America, Bolivia, Cuba, and Venezuela between 1950 and 2020. *Source*: V-Dem Project: https://www.v-dem.net/

---

[12] The liberal principle of democracy emphasizes the importance of protecting individual and minority rights against the tyranny of the state and the tyranny of the majority, and therefore emphasizes free and fair elections and a limited government and guarantees to protect those rights.

The rise of authoritarianism in the region is in itself problematic. But the problem is further compounded by clear signs of support for authoritarian leaders in the region from the Mexican government. The literature on democratization has underscored the importance of the regional political environment as a factor in strengthening this process; in particular, strong international support for democracy increases the probability of democratic transitions and reduces the risks of democracy breakdowns (Mainwaring and Pérez-Liñán 2013). One mechanism through which this process operates is the allocation of resources from international actors to empower domestic ones; foreign countries can offer material aid, technical assistance, or moral support to some domestic groups as a mechanism to alter the domestic balance of power in favor of the coalition that embraces the preferences of external allies (Mainwaring and Pérez-Liñán 2013). Previous examples of this strategy can be found in U.S. efforts to boost democracy in Latin America after 1977, by selectively lowering dictatorships' annual ratings on human rights to justify U.S. prohibitions of foreign assistance and trade (Schenoni and Mainwaring 2018). At the other end of the spectrum, Venezuela breathed fresh life into the Cuban dictatorship through material benefits included in ALBA, such as the removal of all tariffs and other trade barriers on Cuban goods, and low-priced oil and oil purchasing facilities (Anderson 2014). Additionally, many scholars have argued that membership of regional organizations could increase the likelihood of democratization; however, recent scholarship has shown that authoritarian regimes "are often members in 'Clubs of Autocrats' that supply material and ideational resources to strengthen domestic survival politics and shield members from external interference during moments of political turmoil" (Debre 2021: 1).

Selectively rejecting the principle of not interfering in other countries' affairs, López Obrador gave refuge to Evo Morales after he resigned from the presidency of Bolivia in 2019. This resignation came as a consequence of a wave of popular protests that accused Morales of capturing the electoral authority and committing fraud against the opposition to achieve his fourth reelection.[13] In 2016, Morales reneged on his promise to respect the results of a referendum, where a majority had refused to support his proposal to lift the constitutional ban on consecutive reelection.[14] Then, taking advantage of the fact that the Constitutional Court had been packed with loyalists, he demanded it decide whether the constitutional prohibition of reelection was violating his human right to be elected under Article 23 of the American Convention on Human Rights. The Bolivian Court ruled in his favor, so the path was cleared for his fourth reelection.[15] In 2019, the Colombian government requested the Inter-American Court of Human Rights issue an advisory opinion on this topic and, of course, the Court denied that there is such a thing as the human right to indefinitely run for reelection,[16] making clear the illegality of Morales's actions.

However, the Mexican government denounced Morales's resignation as a coup d'état[17] plotted by the conservative right in Bolivia, with the support of the OAS. This narrative comes from the fact that the Electoral Observation Mission of the OAS issued a tech-

---

[13] Aparicio-Otero, Jaime, "Will Bolivia's Elections Usher in a New Wave of Socialism in Latin America?" *Foreign Policy*, October 16th, 2020, https://foreignpolicy.com/2020/10/16/bolivia-elections-morales-socialism-left-liberals-democracy/ (accessed on November 10th, 2021).

[14] Anria, Santiago, "Evo Morales wants to change the law so he can remain president. Is Bolivia's democracy in danger?" *Monkey Cage by the Washington Post*, November 28th, 2017, https://www.washingtonpost.com/news/monkey-cage/wp/2017/11/28/bolivias-president-thinks-hes-irreplaceable-what-does-this-mean-for-democracy-there/ (accessed on November 10th, 2021).

[15] Reuters Staff, "Bolivian court clears way for Morales to run for fourth term." *Reuters*, November 28th, 2017, https://www.reuters.com/article/us-bolivia-politics-idUSKBN1DS2ZX (accessed on November 10th, 2021).

[16] Corte Inter-Americana de Derechos Humanos, "Solicitud de Opinión Consultiva relativa a la figura de la reelección presidencial indefinida en el contexto del Sistema Inter-Americano de Derechos Humanos." October 21st, 2019, https://www.corteidh.or.cr/docs/opiniones/soc_04_19_es.pdf (accessed on November 10th, 2021).

[17] Ebrard, Marcelo, "Position of the Government of Mexico on the Events in Bolivia." November 11th, 2019, https://www.gob.mx/sre/prensa/position-of-the-government-of-mexico-on-the-events-in-bolivia (accessed on November 10th, 2021).

nical report in which it pointed out that the irregularities in the Bolivian election were grave enough that they suggested calling for a new electoral process, a point with which Morales had initially agreed.[18] Since then, the Mexican government has accused the OAS of interfering in the internal affairs of Latin American countries and has thus called for replacing the OAS with the CELAC. This is a clear example of how membership of regional organizations originally created by Chávez, such as the CELAC, and the selective use of the principle of non-intervention have been used as an attempt to shield from criticism of authoritarian governments that tilt the electoral playing field in their favor, undermining the constitutive principles of democracy.

At the 2021 CELAC summit in Mexico City, where the Mexican government had planned to discuss its proposal to replace the OAS with this Latin American organization, the presence of Nicolás Maduro and Cuba's President Díaz-Canel caused an uproar. Regarding the OAS, Uruguay's President Luis Lacalle Pou said in his initial remarks that his participation at the CELAC summit in no way represented his support for the plan to replace the OAS. Regarding Mexico having invited authoritarian leaders to the summit, he also added: "Participating in this forum does not mean being complacent. And with due respect, when one sees that in certain countries there is not a full democracy, when the separation of powers is not respected, when the repressive apparatus is used to silence protests, when opponents are imprisoned, when human rights are not respected, we, in a calm but firm voice, must say that we see with concern what is happening in Cuba, Nicaragua and Venezuela."[19] Cuba's president replied that

---

[18] Organization of American States, "Press Release on Disinformation Campaign Regarding the Role of the OAS in the Bolivian Elections." January 16th, 2020, https://www.oas.org/en/media_center/press_release.asp?sCodigo=E-064/20 (accessed on November 10th, 2021).

[19] BBC News, "CELAC: el duro choque verbal entre los presidentes de Uruguay y Cuba, y otros mandatarios, durante una cumbre en México." *BBC News Mundo*, September 19th, 2021, https://www.bbc.com/mundo/noticias-america-latina-58612780 (accessed on November 10th, 2021).

Lacalle's remarks reflected his lack of understanding of Cuba's situation. Along the same lines, Paraguay's President Mario Abdo Benitez opened his speech at the CELAC summit by reiterating that he doesn't regard the Venezuelan leader's rule as legitimate: "My presence at this summit in no way represents an acknowledgment of the government of Nicolás Maduro. There is no change in my government's stance on this point and I believe that the gentlemanly thing to do is to tell you that to your face".

López Obrador had also planned that, in the final declaration of the CELAC summit, the participating countries could request that the international community lift the economic sanctions on the Venezuelan Government. However, Colombian President Ivan Duque refused to participate in the summit as a sign of protest against López Obrador's proposal and, as a result, Colombia broke the consensus to include López Obrador's petition in the final declaration.[20] Despite López Obrador's efforts to help authoritarian leaders in the region, this summit demonstrated that other countries like Uruguay, Paraguay and Colombia openly rejected this strategy based on a commitment to democratic norms. This episode exemplifies how, in Latin America, the positioning that countries take regarding democracy can become a factor that explains geopolitics in the region and adherence to or rejection of different projects of regional integration.

Additionally, Mexico's position towards the Nicaraguan crisis has also been criticized by human rights activists. For instance, José Miguel Vivanco, executive director of the Human Rights Watch for the Americas, tweeted that "President López Obrador's response to the brutal repression against opponents and critics orchestrated by Ortega in Nicaragua has been shameful and disappointing".[21] In December 2021, the OAS General Assembly

---

[20] Pretelin Muñoz De Cote, Fausto, "Colombia rompe consenso en documento final de la CELAC." *El Financiero*, September 16th, 2021, https://www.eleconomista.com.mx/internacionales/Colombia-rompe-consenso-en-documento-final-de-la-Celac-20210916-0077.html (accessed on November 10th, 2021).

[21] Mexico Daily Post Staff, "'Shameful' AMLO's response to the Nicaraguan crisis says Human Rights Watch." *Mexico Daily Post*, November 9th, 2021, https://mexicodai-

rejected the legitimacy of the November 7 elections in Nicaragua, saying that the democratic institutions in that country were 'seriously undermined' by Ortega's government; however, the Mexican government abstained from voting on this resolution and covertly attacked Almagro by saying: "We regret that the approved resolution is destined to be another resolution without results since it ignores that the designated interlocutor [OAS] does not have the minimum credentials necessary to ensure a constructive and viable dialogue".[22] Since then, repression of the opposition and limits on freedom of speech have intensified in Nicaragua, and this has reached the point of restricting academic freedom by taking control of five private universities: "Opposition activists and academics fear more such takeovers are imminent, and that the growing crackdown will force universities to censor professors or students who are not afraid to express their opinion. Academics also fear that the quality of education will decline as government loyalists, unskilled and hostile to education, fill the ranks."[23] Recently, hate speech by Ortega and his wife Rosario Murillo towards the Catholic Church has caused physical and verbal aggression against priests, and desecration and theft of temples have been on the rise since Ortega declared the Church as a public enemy of his regime in 2018.[24]

More recently, in May 2022, López Obrador completed a four-day, five-nation international tour that began in Guatemala, then

---

lypost.com/2021/11/09/shameful-amlos-response-to-the-nicaraguan-crisis-says-human-rights-watch/ (accessed on May 26th, 2022).

[22] AFP, "México reitera indolencia frente a crisis en Nicaragua." *El Economista*, December 8th, 2021, https://www.eleconomista.com.mx/internacionales/OEA-concluye-que-Nicaragua-incumple-con-la-Carta-Democratica-Interamericana-20211208-0089.html (accessed on May 26th, 2022).

[23] Mendoza, Yubelka and Maria Abi-Habib, "El gobierno de Nicaragua confisca universidades privadas y avanza hacia la dictadura." *New York Times*, February 14th, 2022, https://www.nytimes.com/es/2022/02/14/espanol/nicaragua-ortega-universidad.html (accessed on May 26th, 2022).

[24] Voces en libertad, "Iglesia católica en Nicaragua bajo ataque: hasta tres agresiones por día en cuatro años." *Coyuntura*, May 26th, 2022, https://www.coyuntura.co/post/iglesia-cat%C3%B3lica-en-nicaragua-bajo-ataque-hasta-tres-agresiones-por-d%C3%ADa-en-cuatro-a%C3%B1os (accessed on May 26th, 2022).

went on to El Salvador, Honduras, Belize and Cuba. This was his first international tour to somewhere other than the U.S. Except for Belize, the other four countries have been criticized for actions that could fit Levitsky and Ziblatt's criteria for identifying authoritarian leaders. On this tour, López Obrador:

> "[…] visited the Guatemala of his counterpart Alejandro Giammattei, where justice has been dismantled in recent years to the point that today there is a systematic persecution of prosecutors; Nayib Bukele's El Salvador, which continues to have absolute powers after extending a state of emergency in the country; the Honduras of Xiomara Castro, who has served 100 days as president with the promise of removing the country from criminal governance, while her family has intervened in the Legislative and Judicial powers, and has promoted pardons for former officials of her husband, the former president Manuel Zelaya, accused of corruption. And, although he skipped the Nicaragua repressed by Daniel Ortega, the last stop on the tour was Cuba, the oldest dictatorship in the Americas".[25]

It is noteworthy that, in this visit to Central America, López Obrador chose to visit these countries with dubious democratic credentials and excluded Costa Rica, one of the most consolidated democracies in the region, especially since Rodrigo Chaves took his oath of office as president of Costa Rica that same week; neither López Obrador nor his chancellor Marcelo Ebrard attended this ceremony. Why did López Obrador not take advantage of his tour to attend the swearing-in ceremony of a democratically elected neighbor? That very same day, López Obrador was instead arriving in Cuba.

During his stay in Havana, López Obrador harshly criticized the U.S. embargo on Cuba and condemned Joe Biden's decision not to invite the dictatorships of the region (Cuba, Venezuela, and

---

[25] Valencia, Daniel, Jennifer Ávila Reyes and José Luis Pardo Veiras, "AMLO y su mirada ciega hacia América Central." *El País*, May 12th, 2022, https://www.washingtonpost.com/es/post-opinion/2022/05/12/amlo-cuba-gira-centroamerica-bukele-sembrando-vida-cumbre-americas/ (accessed on May 26th, 2022).

Nicaragua) to the Americas Summit.[26] In this case, López Obrador was not shy about criticizing U.S. foreign policy decisions and did not invoke the principle of non-intervention to avoid taking a stance. One week later, López Obrador declared that he would boycott the 2022 Summit of the Americas if the Biden administration failed to invite Cuba, Venezuela, and Nicaragua. Meanwhile, López Obrador's decision to boycott the summit was applauded by Beijing; Chinese Foreign Ministry Spokesman Zhao Lijian took advantage of Mexico's diplomatic snub to emphasize that the Monroe Doctrine "has no audience in Latin America today".[27] With these actions, López Obrador showed that he was willing to escalate his differences with the Biden administration with the ultimate purpose of giving his political support to the continent's three fully authoritarian regimes.

Taking these examples together, there is clear systematic reluctance by Mexico's government to condemn attacks on political rights and civil liberties, or to denounce cases of fraudulent elections under the Inter-American Democratic Charter, allegedly based on the principle of non-intervention in other countries' domestic matters. However, the Mexican government has openly given material, economic and moral aid to the governments of Cuba, Venezuela, and El Salvador, and has actively fought for the inclusion of these countries in regional organizations such as the OAS and the CELAC. The Mexican government has also failed in the principle of Latin American brotherhood by violently repressing Central American immigrants in Mexico's territory under the auspices of Trump's migratory policies. In contrast, in the face of more democratic leadership in the U.S., López Obrador has criticized and

---

[26] Vicent, Mauricio, "López Obrador condena en La Habana el embargo de EEUU y pide a Cuba que la revolución sea capaz de renovarse." *El País*, May 8th, 2022, https://elpais.com/mexico/2022-05-08/lopez-obrador-condena-en-la-habana-el-embargo-de-eeuu-y-pide-a-cuba-que-la-revolucion-sea-capaz-de-renovarse.html (accessed on May 26th, 2022).

[27] Zilli, Renata, "La nueva doctrina Monroe: América ¿para los chinos?" *El Universal*, May 26th, 2022, https://www.eluniversal.com.mx/mundo/una-mirada-global-6 (accessed on May 26th, 2022).

opposed U.S. foreign policy to the point of boycotting the 2022 Summit of the Americas. This last point lends credence to a hypothesis of a Mexican foreign policy that is particularly friendly to authoritarian leaders. Under Trump's leadership, López Obrador exchanged mutual flattery with his U.S. counterpart and closely collaborated with him on issues that hurt the integrity of Central American immigrants, but under Joe Biden's administration, he has chosen confrontation and criticism of his foreign policy.

Conclusion

In a period of reconfiguration of the world order, Mexico has displayed what seems to be a paradoxical foreign policy strategy: supporting Latin Americanism and denouncing U.S. imperialism but simultaneously bowing to Trump. This apparent paradox could be understood if we think of López Obrador's actions as an effort to support authoritarian leaders in the Americas. By selectively deciding when to adhere to the principle of non-intervention, López Obrador has been able to avoid taking a stand against authoritarian leaders, but on the other hand, he has been swift to give moral and material support to other authoritarian leaders with whom he identifies more. This strategy could be potentially damaging to the whole region because, by giving support to authoritarian governments, López Obrador could contribute to shifting the domestic balance of power in those countries in favor of the authoritarian coalition, and thus contribute to the acceleration of democratic backsliding in Latin America.

Mexico has traditionally followed a strategy of building coalitions with countries that share its interests, preferences, and values, "to maximize their relevance and international impact" (Schiavon 2022: 16). Considering that, what would be the long-term benefits for Mexico or López Obrador of building a coalition with authoritarian leaders? Why is Mexico going back to foreign policy that gives preeminence to the principle of non-intervention, which was the rule under the PRI governments? Why is Mexico moving away from a policy of openness to international scrutiny that was the norm under the last three democratic governments?

These are open questions whose answers go well beyond the scope of this article. Meanwhile, I hope that the description of the facts presented here contributes to an open debate that analyzes the contradictions in the foreign policy of this administration and assesses its goals and regional repercussions.

References

Aguirre I. L., "El Congreso de Panamá: Bolivarismo y Monroísmo", *Desarrollo Económico* 8, 30/31, 1968: 193–241. https://doi.org/10.2307/3466009.

Anaya Múñoz A., "Política exterior y derechos humanos durante el sexenio de Enrique Peña Nieto", *Foro Internacional* LIX, 3–4, 2019: 1049–75. https://doi.org/10.24201/fi.v59i3-4.2651.

Anderson T., "Chávez and American Integration", Angosto-Ferrandez L. F. (ed.), *Democracy, Revolution, and Geopolitics in Latin America: Venezuela and the International Politics of Discontent*, Routledge Studies in Latin American Politics 9, Routledge, 2014: 13–46. https://doi.org/10.4324/9781315890111.

Casullo M. E.,*¿Por qué funciona el populismo?: El discurso que sabe construir explicaciones convincentes de un mundo en crisis*, Siglo Veintiuno Editores, 2019.

Davis H. E., "The Charter of the Organization of American States", *The Western Political Quarterly* 1, 4, 1948: 439–48. https://doi.org/10.2307/442943.

Debre M. J., "Clubs of Autocrats: Regional Organizations and Authoritarian Survival", *The Review of International Organizations*, June 2021. https://doi.org/10.1007/s11558-021-09428-y.

Economist Intelligence Unit, *Democracy Index 2021: The China challenge*, Economist Intelligence Unit, 2022.

Haggard S., *Backsliding: Democratic Regress in the Contemporary World*, Cambridge Elements. Elements in Political Economy, Cambridge University Press, 2021.

Levitsky S. - Way L., "Elections Without Democracy: The Rise of Competitive Authoritarianism", *Journal of Democracy* 13, 2, 2002: 51–65.

Levitsky S. - Ziblatt D., *How Democracies Die*, Crown, 2018.

Linz J., "Totalitarian and Authoritarian Regimes", Greenstein F. - Polsby N. (eds.), *Handbook of Political Science* 3, Addison-Wesley, 1975:175–91.

Mainwaring S. - Pérez-Liñán A., "Latin American Democratization since 1978", Hagopian F. - Mainwaring S. (eds.), *The*

Third Wave of Democratization in Latin America: Advances and Setbacks, Cambridge University Press, 2005: 14–59.

——, *Democracies and Dictatorships in Latin America: Emergence, Survival, and Fall*, Cambridge University Press, 2013.

McCarthy-Jones A., "'Ploughing the Sea' in a World of Regions: Venezuela's Role in Reviving Latin American Regionalism for the Twenty-First Century", Angosto-Ferrandez L.F. (ed.), *Democracy, Revolution, and Geopolitics in Latin America: Venezuela and the International Politics of Discontent*, Routledge Studies in Latin American Politics 9, Routledge, 2014: 13–46. https://doi.org/10.4324/9781315890111.

Norris P. – Inglehart R., *Cultural Backlash: Trump, Brexit, and Authoritarian Populism*, Cambridge University Press, 2019.

Schenoni L. L. – Mainwaring S., "US Hegemony and Regime Change in Latin America", *Democratization* 26, 2, 2019: 269–87. https://doi.org/10.1080/13510347.2018.1516754.

Schiavon J. A., "Mexican Foreign Policy", *Oxford Research Encyclopedia of International Studies*, February 24, 2022. https://doi.org/10.1093/acrefore/9780190846626.013.684.

Lecture n. 5

INSTITUTIONS
Democracy in Mexico:
In the Context of Ethnic and Social Differences

*A Historical Reflection
on Decent Democracy*

Dr. Luis Felipe Bravo Mena –
Former Ambassador of Mexico
to the Holy See – Naucalpan,
State of Mexico

Introductory words

I am grateful for the invitation from the Center for Faith and Culture *Alberto Hurtado* of the Gregorian University to share with you, *Scuola Sinderesi*, this reflection on Democracy in Mexico: in the context of ethnic and social differences.

I greet Samuele Sangalli and Antonella Piccinin, coordinators of the *Scuola*, as well as the friends of the Konrad Adenauer Foundation in Italy and Mexico: Silke Schmitt and Hans Blomeier, who were the kind conduit of the proposal to be with you this afternoon.

This year we Mexicans remember two fundamental events in our history. Five hundred years ago, on August 13, 1521, the world that the ancient native peoples had built collapsed. The capture of Tenochtitlan, capital of the Mexica empire, through the alliance between the Spaniards and the indigenous clans rebelling against oppression, was not only a local cataclysm, but an event of universal impact.

It marked the beginning of the first stage of globalization; suffice it to say that four decades later, in 1565, New Spain had already become the epicenter of international trade at the time. It linked, with navigation between the port of Acapulco and Manila, the economies of two empires: that of the Habsburgs and that of the Ming Dynasty.

The other event is the consummation of independence on September 27, 1821, which untied New Spain from the Spanish Crown. The new nation, forged over 300 years, was constituted as a sovereign state, and began its exciting and eventful journey.

Both commemorations have not led to a thoughtful reflection that would contribute to think of a better Mexico; on the contrary, they have been taken as an occasion to revive grievances and feed stale divisions. We live in times of anger.

In this environment of polarization, making judgments about political and social realities without sufficient information and study has become a common practice. Historical episodes, people, institutions, and norms are sacralized or demonized.

Reasoned argumentation has almost disappeared; the fashion is to disqualify and sectarian exacerbation. Political and parliamentary debate is now a spectacle of quarrels in which slogans and ideological clichés are repeated ad nauseam, all of which takes us back to an incivility that seemed to have been overcome.

To understand the situation of Mexican democracy and its specific relationship with ethnic and social differences, it requires a historical journey, where some of the keys to its current problems can be found.

I will approach the subject from a personal perspective that combines history, political science and my experience as a politician and civil servant.

These are subjects that have interested me for a long time. I graduated with an essay on the *Problems of the Mexican State Organization* (1976).[1] Professionally, I am dedicated to political analysis, I am greatly involved in a political party: I have been its national president, deputy, senator, civil servant and ambassador to the Holy See.

52 years in these tasks have allowed me to know all the regions and the character of its people; I have witnessed the fourth part of the life of the Mexican State, and as an activist I participated in the peaceful transition from authoritarianism to democracy.

I am self-critical, I recognize the failures and mistakes of our political generation. With this experiential baggage I composed this reflection divided into three parts.

In the first part, The Democratic Question in Mexico, I propose

---

[1] See: Bravo Mena L.F., *Problemas de la Organización Estatal Mexicana*, professional thesis, School of Law, University of Guanajuato, private ed., 1976.

to compare the reality of the country with the concept of democracy, complementing it with Avishai Margalit's notion of a Decent Society (Margalit 2010). I believe that the product of this fusion, which I call Decent Democracy, is useful for our reflection and thus we may approach the question of how to achieve it in such a diverse country.

One of the main characteristics of Mexico is its diversity, starting with its fantastic biodiversity and its cultural, ethnic, and geographical differences. Alongside these are the long-standing and abysmal social and regional inequalities. The evolution of the World Bank's Gini Index on inequality over the last 30 years places our society in the barrier between 50.6 in 1989 and 45.4 in 2018.[2]

In search of solutions to these disparities, several generations have experienced proposals coming from a wide range of colorful doctrines and ideologies, without reaching the ideals proclaimed by one or the other.

The second part, *Great ideals and difficult realities*: "You already know the way to be free, it is up to you to point out the way to be happy", is a historical synopsis of the various attempts to implant sociopolitical structures on the Mexican nation with libertarian and vigilante purposes. The journey culminates with the new experiment underway, detonated by the political process of 2018.

The final section, "From philanthropic ogre to anthropophagous ogre, where are we?" seeks to describe the current situation of Mexican democracy under the lens of a Decent Democracy.

I close this introduction with an optimistic quote from *Evangelii Gaudium*:

"People in every nation enhance the social dimension of their lives by acting as committed and responsible citizens, not as a mob swayed by the powers that be [...] becoming a people demands something more. It is an ongoing process in which every new generation must take part: a slow and arduous effort calling for

---

[2] In the Gini Index of wealth distribution, 100 is the maximum inequality and 10 corresponds to perfect equality.

a desire for integration and a willingness to achieve this through the growth of a peaceful and multifaceted culture of encounter". "In every nation, the inhabitants develop the social dimension of their lives by shaping themselves as responsible citizens within a people, not as a mass dragged along by dominant forces... Becoming a people is still more, and requires a constant process in which each new generation is involved. It is a slow and arduous work that requires wanting to integrate and learning to do so until a culture of encounter in a pluriform harmony develops" (EG 220).

The democratic question in Mexico

Theoretical framework: decent democracy

Norberto Bobbio, in his *Dictionary of Politics*[3] points out the following regarding democracy: "the problem of democracy, its characteristics and its reputation (or lack of such) is [...] as old as the reflection on politics itself , and has been reproposed and reformulated throughout history…".

Bobbio argues that in countries with a liberal-democratic tradition, the definition of democracy tends to be exhausted in a list of 'game-rules' or plain procedures: free elections, universal secret ballot, effective pluralism, majority principle, among others.

Along with the procedural notion of democracy, the author continues, in political language a qualifying attribute was introduced to the generic concept [of democracy]: "It is thus called… **formal** – characterized by procedural universals, by which decisions can be taken… and **substantial** which refers primarily to certain matters *in primis* egalitarianism is above all a government for the people".

Bobbio concludes: "it is necessary to recognize that in the two expressions (formal and substantial democracy) the term democracy has entirely different meanings. In the former it suggests a set of means totally apart from the ends; in the latter it implies a

---

[3] The following is a summary of the word Democracy (Bobbio – Matteucci – Pasquino 2011: 441-453).

certain set of ends, above all, the equality not only juridical but also social when not economic, independent of the consideration of the means adopted to achieve them...".

"The only point on which the one and the other could meet is that a perfect democracy – so far nowhere accomplished, and therefore utopian – should be at the same time formal and substantial" (Bobbio – Matteucci – Pasquino 2011).

Bobbio's realism leads us to the considerations of the philosopher Avishai Margalit, on the relations and differences between a just society and a decent society (Bobbio – Matteucci – Pasquino 2011: 441-453): "A decent society is one in which its institutions do not humiliate people; and I distinguish between a decent society and a civilized society. The former is one in which its institutions do not humiliate people, the latter is a society in which its own members do not humiliate each other" (Bobbio – Matteucci – Pasquino 2011).

In his view, a non-decent society can exist in a civilized society, and at the same time, it would be possible to have a decent but less civilized society. However, for Margalit this distinction is not much relevant, because "the idea of a civilized society is a micro-ethical concept that concerns the relations between individuals, while the idea of a decent society is a macroethical concept, linked to the social organization as a whole". The philosopher specifies, "the most important comparison of all is that between a decent society and a just society" (Bobbio – Matteucci – Pasquino 2011). In his conclusion, he argues with the principles of Rawls' *A Theory Of Justice* (1971), according to which;

1. Each person must have an equal right to the broadest system of basic freedoms, compatible with a similar system of freedoms for all.

2. Social and economic inequalities must satisfy two conditions: a) they must benefit the most disadvantaged members of society; b) positions and functions must be accessible to all, under conditions of fair equality of opportunity.

Margalit notes that Rawls distinguishes, in the relationship between a decent society and a just society, "two aspects in the distribution of the economic pie. One is the 'pattern', i.e., that the portions be equal for all. The other is the 'procedure' used to ensure that the distribution is fair" (Rawls 1971: 214).

The above is fundamental, because it alludes to the possibility that the distribution may be procedure – wise humiliating, which raises the question whether a just society is necessarily a decent society. Margalit, like Bobbio, is realistic in his conclusion: "It is highly probable that the political strategy aimed at achieving a decent society has little to do with the one to be followed to achieve a just society, even if this is, necessarily, a decent society" (Rawls 1971: 217-218).

With these elements, I propose the next definition for 'Decent Democracy', namely: it is one in which its formalities – the procedural universals and its institutions – do not humiliate people, because they are aligned, articulated and consistent with three principles: 1.- Recognition of the equality of all members of the community; 2.- Respect for their freedom; 3.- Abatement of inequalities through a fair distribution, with guidelines and mechanisms respectful of human dignity.

Following Margalit, its essential being for a decent democracy lies in avoiding the humiliation that governments and institutions can inflict on people by promoting or allowing discrimination, exclusion and 'a throw-away culture'[4] for various reasons: political, ideological, religious, ethnic, social and economic differences, cultural, gender, age, nationality.

Political regimes, even those that proclaim purposes inspired by the highest humanitarian, libertarian and egalitarian principles, despite being based on formally democratic procedures and deploying distributive social policies, can be, and many are, structurally humiliating.

---

[4] Term used by Pope Francis: "Some parts of our human family, it appears, can be readily sacrificed for the sake of others considered worthy of a carefree existence. Ultimately, "persons are no longer seen as a paramount value to be cared for and respected, especially when they are poor and disabled, 'not yet useful' – like the unborn, or 'no longer needed' – like the elderly. We have grown indifferent to all kinds of wastefulness, starting with the waste of food, which is deplorable in the extreme" (FT 18).

Diversity and inequality

How to build a decent democracy in a country in which one of its main characteristics is diversity and one of its biggest problems is inequality?

In its 2 million kilometers of territory, Mexico holds the treasure of one of the greatest biodiversities of the planet, housed among the forests, jungles, deserts, volcanic chains, valleys and coasts that form its multiple geographic regions.

Diverse human groups have settled in them: first their native peoples and since 500 years ago, settlers who arrived from other latitudes, mostly Europeans, but Africans as well, and later immigrants from the Middle East and Asia.

The process of Spanish occupation of the territory was carried out in several stages which lasted almost a century 1521-1611. It began in Mesoamerica[5] with the fall of Tenochtitlan, favored by the presence of organized indigenous societies[6]. It then advanced to Yucatan, Michoacan, Colima and New Galicia (today Jalisco).

Once consolidated, Spanish power began to expand northward, 'the march to the interior', sparsely inhabited by nomadic groups, stimulated by the possibilities of exploiting natural resources – the silver of Zacatecas, San Luis Potosí, Guanajuato – and establishing

---

[5] Term created by anthropologist PAUL KIRCHOFF to identify a cultural region, not geographic; delimited from the southwest of the United States to the west of the Central American isthmus. This cultural region was inhabited by several ethnic groups: *Nahua, Maya, Zapotec, Mixtec, Purepecha*, among others, in which diverse cultures and civilizations flourished, such as the *Mexica*, which became hegemonic.

[6] Pedro Carrasco: "The nature of Mesoamerican society and its geographical distribution form a fundamental antecedent to explain the process of Spanish conquest and colonization..". It was facilitated by several features of the pre-Hispanic political organization: stratified societies, peasant masses accustomed to obeying, and organism of domination. Mesoamerica was politically unified and the divisions between lordships made it possible to find allies to disrupt the *Tenochca* power. The Spaniards were able to use the dominant indigenous estate to rule indirectly through the Indian caciques. "It can be said that Mesoamerica, under the conditions of the 16th century, was an eminently conquerable country for the Europeans". *Cultura y sociedad en el México antiguo; Mesoamérica ante la Conquista, Historia General de México*, El Colegio de México, 2001: 232-233.

agricultural activities – and no less encouraged by the evangelizing impetus of the religious orders.[7]

Such multiplicity of human groups was integrated into the Spanish Empire as the 'Viceroyalty of New Spain'. It was territorially structured and governed under the legislation dictated by the Crown and the Council of the Indies, with norms based on the experience of unprecedented set of cases [casuistica] and unknown situations, as well as to mitigate the humiliation of the conquerors' atrocities and abuse caused by emigrants.

For this purpose, the 'Republic of *Indios*' was created, with town councils in the style of the municipalities of the Iberic peninsula, and the 'Republic of Spaniards', cities and towns founded by emigrant families, governed by city councils. All were vassals of the king and had his protection, but not all had the same obligations, since the Spaniards were exempt from tax burdens and only they enjoyed the privilege of occupying positions in the public office, which were forbidden to Indians, *mestizos*, black and castes.

This dual model was theoretically intended to protect the indigenous people, but humiliation took root, since, as Carrasco points out, "the growth of the Creole and *mestizo* population and the assimilation of a large part of the indigenous population downgraded the strictly-speaking Indian population to a marginal role" (Carrasco 2001: 235).

Nevertheless, this differentiation was the hotbed of new local cultures. In 300 years, a *mestizo* nation with a strong indigenous substratum was formed. An extensive mosaic of communities, cities and regions with their own idiosyncrasies, cultures, and varied personalities.

I must emphasize that at the origin of such cultural and socioeconomic variety, there was another determining factor for diversity and inequality: the density and forms of indigenous presence in the territory before the conquest; by sedentary indigenous societies, with varying degrees of organization or by unstructured tribal

---

[7] On the process of territorial occupation, see: García Martinez 2001: 257-306; O'Gorman 1976: 2-26.

groups. This factor defined the character of society that developed in each place and is still present in our social reality.

John Tutino[8] distinguishes two processes: the one that occurred in Spanish Mesoamerica, different from the one that took place in Spanish North America. In the former, Europeans implanted themselves "onto the enduring customs of Mesoamerica. Mesoamerican communities, cultures, languages, and beliefs adapted and persisted for centuries under Spanish rule. Mesoamerica was an old world, a world that adapted, changed, and endured despite conquest and colonial incorporation". Spanish Mesoamerica was "an inevitably limited attempt" (Tutino 2016: 58-59).

Spanish North America was different: "When the Europeans arrived in the 1530s [...] El Bajío (actual center of Mexico) was a sparsely populated frontier... they developed as the first new world in America... it was neither a variant nor an appendix of Spanish Mesoamerica; the two developed in parallel as distinct colonial orders: the kingdom of New Spain governed both and from their combination obtained dynamism and durability" (Tutino 2016: 60).

Tutino goes on: "Beginning in the 16th century, the Bajío and Spanish North America developed as commercial societies. The profitable production of silver and commercial goods organized almost everything [...] a diverse population, almost all displaced, struggled to live and produce with few community rights and few land rights for sustainable agriculture. The result was a versatile capitalist society in the interior of America..." (Tutino 2016: 68-69).

Thus, it is possible to have a deeper understanding of the complex social, economic and ethnic fabric that emerged then, whose traits survive to this day.

---

[8] Jonh Tutino (1947), a specialist in Mexican history at Georgetown University, has focused his research on the emergence, development, and importance of the *Bajío* region, formed by the current states of Querétaro, Guanajuato, and Aguascalientes. He contributes to the historical analysis the identification of Spanish North America, differentiating it from Spanish Mesoamerica.

Let us look at the geographical regions of the country. Specialists – I follow the study of Bernardo García Martínez (2001: 25-91) – identify six geographic groups subdivided into 89 regions in Mexico's territory, which, it is worth mentioning, do not correspond to the boundaries of the political division.
1-Central Mexico; 15 regions, in the current states of Puebla, Tlaxcala, Mexico City, State of Mexico, Hidalgo, Queretaro, Michoacan, Guanajuato, Jalisco, Oaxaca.
2-Gulf slope; 13 regions in what today are the states of Veracruz, Puebla, Oaxaca, Hidalgo, San Luis Potosí, Querétaro and Chiapas.
3-Pacific slope; 15 regions, in the states of Morelos, Oaxaca, Guerrero, Michoacán, Colima, Jalisco and Nayarit.
4-Northern slope; 29 regions in the states of Zacatecas, Coahuila, San Luis Potosí, Durango, Chihuahua, Sinaloa and Sonora, the peninsula of Baja California, Nuevo León and Tamaulipas.
5-Central American Chain; 9 regions located in Oaxaca and Chiapas.
Caribbean Chain; 8 regions in Veracruz, Tabasco, Campeche, Yucatan and Quintana Roo.
Next, the composition of the country's indigenous population. There are 68 indigenous peoples with their own native languages, which are organized into 364 dialectal varieties. According to the National Institute of Statistics and Geography (INEGI), 27.7 million people (21.5% of the population) self-identify as indigenous. Meanwhile, 12 million inhabitants (10.1% of the population) reported living in indigenous households. 6.5 percent of the national population is registered as speaking an indigenous language, representing 7.4 million people[9].
The 20 most numerous peoples are concentrated in the following geographic groups:

---

[9] See: *Atlas de los Pueblos Indígenas de México,* Instituto de los Pueblos Indígenas, atlas. inpi.gob.mx *El Mundo Indígena 2020:México,* Grupo de Trabajo Internacional para Asuntos Indígenas (IWGIA)iwgia.org

[20] *pueblos y grupos indígenas de México con mayor población, htpps//www.mexicodesconocido. com.mx*

Nahuas: in Central Mexico, the Gulf, Pacific and Northern slopes.
Mayas: in the Central American and Caribbean chain.
Zapotecas: in the Pacific slope and the Central American chain.
Mixtecas: in Central Mexico.
Otomí:in Central Mexico,
Totonacas: Gulf Coast.
Tsotsiles: in the Central American Chain.
Tzeltales: in the Central American Chain.
Mazahuas: in Central Mexico.
Mazatecos: in the Gulf Coast.
Huastecos: in the Gulf Coast.
Choles:in the Central American Chain.
Purépechas: in Central Mexico.
Chinantecos: in the Gulf Coast.
Mixes: in the Central American Chain.
Tlapanecos: in the Pacific Coast.
Tarahumaras: in the North Slope.
Mayos: in the North Slope.
Zoques; in the Central American Chain.
Chontales de Tabasco: in the Caribbean Chain.

Special mention should be made of the **Afro-descendant** ethnic group. They were incorporated into Mexico's multiethnic landscape, which began to take shape in the 16th century, at the same time as the Europeans, and are a component of the social diversity that has been developing since then.
It says a lot about their exclusion that until very recently an institutional effort began to make them visible and protect them (CNDH Mexico 2016)[10]. Studies indicate that Afro-descendant communities are located in coastal areas and in villages on the banks of rivers in the states of Guerrero, Oaxaca, Tabasco, Veracruz, and in the '*tierra caliente*' region of Michoacán.

---

[10] *Afrodescendientes en México. Protección Internacional de sus Derechos Humanos*, National Human Rights Commission. Coordinator Helen Patricia Peña Martínez, Research and text Ariadne García Hernández, 2016.

In the municipality of Múzquiz, in the northern state of Coahuila, are the descendants of the black tribe of the **Mascagogos**, a people that resulted from the coexistence and mixed race between the Seminole Indian communities and slaves from the plantations in the North American colonies, to whom in 1850 the Mexican government granted refuge on the northern border of the country (CNDH Mexico 2016: 19-21).

Unfortunately, the beauty of ethnic and cultural diversity is transformed into human, social and economic tragedy:

The report *El Mundo Indígena 2020: Méxic*, by IWGIA, already referred to above, points out, "The original communities continue to be the most vulnerable to the situation of inequality, since according to the National Council for the Evaluation of Social Policy (CONEVAL), 69.5% of the indigenous population, 8.4 million people, experience a situation of poverty, and 27.9%, 3.4 million people, of extreme poverty...". [11]

For its part, the research on Ethnic-Racial Diversity in Mexico and its influence on social mobility, by the Inter-American Development Bank IDB, reveals:

1. "We found that in Mexico the simple fact of self-identifying as indigenous or Afro-descendant is associated on average with a decrease between 2 percentiles (indigenous peoples) and 4 percentiles (Afro-descendants) in wealth, as well as with 0.4 (indigenous peoples) to 0.9 (Afro-descendants) fewer years of education completed on average, even taking into account other factors such as rurality, age, language and gender".

2. We observed evidence that points to the existence of differences in the generational transmission profile of wealth and education among indigenous peoples and Afro-descendants, compared to the rest of the population. We found that among indigenous peoples and Afro-descendants there is a high heritability of poverty and low transmission of wealth, while among the rest of the pop-

---

[11] Poverty measurement 2018. *Población según pertenencia étnica*, CONEVAL, Mexico 2018. Available at http///www.coneval,org.mx./evaluación/publishin-l glmages/Pobreza 2018/POBLACIÓN PERTENENCIA ETNICA.ipg.

ulation there is a low persistence of poverty between generations but a high heritability of wealth".

"In other words, for both the indigenous and Afro-descendant populations, immobility is aggravated among those who have the least wealth, while at the same time increases the downward mobility. This implies that in Mexico it is more difficult for indigenous and Afro-descendant people to escape poverty and much easier to fall into poverty even when they come from a household with greater resources. A parallel phenomenon is observed in the case of the level of schooling measured by years of study" (Rojas – Aguad – Morrison 2019).

After 500 years of *mestizaje* and 200 years of being an independent nation, it is worth asking: why the social and political structures of Mexicans place us so far from a decent and just society?

II. great ideals and difficult realities: "you know how to be free, it is up to you to point out how to be happy".

Illusions, utopias and paradigms

The Mexican national state was born with optimism and great expectations.

Agustín de Iturbide, a general in the service of the Crown who fought against the pro-independence insurgents after 10 years of revolts and destruction, led a successful negotiation that involved all the fighting military forces: insurgents and royalists, the Novo-hispanic ruling classes and Viceroy O'Donojú himself – a representative of King Ferdinand VII – to emancipate the opulent and immense kingdom of New Spain from the Iberian metropolis.[12]

The great agreement among all factions was called the "Plan for the Independence of North America", popularly known as the "Plan

---

[12] The natural and cultural riches of New Spain, as well as the development achieved and its potential for the future, were analyzed and described at the dawn of the 19th century by one of the most representative explorers of the European enlightenment (Humboldt 1966).

of the Three Guarantees" – Religion, Union, Independence. The Army of the Three Guarantees was formed, commanded by Iturbide, who victoriously entered the capital on September 27, 1821. In the proclamation he addressed to the nation, he pronounced an unfinished prophecy: "You already know the way to be free, it is up to you to point out the way to be happy" (De Iturbide 1921). The agreement between the forces outlined the program to constitute the Mexican Empire based on principles and purposes of equality and freedom. For the reflection that concerns us, the Union guarantee expressly sought the unity of all social classes. In Iturbide's words, "the general union between Europeans and Americans, *Indios* and Indigenous people, is the only solid foundation on which our common happiness can rest" (Cuevas 1947: 192). This was stated in the Plan, according to its clause XII: "All its inhabitants, with no other distinction than their merits and virtues, are ideal citizens to opt for any job" (Cuevas 1947: 193). This provision repealed the discriminations established during the viceroyalty between *penisulares*, Creoles, Indians, *mestizos*, and castes, including those of African descent. Historians notice that such inclusion was more advanced than the liberal Constitution of Cadiz in granting citizenship without racist exclusions (Jiménez Codinach 2001: 248-252).

Paradigms: state and democracy

What happened afterwards was not very pleasant. The novo-Hispanic people found the way to be free, to be an independent Mexican nation and sovereign state, but the way to become happy has been a bumpy exploration.

Two paradigms dominate this persistent search: the construction of a strong State as guarantee of political order; and democracy – according to the criteria of each era – motivated by justice and equality. In 200 years, we have experienced a wide repertoire of modalities mixing both paradigms.

The Mexican State has gone through five periods:[13] 1) Constitu-

---

[13] In the division by periods, I have modified and expanded the methodology of the

ent 1821-1867; 2) Constitutional 1867-1911; 3) Revolutionary Constitutional 1911-1917; 4) Post-revolutionary Constitutional 1917-2000; 5) Democratic Constitutional 2000.

The constituent or establishing period 1821-1867: it is distinguished by its indefiniteness and inconsistency, which took the monarchic form on two occasions: First Empire 1821-1823 with Agustín de Iturbide and the Second Empire 1863-1867 with Maximilian of Habsburg.

There were six experiments with the republican model: four with the federal formula and two with the centralist.

The sign of this period is the civil war between the liberals, who wished to erase the old vice royal order, and the conservatives who proposed to reformulate the institutions already existing in the new independent state. Reconfiguring the State-Church relationship with radical and moderate laicism was a destabilizing factor.

No less destructive were two foreign wars, namely, with the United States (1835-1847); first, for the independence and annexation of Texas to the American Union and then for the invasion that took away half of the territory. And the second war with France (1861-1867), because of Napoleon III's adventure as the sponsor of the Second Empire with Maximilian.

No one could expect that in these four decades of permanent disorder and confrontations, justice and equality would have advanced in Mexican society, or that humiliations would have diminished.

In the **constitutional period** the form of organization was consolidated. A secular, republican, federalist State came to be. It had two stages: The restored Republic from 1867-1876, and the *Porfiriato* from 1876-1911.

The liberal victory abolished privileges and exemptions, and radically executed the separation between Church and State, disentailed -that is to say expropriated and took out to the market- the goods of the clergy and religious orders, and also promoted the capitalist economy in an agrarian society.

---

historian José Bravo Ugarte (1946). He recognizes two: constituent/establishing period 1821-1867 and constitutional from 1867 onwards. For my part, I divide the second into three periods: constitutional, revolutionary, post-revolutionary and democratic.

Among the social sectors that lost out from the liberal reform were the indigenous communities; the new agrarian statute also put their communal lands on the market, those that had been protected for the Indian peoples by the laws of the viceroyalty.

During the *Porfiriato*, political stability was achieved through a dictatorship with republican formalities. The tensions with the Church moderated without making juridical concessions. Also, in this period the promotion of foreign investment was encouraged through infrastructure works, railroads, and although late, the industrial revolution arrived in the country.

The period ended abruptly when a multi-class rebellion broke out, with demands for political freedom, social justice and restitution of land to the people. The middle class had grown, but inequalities increased. It became evident that in that period humiliations had increased.

The revolutionary constitutional period began with the 1910 revolution. The democratic demand 'Sufragio efectivo no reelección' (*Effective suffrage, not reelection*) demanded the fulfillment of the 1867 constitution, satisfying the grievances of the peasant communities and workers.

In 1911 the first elections in the history of the country were held with universal standards of democratic procedure. It was a brief spring; in 1913 President Madero was assassinated.

An armed uprising of social and political leaders from different regions and with diverse profiles followed. First, they were united to overthrow Madero's assassin, but soon after they confronted each other.

In 1917 a Constituent Congress was called. The new Magna Carta ratified the republican and federal principles, strengthened the Executive Branch over the Legislative, incorporated social rights, agrarian reform, established the nation's ownership of its natural resources and reinstated radical Jacobinism.

This period opened, legislative wise, the possibility of healing some old social humiliations, but deepened the religious ones.

Post-revolutionary constitutional period. First stage 1917-1929: authoritarianism of the caudillos. With the new constitution, a new period of stability and economic reconstruction was expected. This was not the case, since the dispute for power divided the leaders of the revolution once again.

Generals from the state of Sonora (northern mexico) came to power and began to apply the revolutionary, social, political and anti-religious program. On the one hand, economic life began to resurge; on the other hand, an absurd harassment of the Church and Catholics escalated, which gave rise to a civic resistance movement demanding respect for religious freedom.

The government's response was humiliating and persecutory; the aggrieved, using the argument of a just war, took up arms, giving rise to what is known as the '*Cristero War*', whose theater of operations was the central states of the country (1926-1929).

President Calles, the only survivor of the revolutionary caudillos who had become 'the maximum leader', stopped the bloody dispute for power by grouping all the revolutionary factions into a state party: the National Revolutionary Party (PNR).

Thus began the second stage of this period: corporate authoritarianism 1929-1968. The state party pyramidally structured the political-administrative apparatus and the social organizations. In the format of federalist republicanism, a vertical, rigid, and hierarchical system was developed, in whose highest point was placed the Federal Executive Power.

Its holders concentrated constitutional and meta-constitutional powers, with very few limitations: no reelection, negotiating stability among the groups of the revolutionary family, and the relationship with the United States. They held four leadership positions: head of state, head of government, head of the army and head of the hegemonic party (Carpizo 1978).[14]

During 70 years, fifteen presidents succeeded each other peacefully. Historians have baptized it with different names: sexennial hereditary absolute monarchy by transversal route (Cosío Villegas

---

[14] Classic text that unravels from the legal perspective the concentration of power in the hands of Mexican presidents.

1972); imperial presidency (Krauze 1997), and perfect dictatorship (Vargas Llosa 1990).

Each one of the fifteen presidents imprinted his personal style and orientation. President Cárdenas (1934-1940) reformed the party as an organization of social sectors, including the military; this was a form of popular front with the ideology of revolutionary nationalism (Party of the Mexican Revolution PRM).

Presidents Avila Camacho and Miguel Alemán, in the context of the Second War and the post-war period, moved the ideological pendulum to the center: they airbrushed the party (Partido Revolucionario Institucional PRI), disassociated the military sector from its ranks and initiated an industrialization program with import substitution within the framework of a mixed economy.

It achieved its best moment during the years of the Stabilizing Development of 1954-1970, which was called the 'Mexican miracle' with high growth. This period was successful in achieving the maximum level of production with price stability (Llerenas Morales 2018).

But the model suffered from serious structural disparities and entrenched historical inequalities. It was recognized that "in the Mexican economy there are mechanisms that favor a marked and growing concentration of income, originating in sectoral and intrasectoral inequities and regional and intraregional differences in the development process, as well as in the concentration of ownership of the means of production, and various social and political factors, connected with the poor preparation (schooling) of the labor force, the impoverishment of marginalized urban and rural groups and the scarce increase in unionized workers..." (Banco Nacional De Comercio Exterior 1971: 33-64; Carmona – Montaño – Carrión – Aguilar 1970).

If, in the economic sphere the model exhibited its counterfeit, in the political sphere its revolutionary legitimacy had been consumed. Just when it was boasting its best numbers, political contestation erupted, marking the beginning of its decline (1968-1988).

Independent trade unionism began to express itself with greater force, the university movement was bloodily suffocated by the military forces (1968), the civic-electoral action of the partisan opposition increased in various parts.

The criticisms of the system multiplied; they proposed a profound change. From the Marxist perspective, a classic text was 'Democracy in Mexico' by Pablo Gonzalez Casanova (1967). From Christian humanism, the document 'Democratic Change of Structures' emerged, proposed by two Catholic intellectuals and politicians: Efrain Gonzalez Morfin and Adolfo Christlieb Ibarrola.[15]

The regime's responses to recover legitimacy and respond to nonconformity failed. They were economically destructive and sustained its traditional mechanisms of domination.

From 1970 to 1982 it practiced a fiscally irresponsible populism that destroyed economic stability. Currency devaluations caused capital flight, reduced the savings of the population to ashes and made the poor poorer. Wastefulness consumed the resources of the oil boom of those years: "Instead of being the lever of development, oil became the way back to indebtedness and financial problems" (Ravasa Kovaks 2013).

This made the citizens even more angry and the regime was forced to liberalize the political system (Linz 1990; O'Donell – Shimitter 1986: 20-21; Woldenberg 2012: 18-46; Bravo Mena 1992); this new opening seemed to be a gatopardist maneuver to disguise the dictatorship as democracy. Nonetheless, this incited political competition, which led to an increase in electoral conflict. The political reform encouraged party plurality but in real terms it did not mean power sharing: the imposition of authorities through electoral fraud was the real law in the electoral processes in the municipalities and states.

Thus began the stage of the transition to democracy 1988-2000: the accumulation of social, economic, and political tensions was expressed in all its magnitude in the 1988 presidential elections.

The PRI (Institutional Revolutionary Party) was divided: the official candidate, Salinas de Gortari, represented the technocratic

---

[15] *Cambio Democrático de Estructuras, Memorias de la XX Convención Nacional, feb. 7 1969,* Ediciones del Partido Acción Nacional, N. 12, 1969.

sector with a proposal of economic modernization in tune with the neoliberal world trend, without democratization: "perestroika without glasnost"[16]. The revolutionary nationalist wing of the PRI represented by Cuahutémoc Cárdenas – son of former President Cárdenas – formed a front with all the parties of the left. For its part, the center-right middle class rallied around the National Action Party candidate, Manuel Clouthier.

The triple clash of forces broke the system. The post-electoral crisis of 1988 achieved a great transformation potential. President Salinas assumed power without legitimacy of origin. In order to move forward with his economic reform plan, he had to incorporate proposals from the opposition parties on various issues into his government program, give guarantees that his electoral victories would be respected and negotiate new rules of the game[17].

Special mention should be made of the negotiations with the Catholic Church to reform the constitution and grant legal recognition to the churches (1992). Diplomatic relations were established with the Holy See and progress was made in religious freedom. The historical humiliation in this matter began to heal.

At the end of Salinas' six-year term, the country's economic model was immersed in a profound metamorphosis, following the recommendations of the Washington Consensus[18] and under the rules of the North American Free Trade Agreement Mexico-United States-Canada, in force since January 1994.

On the same date the Trade Agreement started, the Zapatista Army of National Liberation (EZLN) began a rebellion of indigenous communities in the state of Chiapas, unleashing a process –still unfinished – for their visibility and vindication of their historically postponed rights.

---

[16] Reference to the reform program implemented in the Soviet Union between 1985 and 1991 by President Gorbachev. In general terms: *Perestroika*, economic restructuring; *Glasnost*, political opening.

[17] Partido Acción Nacional, *Compromiso nacional por la legitimidad y la democracia*. November 16 1988. http//www.memoriapoliticademexico.org

[18] *Medidas del Consenso de Washington*, economipedia.com

The presidential succession of that year was traumatic, the group in power lost cohesion. Its candidate, Colossio, was assassinated. This set of events led the government to maintain investor confidence with high interest rates and win the elections by increasing public spending. The elements for a new economic crisis were in place.

The collapse occurred in the first months of President Zedillo's administration. Banco de México describes it as "the most severe since the 1930's". It dragged down banks, businesses and families, inequalities deepened, GDP fell 6.9 percent.[19]

In January 1995, while managing the economic crisis, President Zedillo sought a way out of the political pressure by calling the parties to a National Political Agreement to take definitive steps towards a democratic transition. In October 1996, after laborious negotiations, a consensus was reached which resulted in a robust legislation with norms and institutions in accordance with the 'procedural universals' of free and democratic elections.

In March 1995, the Congress approved the Law for Dialogue, Conciliation and Peace in Chiapas, and created the Commission for Concord and Pacification (COCOPA), as an intermediary body of the Legislative Power between the EZLN and the Federal Government. On January 16, 1996, the 'San Andres Agreements' were signed, recognizing the need for a new relationship between the State and society with the indigenous peoples of the country. It was agreed to establish a "new pact to eradicate the daily forms of public life that generate subordination, inequality and discrimination and to make effective the rights and guarantees that correspond to them: to their cultural difference, to their habitat, to the use and enjoyment of their territory, in accordance with ILO (International Labor Organization) Convention 169, to community self-management, to the development of their culture, to their traditional production systems, to the management and execution of their own development projects".[20]

---

[19] On the causes, dimensions, consequences and measures to overcome this crisis, see Banco de México, Annual Report 1995.
[20] *Acuerdos sobre derechos y cultura indígena.* Joint statements that the Federal Government

The process that began with the irruption of the EZLN in the political scenario is unfinished, the agreements were not fulfilled, the constitutional reform sent by President Zedillo in 1998 did not receive the approval of the indigenous movement. Its fulfillment is still being demanded.

The democratic Constitutional period 2000 began with the first elections held under the new democratic rules. In 1997 the Federal House of Representatives (lower house) was renewed and the PRI, the former hegemonic party, did not obtain a majority, the President lost control of the Legislative Branch. The transition to democracy had begun.

In the 2000 presidential elections, the trend was consolidated; Vicente Fox, nominated by the PAN, inaugurated the history of alternation, six years later Felipe Calderón, from the same party, won the election again.

When PAN won the Executive Power, it did not achieve a majority in Congress but dismantled the imperial presidency. Presidentialism, as described by Carpizo,[21] ceased to exist. The division of powers and federalism became effective, although it later degenerated into feudalarism.[22] Autonomous constitutional bodies developed, and new ones were created to deconcentrate power.[23]

---

and the EZLN will send to the national debate and decision-making bodies. Chiapas. iiec.unam.mx

[21] *Ibid.*

[22] The neologism *feudalarism* defines the process by which state governors, freed from the yoke of imperial presidency, became feudal lords with high degrees of mind-boggling corruption.

[23] The autonomous constitutional bodies are: *Banco de México* BM (Mexican Banc); *Instituto Nacional Electoral* INE (National Elections Institute)*; *Comisión Nacional de los Derechos Humanos* CNDH (National Comission for Human Rights); *Instituto Nacional de Estadística y Geografía* INEGI (National Institute of Statistics and Geography); *Comisión Federal de Competencia Económica* (Federal Comission for Economic Development)COFECE; *Instituto Federal de Comunicaciones* IFT (Federal Institute of Communication); *Instituto Nacional de Transparencia* (National Institute for Transparency), *Acceso a la Información y Protección de datos personales* INAI (Access to Information and Protection of personal data); *Fiscalía General de la República* FGR (General Prosecutor's Office); Consejo Nacional de Evaluación de la Política de Desarrollo Social CONEVAL

The multiparty landscape in local and municipal governments neutralized.

The PRI's return to the presidency in 2012 did not have the conditions to rebuild the presidency of its ancestors. However by political culture, style, and corruption mechanisms it was able to colonize some of these institutions.

During this period, the full recognition of the rights of indigenous peoples did not undergo significant changes. Fox promoted a new constitutional reform (2001) that did not meet the expectations of a substantive change either. The demand to comply with the San Andres Accords with a far-reaching reform was maintained.[24] Nevertheless, a public policy was designed with the creation of the National Commission for the Development of Indigenous Peoples (CNDPI) and there was a renewed focus of social policies, but the levels of inequality were not significantly reduced.

In 2018, the current President López Obrador won the election, nominated by the National Renewal Movement, MORENA. Under the paradigm of carrying out a Fourth Transformation - the first, independence; second, the reform of the 19th century; third, the revolution of 1910 - and with the slogan 'the poor come first', he applies a program with similarities to the revolutionary nationalism of the 1940s.

His political party, MORENA, has the majority in both Houses of Parliament and is advancing constitutional reforms to reverse part of the legal scaffolding built during the 'neoliberal' governments to reposition the State as the rector of the economy. The federal budget is available to carry out a massive transfer of resources to its strategic priorities: to social programs, with direct cash deliveries to registered beneficiaries through networks under presidential control called 'Servants of the Nation', and to costly infrastructure works in the southeastern states.

(National Counsel for the Political of Social Development Evaluation); *Instituto para la Evaluación de la Educación* INEA (Institution for the Evaluation of Education). See en.m.wikipedia.org

[24] "La reforma constitucional en materia indígena de México", *Revista Lex* 79, January 2002. Archivos.juridicas.unam.mx

A redistributive purpose is presumed in this since the target population of the social programs and the southeast concentrate the greatest social and economic backlog. However, it is not yet possible to draw definitive conclusions about their effectiveness.

Where palpable changes can be seen, with serious unknowns about their political outcome, is in the reconcentration of power in the Presidency and the impulses to return to the hegemonic party.

This is accompanied by ideological overload in decision-making; intolerance to pluralism, to the protagonism of civil society, to autonomous bodies, to the press, as well as disregard for social protests demanding attention: women and the lack of medicines in the public health system.

The health system underwent a total reconfiguration: *Seguro Popular* was cancelled and the *Instituto de Salud para el Bienestar* INSABI was created; to eradicate corruption, the system for purchasing medical supplies and medicines was dismantled, all under centralized control. There have been serious shortages and medical facilities have increased their inhuman precariousness.

The COVID-19 pandemic is managed with political criteria. The country registers 288 thousand deaths, 5th place in the world in the mortality rate for confirmed cases.[25] Vaccination did not use the effective vaccination system created during decades and is executed with guidelines and channels without clear logic.

No less disconcerting is the new role assigned to the armed forces, which are seen as 'people in arms', commissioning them with public security functions, with the National Guard under their command. It has been transformed into an infrastructure construction corporation that controls ports and customs, and receives additional commissions for work that is not of its nature. The greatest contrast with the army's growth and the political will to rebuild a strong state is the reluctance to confront the organized crime that plagues many regions of the country.

There is no evidence of the results of the policy of 'hugs, not bul-

---

[25] See: JHU CSS COVID, Universidad Johns Hopkins, which assesses the performance of the Mexican health system in the COVID-19 pandemic; available at: htpp://www.arcgis.com/apps/dashboard/85320e2ea5424dfaaa75ae62e5c06e61

lets' and not fighting violence with violence, addressing its causes and fighting the cartels in other ways. Criminal groups have taken over several areas and hundreds of families live under their terror and abuses; in last June's electoral process they proved to be a determining factor in defining the outcome in several regions.

We are facing the deepest hell of humiliation, from December 2018 to last November 3rd 83,596 homicides[26] have been accumulated, the disappearances of people are daily, and the discovery of clandestine graves is permanent news… In the face of this horror: impunity.

President Lopez Obrador incorporated an indigenous ritual into his inauguration ceremonies, in which he was handed the baton of command. From the speech and the *paraphenalia*, it seemed that the expected new relationship between the State and the indigenous peoples was at the door with the fulfillment of the San Andres Accords.

In three years, beyond the claim to Spain and the Church for the conquest and Christianization, and some actions in favor of the Yaqui People in Sonora, there is no evidence of significant variations in the condition of exclusion in most of the communities.

The CNPDI, created by President Fox, was renamed the National Institute of Indigenous Peoples (Instituto Nacional de los Pueblos Indígenas INPI), but the major change does not appear.

Among the social actors most critical of the Morena government are the indigenous movement and the EZLN. In fact, they have never been part of their cause. The 4th Transformation

has not had, until now, a specific policy for them that satisfies their repeated demands. For the construction of the Mayan Train and other gigantic works in the southeast, the obligatory consultation of the peoples has not respected the point of view of the non-conforming communities.

---

[26] INS, Prosecutor's Office Report, homicides_03112021_v2(1).pdf; see also: http://www.informeseguridad.cns.gob.mx/

III. From the philanthropic ogre to the anthropophagous ogre. Where are we?

Octavio Paz published in 1978 an essay on the Mexican State: *El ogro filantrópico* (The Philanthropic Ogre). In that year, the central issue in the public discussion was the political reform proposed by the government.

He argued: "the modern State is a machine that reproduces itself incessantly" and "the State created by the Mexican revolution is stronger than in the 19th century... it completed its evolution with the creation of two parallel bureaucracies": administrators-technocrats and political professionals. In Mexico, "the central power resides neither in private capitalism, nor in the unions, nor in the political parties, but in the State. Secular Trinity; the State is Capital, Labor and the Party. However, it is neither a totalitarian State nor a dictatorship".

He described the apparatus of domination that had been placed, heavily, on top of people and society. Thus, the poet was critical of the political reform underway. Given the persistence of the courtly patrimonialist morality within the State and its corruption. "The State should begin with its self-reform" and look at the traditional democratic practices of peoples and communities". If democracy is pluralism, the first thing to do is to decentralize (Paz 1978: 85-100).

Ten years later, in 1989, the philosopher and politician Carlos Castillo Peraza wrote El ogro antropófago (The Anthropophagous Ogre), about the irrepressible tendency of the State to expand, assuming functions of various kinds with a tendency to monopolize them.

Such a State "does not usually present itself as the representative of the privileged sectors, sometimes not even of the marginalized or the weak, but as the superior instance depositary of the definition and realization of the common good...".

"Overgrown, the State will become at the same time capable of being violent as a cruel and omnipotent monster, and kind, if on its altar every man and every social group accepts to become habitual accomplices or eventual victims... Lost its possible philanthropic facet, especially in times of economic or political crisis, the ogre shows itself for what it is: a voracious being that does not hesitate to crush men, an anthropophagous creature".

He continues that at the bottom lies a crisis of culture: "The State must be recovered by civil society, yes, but a civil society that is capable of rediscovering, creating, developing, disseminating and assuming democratic culture, as well as giving itself the instruments to do so" (Castillo Peraza 1989: 328-350).

Beyond the title of the two texts, the reflections of both Mexican thinkers complement each other and can be combined with the proposal of Decent Democracy. The post-revolutionary state described by Paz was in the first phase of liberalization, without the will to democratize; but he finds it philanthropic because, in his view, it is neither totalitarian nor a dictatorship. Castillo warns of the danger of the gigantic State, capable of devouring the will and power of society, whether 'democratically' consented or kidnapped in a authoritarian or totalitarian way.

Paz recommends to the Mexican State to self-reform. To resume the democracy of the communities and peoples and therefore decentralize. Castillo bets on the strength of civil society, on the participatory and responsible democratic culture of citizens.

We have seen the periods through which the Mexican State has passed, from its birth to the present day. It does not seem that our bicentennial ogre has taken firm steps to become a 'decent ogre'.

I will conclude with a balance. I make use of a relevant study to compare our reality with the paradigm of Decent Democracy: the Index of Democratic Development of Mexico IDD-Mex, elaborated every year since 2010, and published with the support of the Konrad Adenauer Foundation and other institutions.[27]

The IDD-Mex is compatible with the concept of Decent Democracy, because it follows the criterion of 'maximalist democracy' based on authors such as Gerardo Munck (2009), who warns that

---

[27] *Índice de Desarrollo Democrático de México, IDD-México 2020,* Konrad Adenauer Foundation KAS, Polilat, S.A, Instituto Nacional Electoral INE, Confederación USEM, Centro de Estudios Políticos y Sociales CEPOS, available www.idd-mex.org / info@idd-lat.org

research on democracies should include aspects that go beyond the electoral process and the electoral connection between voters and their representatives. It is a multidimensional study that presents national and state aggregates, which allows for a deeper and more detailed analysis.

In its national chapter the IDD-MEX 2020 with data referring to 2019 statistics points out:

"Compared to the previous year all dimensions present lower averages, evidencing that a greater number of states obtained lower results".

1st Dimension Citizens' Democracy: measures respect for civil rights and freedom; citizen exercise of commitment to the values of democracy, indigenous exclusion, and gender violence.

"It worsens again this year, with a drop in the order of 4% with respect to IDD-Mex 2019".

2nd Dimension Democracy of Institutions: measures institutional quality and political efficiency; perception of corruption, participation of political parties, legal and political accountability, social accountability, destabilization, federal intervention in powers, government crisis.

"The national average falls again and continues the trend of the previous year, registering the second worst value, only higher than in 2018".

3rd Dimension Social Democracy: measures capacity to generate policies that ensure well-being; unemployment, population under poverty line, performance in health: infant mortality and spending, performance in education: illiteracy rate, secondary terminal efficiency.

"It falls on average with respect to the previous report".

4th Dimension Economic Democracy: Capacity to generate policies that ensure economic efficiency; GDP per capita, inequality, competitiveness State-Society, financial autonomy, investment.

"Falls on average with respect to the 2019 report.[...]" At the federal level, the differences in democratic development between the regions of the country continue. In 2019, 21 of the 32 entities had advanced in their development index. On the other hand, in 2020 only 11 states achieved a better result compared to the previous year.

In the ranking by states; high DD : Yucatán, Baja California Sur, Aguascalientes, Querétaro, Hidalgo, Tlaxcala, Tamaulipas, Sonora, Nuevo León.
Medium DD: Coahuila, Sinaloa, San Luis Potosi, Jalisco, Mexico City, Campeche, Durango, Quintana Roo, Tabasco, Guanajuato, Nayarit, Colima, Zacatecas.
Low DD: Baja Califiornia, Chihuahua, Puebla, State of Mexico.
Minimum DD: Chiapas, Oaxaca, Michoacan, Veracruz, Morelos, Guerrero.
In view of the specific topic that concerns us here, let us look in to the GDP per capita of the states, measuring their economic capacity in relation to their population, measuring the value of the product (total value of the production of goods and services of a state) in relation to its distribution among the population. It is a suitable indicator to characterize the generation of economic capacity for a decent life.
High GDP-Development. "Mexico City leads the national ranking, Campeche has an enormous difference with respect to the rest of the states. The economic potential of the country's capital is far superior to any state. In the case of Campeche (southern state), a good part of its economic capacity comes from the oil income, we have applied a correction factor, since according to all studies, most of this wealth, although it originates in that state, has not been a powerful tool for the transformation of the economic reality of that state. These two states are accompanied by Nuevo León".
Five states have **medium GDP development**: Baja California Sur, Coahuila, Sonora, Querétaro and Tabasco. Eight with **low development:** Quintana Roo, Aguascalientes, Baja California, Chihuahua, Jalisco, Colima, Tamaulipas, San Luis Potosí. Sixteen entities show **minimum GDP-development**: Sinaloa, Guanajuato, Yucatan, Durango, Morelos, Veracruz, Nayarit, Zacatecas, State of Mexico, Puebla, Michoacan, Hidalgo, Tlaxcala, Guerrero, Oaxaca and Chiapas.
Income Inequality is one of the factors that limits social and economic development since a less egalitarian society conditions the possibilities of individuals to develop and generate value. The

indicator allows us to review how the wealth generated in each entity is distributed and whether this distribution contributes to reversing situations of inequality.
The study ranks 18 entities with high development: Nuevo León, Baja California Sur, Mexico City, Coahuila, Quintana Roo, Colima, Querétaro, Sinaloa, Chihuahua, Jalisco. Sonora, Aguascalientes, Nayarit, Campeche, San Luis Potosí, Tabasco, Yucatán, Michoacán. 10 are in the medium development group: Guanajuato, Durango, Puebla, State of Mexico, Tamaulipas, Zacatecas, Hidalgo, Tlaxcala, Veracruz and Chiapas. Only one state, Oaxaca, shows low development.
The study points out: "Mexico suffers from extreme inequality, with 44% of its inhabitants living in poverty, and 7.5% in extreme poverty. The richest 10% of the population receives 36% of the country's income; in contrast, 50% of the population divides 20% of the country's income. The poorest 10% receive only 1.8% of the income."
"In Mexico there are around 12 million 'rich' people who concentrate the economic resources of more than 84 million people with low or very low incomes. In 2002 the wealth of the four most affluent Mexicans represented 2% of GDP and in 2018 it was equivalent to 10%."
"Vulnerability in Mexico is structural so it needs structural and not gradual changes, not only transference programs to particular sectors. It requires policies of inclusion, of deep transformation, not only economic but also social. All of this also translates into environmental vulnerability, as there is less access to key resources such as water".
Regarding the exclusion of indigenous rights and freedoms, the IDD-Mex 2020 coincides with what has already been exposed above in the section Diversity and Inequality (p.11) with what is pointed out in the IWGIA report (quote 23 p.11), and by the CONEVAL (quote 26 p.12) and the IDB Study (quote 27 p.12). The indices of exclusion and inequality associated with ethnic diversity call for a structural change that has not been achieved at any stage of the Mexican State. Among others, this is the most pressing issue in the paradigm of a Decent Democracy.

Final reflection

For 200 years, 13 generations of Mexicans have sought freedom, justice, and democracy as formulas for happiness. We have done it, repeatedly disunited, humiliating each other; either by ethnic, cultural, social, and economic differences, or by religious causes; sometimes by ideologies; other times by party radicalism and power fever. What some do, others undo; and this is the vicious circle in which we have been going around for two centuries.

Episodes of dialogue and consensus are scarce. Our troubled history is written and rewritten in a Manichean key. The successes that some boast, standing on the humiliations of others, become crimes in time and the humiliated become humiliators.

We will not achieve a Decent Democracy without the intervention of the new agent of change: a strong civil society, promoter of a culture of responsible participation, seedbed of a political class committed to respect the dignity of people, and to the solution of their problems through dialogue, social friendship, solidarity, and subsidiarity. To follow the four criteria proposed by Francis to achieve the common good and peace: 1º time is superior to space, 2º unity prevails over conflict, 3º reality is more important than the idea and 4º the whole is superior than the part (EG 217-237). Above all, we need activists to approach each other, express ourselves, listen to each other, look at each other, get to know each other, try to understand each other, and look for points of contact. In short, to incarnate in our lives and sculpt in the soul of our social and political institutions the verb dialogue (FT 198-223), and to travel together, with courage, the paths of reunion, starting from the truth, as artisans and architects of peace, to heal wounds and avoid new humiliations.[28]

---

[28] *Ibid.*, Paths of renewed Encounter, n. 225-253.

References

Banco Nacional De Comercio Exterior, S.A., *México: La política económica del nuevo gobierno,* Chapter 2: La situación económica al iniciarse los años setenta, 1971.
Bravo Mena F.L., *Los Cambios Políticos en México ¿ dónde estamos?,* Folleto Alternativa 6, Secretaría de Estudios del Partido Acción Nacional, 1992.
Bravo Ugarte J., *Compendio de Historia de México,* Editorial Jus, 1946.
Bobbio N. – Matteucci N. – Pasquino G., *Dizionario di politica,* 1983. Trad.English; Dictionary of Politics, Mexico, Siglo XXI editors, 2011.
Carmona F. – Montaño G. – Carrión J. – Aguilar A. M., "El Milagro Mexicano", *Editorial Nuestro Tiempo,* 1970.
Carpizo J., *El Presidencialismo Mexicano,* Siglo XXI editores, 1978.
Castillo Peraza C., *El Ogro antropófago,* Epessa, 1989.
CNDH Mexico, *Afrodescendientes en México. Protección Internacional de sus Derechos Humanos,* National Human Rights Commission, 2016.
Cosío Villegas D., *Sistema Político Mexicano,* Cuadernos de Joaquín Mortiz, 1972.
Cuevas M., *El Libertador,* Selected Documents of Don Agustín de Iturbide; *Iguala* Plan. February 24, 1821, Editorial Patria, 1947.
De Iturbide A., "Speech upon entering Mexico City", September 27, 1821. *Los Presidentes de México ante la nación: informes, manifiestos y documentos de 1821 a 1966* V, Cámara de Diputados, Ediciones de la XLVI Legislatura.
Garrasco P., *Cultura y sociedad en el México antiguo; Mesoamérica ante la Conquista, Historia General de México,* El Colegio de México, 2001.
García Martinez B., *La creación de la Nueva España; Historia General de México,* El Colegio de México, 2001.
——, *Regiones y paisajes de la geografía mexicana, Historia General de México,* El Colegio de México, 2001.

González Casanova P., *La democracia en México*, Ediciones Era, 1967.
Von Humboldt A., *Ensayo político sobre el Reino de la Nueva España* (Political Essay on the Kingdom of New Spain), Editorial Porrúa, Mexico, 1966.
Jiménez Codinach G., *México su tiempo de nacer 1750-1821*, Fomento Cultural Banamex, 2001.
Krauze E., *La Presidencia imperial*, Tusquets, 1997.
Linz J., *Transitions to Democracy*, The Washington Quarterly, Summer 1990.
Llerenas Morales V., "El Desarrollo Estabilizador", *El Economista*, 2018.
Margalit A., *The Decent Society*, Harvard University Press, 1996. trad. Esp. *La Sociedad Decente*, Paidós, 2010.
O'Donell G. – Shimitter P. C., *Conclusiones tentativas sobre las democracias inciertas*, Paidós, 1986.
O'gorman E., *Historia de las divisiones territoriales de México, Introducción histórica*, Editorial Porrúa, 1976.
Paz O., *El ogro filantrópico, historia y política, 1971-1978*, 1979, in *Vuelta* 21, August 1978: 85-100.
Pope Francis, *Evangelii Gaudium*, III. The common good and Peace in society, 2013.
——, *Fratelli Tutti*, VI. Dialogue and Friendship in Society, 2020.
Ravasa Kovaks T., *Auges petroleros en México: sucesos fugaces; El segundo auge petrolero, 1978-1981*, UNAM Economics, 2013. http:scielo.org.mx
Rawls J., *A Theory of Justice*, Cambridge, Harvard University Press, 1971.
Rojas M. A. – Aguad J. – Morrison J. A., *Diversidad étnico-racial en México y su influencia en la movilidad social*, Inter-American Development Bank, Gender and Diversity Division, June 2019.
Tutino J., *Creando un nuevo mundo, Los orígenes del capitalismo en el Bajío y la Norteamérica española*, Fondo de Cultura Económica, 2016.
Vargas Llosa M., *Encuentro El Siglo XXI, la experiencia de la libertad*, *Vuelta* magazine, August-September,1990.

WOLDENBERG J., *La Transición democrática en México. La Reforma de 1977 y las primeras elecciones después de ella,* El Colegio de México, 2012.

Lecture n. 6

CITIZENSHIP
The Problem of Migration: Separation of Families, Caravans and Remittances.

The Role of Qualified Professional Migrants as Agents of International Development and Corporation

Dr. Celine de Mauleon –
Red Global Mexicanos Calificados – Mexico City

I. Introduction

I.1. International frameworks of reference for migration, and their links with the values of Christian social doctrine.

International organization for migration (IOM)

Founded in 1951, the IOM became an agency of the United Nations (UN) in 2016 and serves as the leading intergovernmental organization in the field of migration. It currently has 174 member states, 8 observers and offices in more than 100 countries, including in Italy. The action of the IOM is based on the principle that an orderly migration with respect for human dignity benefits both migrants and society. Here we find a first alignment with the principles of Christian social doctrine and the ministry of Pope Francis for integral human development.

UN-Migration Global Compact
International framework adopted in 2018 by 152 countries to address migration through shared principles of humanitarian, development, and human rights dimensions, recognizing all the dimensions of international migration with a holistic and comprehensive approach. This is an internationally, non-legally binding intergovernmental agreement that respects the sovereign right of states to determine migration rules in their country but demonstrates commitment to international cooperation and includes concrete objectives and mechanisms to monitor enforcement. The negotiations that led to the adoption of this pact were co-chaired by Mexican Ambassador Juan Jose Gomez Camacho together

with Swiss Ambassador Jurg Lauber. The principles underlying this instrument are: 1) Human Rights; 2) Sovereignty and International Cooperation; 3) Gender awareness and sensitivity; 4) People-centered; 5) multi-stakeholder approach; 6) Integrality.

Agenda 2030 for Sustainable Development

The 2030 Agenda, adopted by 193 countries in 2015, is the most ambitious international policy document since the adoption of the United Nations Charter in 1945. The 2030 Agenda recognizes that poverty and development are not one-dimensional phenomena merely linked to economic growth, industrial development, or technological progress, but to multidimensional and interconnected phenomena with a strong predisposition for the achievement of integral human development. In fact, the dimensions of sustainable development are three: social, economic, and environmental.

The 2030 Agenda is organized around the so-called '5Ps Framework' (People, Planet, Prosperity, Peace, and Partnerships) and establishes 17 Sustainable Development Goals (SDG)[1], which are the global roadmap towards a new development model of universal scope that aims at sustainability and places the person and human dignity – no longer governments – at the center of development efforts. The ODS are:

GOAL 1: No Poverty
GOAL 2: Zero Hunger
GOAL 3: Good Health and Well-being
GOAL 4: Quality Education
GOAL 5: Gender Equality
GOAL 6: Clean Water and Sanitation
GOAL 7: Affordable and Clean Energy
GOAL 8: Decent Work and Economic Growth
GOAL 9: Industry, Innovation and Infrastructure
GOAL 10: Reduced Inequality

---

[1] See: https://sdgs.un.org/goals

GOAL 11: Sustainable Cities and Communities
GOAL 12: Responsible Consumption and Production
GOAL 13: Climate Action
GOAL 14: Life Below Water
GOAL 15: Life on Land
GOAL 16: Peace and Justice Strong Institutions
GOAL 17: Partnerships to achieve the Goal

I.2. The notion of development in the light of the encyclicals Laudato Si' and Fratelli Tutti

In his beautiful and prophetic Encyclical Laudato Si', Pope Francis proposes the concept of *integral ecology* and invites all men and women of good will on earth to reflect on the beauty and suffering of creation in the light of this revolutionary concept. Now, to talk about sustainable development from an integral ecology perspective, it is important to understand what sustainable development is. In 1987, the World Commission on Environment and Development published the so-called 'Brundtland Report' (which served as the basis for the 1992 Rio Summit – better known as Earth Summit) and defined sustainable development as that which can "satisfy present needs without compromising the ability of future generations to meet their own needs". In other words, it calls to understand that what we do today will impact the future of the new generations and will determine their ability to live in dignified conditions.

From the definition of sustainable development, 5 main highlights can be drawn in line with the spirit of integral ecology in the light of Laudato Si':

1. Fair and sustainable development consists of a global, regional and national strategy that allows future generations to progressively improve their quality of life and protect biodiversity without destroying the planet's natural resources.

2. Sustainable development must take place in conditions of economic and environmental efficiency both in the use of natural resources and in the production of goods and services, while the use of

scientific and technological knowledge must enable the protection of renewable and non-renewable resources and promote less polluting production models.

3. Production must always be cleaner in the use of materials, processes, and transformations. Energy from fossil sources will have to be replaced with other forms and sources of energy that are less contaminating and even entirely clean.

4. Sustainable development must be fair, that is, development policies must aim at reducing the huge inequalities that emerged in the 20th century in all the continents of the world. Unemployment and misery cannot take place in an equitable and sustainable development model.

5. In summary, implementing sustainable development means undertaking an integral and multidisciplinary process, in which real productive investments do not only look at achieving high indices of economic well-being, but which simultaneously take into consideration environmental investment and the need to build social well-being in fair way.

As can be seen, the concept of sustainable development embodies various principles and teachings of the Christian Social Doctrine. Such is the case with the notion of *social equity*, that is, to assess the degree of development, it is necessary to consider all social and economic policies and their real effects on inequality. It also encompasses the principle of *social justice*, which implies achieving fewer inequalities and less extreme poverty. It clearly underlines the principles of *solidarity and human fraternity*: intergenerational solidarity (between present and future generations but also those that precede us), and intra-generational solidarity (between members of the same generation). Finally, and above all, it provides for the *protection of the environment and biodiversity*, that is, solidarity with the planet – our common home – and care for creation.

We clearly see how strongly the principles of sustainable development are linked to the principles of integral ecology and universal brotherhood. So, we see how ecological conversion, human solidarity and Laudato Si' values are fundamental to achieving a new model of socio-economic development and human coexistence in harmony with the common home and with our most vulnerable brothers and sisters.

II. Migration today, what is it?
Migration, migrant workers, and qualified professional migrants

II.1. Migration[2]

Human migration is a movement of individuals from one geographical area to another, done with the intention of temporarily or permanently staying in the new area. This means that migration can be of various types:

a) Domestic: within the same state.
b) Regional: from one country to another, remaining in the same geographical region.
c) Global: the international mobility of people between countries in different continents of the world.

Migration is a historical phenomenon that strongly affects the life of the societies of origin, transit or destination of the populations who decide to migrate or are forced to do so. Therefore, it is important to emphasize that the impact of migration affects all societies in the world, either developed or developing countries.
According to IOM, in 2018 there were about 257.7 million **international migrants** on a global scale (it is important to emphasize that this figure **represents only 3.4% of the world population**), of which **74.6% are economically active**.
Currently, most people think exclusively about the figure of poor migrant workers, whose hypothesis is based on the traditional theory that says that poverty, instability, lack of access to education

---

[2] See: Loreto-Echeverria G. – Pérez-Rodríguez M.A. 2019, available at: https://doi.org/10.17163/ret.n17.2019.09.

and to other basic services in the country of origin are the only factors that push people to emigrate from their country.

Nonetheless, today we see that this theory – even if it unfortunately remains a part of reality – is no longer applicable as the only model at a universal level, since today we do not migrate only for reasons related to poverty, instability, or lack of opportunities. In today's world there are those who migrate for work commitments, higher education or specialized training, there are those who migrate for love, for family reasons, for personal choice of residence, for the desire to reach a higher level of quality of life or for an even greater professional growth in an increasingly globalized and highly interconnected world.

In the contemporary world, globalization has intensified the phenomenon of international migration due to the interdependence of economies, transnational work networks, the growth of ICT (information and communication technologies) and the digital industry, which all together have facilitated physical and virtual mobility permanently and have stimulated the attraction of skilled talent to different geographies of the world (Loreto-Echeverria – Pérez-Rodríguez 2019).

Therefore, I affirm that today, migration is a phenomenon that responds to multiple causes and that has different types, and therefore must be understood and addressed in a broader, creative, human, and multidisciplinary way. It is in this context that the figure of professional and skilled migrants emerges.

To understand this approach, we will analyze two of the main theories of migration:

- The *Theory of Dependence* (Castles – Delgado 2007), which says that migrations in general are due to problems of poverty and lack of opportunities, so they only reinforce the vicious circle of poverty in the territories of origin. Although this vision is partly real, I consider it limited since it is focused only on the category of migrant workers and unskilled labor, or those who sadly escape wars or fragile national contexts.
- The *Co-development Theory* (Lacomba 2004), on the other hand, states that migrants favor investments, entrepreneurship, the transfer

of knowledge and technology, thus making themselves agents and promoters of development. In the light of today's world, this vision is more appropriate since it considers the wide range of benefits and contributions that migrants – in all forms of migration – offer to their societies of origin and destination, including professional and skilled migrants (Kapur – Mchale 2005).

Below are some preliminary considerations to continue to define and better understand the current context of migration, and extract some lessons learned:

1. International migrants are only 3.4% of the world population, and 74.6% of them are economically active (IOM, 2018).
2. The bulk of international migration is made up not of poor people, but of members of the middle class from countries with stable and emerging economies, who are driven by the desire for higher professional growth or to have a better quality of life than the one they already enjoyed in the country of origin.
3. The bulk of international migration, in fact, is made up of people with a certain degree of professional training, with a certain economic level, and therefore with the ability to actively contribute to the economy, scientific and technological development, competitiveness and positive integration in the societies of the host countries.
4. A very high percentage of these migrants remain morally tied to their country of origin, to which they try to reciprocate. Although this traditionally takes place in the form of remittances, on this issue it must be emphasized that professional migration reciprocates by promoting economic exchange, stimulating the transfer of knowledge and technology, or the creation of partnerships and cooperation mechanisms. For this reason, professional migration also has the power to strengthen bilateral relations and promote social integration between countries of origin and host countries.

It is therefore necessary to oppose the political and/or media discourse, sometimes populist, which looks one-dimensionally at migration forgetting the human face, personal dignity, and the creative and courageous character of migrants.

Recognizing the benefits that international migration brings to the economy, culture, education, and human development in our societies is also a way to understand and promote the spirit of integral ecology and integral human development, thus responding to the appeal of Pope Francis in the Encyclicals *Laudato Si'* and *Fratelli Tutti*.[3]

II.2. Migrant workers[4]

Migrant workers are identified with the **theory of dependence**: the traditional view of migration that is motivated only by poverty, lack of opportunities, war or fragile and unstable national contexts. Under this theory, underdevelopment is the main cause of migration, and migrant workers are both the cause and part of a vicious circle of poverty and loss of human talent towards both countries of origin and host.

Below we analyze the characteristics and challenges of the so-called migration of workers and unskilled labor:

- When migrants move with their families, the depopulation process accelerates because return migration becomes less likely and there is no longer a need to send remittances.
- When migrant workers bring their families with them, they reinforce the growth of a second generation in the host countries who grow up in singularly disadvantaged conditions.
- The experience of lower-level assimilation of the second generation reinforces negative stereotypes about the immigrant population in the host countries, thus increasing the likelihood of it becoming an impoverished, caste-like minority.
- When entire populations of migrants take their families away with them, progressively the country of origin becomes a ghost and abandoned population.

---

[3] https://www.vatican.va/content/francesco/it/encyclicals/documents/papa-francesco_20201003_enciclica-fratelli-tutti.html
[4] See: Massey – Arango et al 1998.

- The concept of 'relative deprivation' that would affect non-migrant families when they compare their situation with that of those who have emigrated abroad, states that migration represents a form of security on the part of rural families who use migration as an economic tool and survival strategy.
- This is because the positive effects of migration derive from its ability to compensate for market imperfections by allowing households to participate in productive activities and to have access to credit and futures markets in the rural areas of their countries of origin. Even when remittances are spent for direct consumption, they are said to generate indirect multiplier effects because they create a renewed demand for locally produced goods and services. Although this is a positive assessment, it is questionable when the depopulation of rural areas makes the productive use of remittances impossible.

All this considered, it is important for the migration of workers to be cyclical and not permanent. Since migration inevitably generates a settlement process in the host country and this can generate a risk of depopulation in the place of origin, the main consideration must be whether the cyclical nature of the flow can be preserved.

Cyclical migrations work best for both home and host societies. Returners are more likely to save and make productive investments at home, and they leave their families to which they send substantial remittances. Temporary migrants do not compromise the future of the next generation by putting their children in danger of inferior assimilation abroad.

II.3. Professional migrants[5]

According to the **theory of co-development**, migrants in general, in particular highly skilled professionals and technicians, are engines of the economic competitiveness of the host country and become agents of cooperation and exchange with their countries of origin. Countries with medium – not poor – entrancesare the main

---
[5] See: Portes 2006.

source of skilled migration. The middle class in countries with well-established economies is the heart of professional migration. Achieving 'middle class' status in one's country of origin is the main motivation for professional migration on an international scale: it is not the wage difference that guides the decision but the ability to guarantee a more dignified quality of life and better work conditions and opportunities for their own human development. In this context, it is important to emphasize that in the light of the 2030 Agenda, the Sustainable Development Goal 17 invites the creation of innovative partnerships between different actors to achieve all objectives across the goals. This multi-stakeholder and multi-sector partnership approach also involves civil society. Professional migration is indeed part of civil society, therefore, in this new paradigm, professional migration is called to contribute to international development and to the creation of a more fraternal, more just, more compassionate, more prosperous, more sustainable and more supportive society.

However, the positive relationship between migration and development is not automatic and market forces alone will not be able to establish the link. The positive effects of professional migration depend on two main factors: 1) the actions of the government in the country of origin, and 2) the type of migration.

There are some enabling factors to make the contributions of the qualified diaspora possible and effective in their country of origin and destination. To this end, the active role and intervention of the State are crucial to generate a productive structure in rural areas, and institutional scientific and technological infrastructures capable of innovating. These elements constitute the necessary condition to incorporate and materialize the development potential of migratory flows. Some examples are:

- Official creation of higher education centers.
- Support for international applied research projects.
- Incentives for the establishment of innovative companies and for the development of private high technology industry.
- Institutions able to receive and benefit from the remittances, investments, and transfers of both economic, scientific, and techno-

logical nature that migrants send, in order to effectively support the development of the country.
- Develop protected national industry initiatives, to promote technological development and job creation for any migrants wishing to return to their country.
- Develop transnational networks to involve the qualified diaspora and stimulate economic and industrial dynamism.
- Launch collaboration initiatives with the networks of universities and research centers at national level.

Some examples of government programs launched to promote the attraction of international talent are:

- International talent in India and Taiwan to promote the development of national industries: engineers, scientists, researchers, high technology, doctors, ICT, highly qualified specialists.
- Silicon Valley (CA), Ruta 128 (BO), Research Triangle Park (North Carolina).
- H-1B visa program (USA - India, Canada, Mexico, China, Colombia), Carta Blu (Italy).

III. Case Study: Mexico

III.1. Global overview of country context

Overall national context
Mexico is culturally a Latin American country and geo-politically a North American country. Although for culture, history, and popular tradition it is a country that absolutely identifies itself as Latin-American and part of the Latin American region, geographically Mexico belongs to the North American region along with the United States and Canada – it is not Central America nor South America.
With 126 million inhabitants in 2020 and an average age of 29, Mexico is the 11th most populous country in the world, the 15th economy by GDP globally and the 2nd one in Latin America. Mexico is the 11th exporter worldwide and the 1st in Latin Amer-

ica. It is a member of the G20, IMF, WTO, and OECD, and thanks to its 14 Free Trade Agreements with all regions of the world it has preferential access in 50 countries representing 60% of world GDP.

Mexico is one of the mega diverse countries in the world, with a great wealth of biodiversity and culture, characterized by an important component of indigenous peoples. Nonetheless, the serious problems of social inequality, poverty and inequitable access to basic services strongly affect the country, in particular the southern states and indigenous and rural communities.

National poverty challenges

Since 2015, Mexico has applied the CONEVAL[6] methodology for multidisciplinary measurement of poverty, which considers that it is not only income that determines people's poverty or vulnerability, but the ability to access the various basic services that impact the actual degree of human development in an integral way.

This Mexican vision has also been incorporated into the M&E mechanisms of the 2030 Agenda and considers 9 dimensions of poverty according to social deprivation criteria:

a) entry level,
b) educational backwardness,
c) access to health,
d) access to social security,
e) access to housing quality,
f) suitability of basic services,
g) access to nutritious and quality food,
h) urban conditions, and
i) social cohesion.

CONEVAL statistics show that between 2018 and 2020 the percentage of the population living in poverty at the national level went from 41.9% to 43.9% (increased over 3.8 million people).

---

[6] See: CONEVAL (2021), available at: https://www.coneval.org.mx/Medicion/Paginas/PobrezaInicio.aspx

In the same period, the population living in conditions of extreme poverty went from 7.0% to 8.5% (2.1 million more).
Lack of access to social security shows the highest incidence: 52.0% of the population (i.e., 66 million people). Lack of access to health services increased from 16.2% to 28.2% (over 15.6 million people). Lack of access to nutritious and quality food increased from 22.2% to 22.5% (1+ million people).
The highest growth and incidence of poverty are recorded above all among children under 18 (52.6%). Between 2018 and 2020, total current per capita income decreased by 6.9%.
It is important to consider that these measurements coincide with the Covid-19 pandemic that began in 2020 and is still ongoing at the time of drafting this report, so the outcomes and implications for economic and social development are still uncertain. However, this information offers a first comprehensive overview of the implications of the pandemic on the income and social deprivation of Mexicans in 2020.

The impacts of poverty on the indigenous population
Mexico is a federated republic of 32 states. The states with the highest levels of poverty are Chiapas, Guerrero, Puebla, Oaxaca, and Tlaxcala; while those with the most severe index of extreme poverty are Chiapas, Guerrero, Oaxaca, Veracruz, and Tabasco. Mexico City does not present serious challenges of poverty or extreme poverty.
People who speak an indigenous language live in more severe poverty than people who speak Spanish (the country's official language). Chiapas, Guerrero, Oaxaca, and Tabasco are the states with the largest rural component and indigenous population nationwide. This picture highlights that indigenous peoples and rural communities in the poorest states are the most vulnerable to poverty and social deprivation, hence those who suffer the most.
The population aged three and more who speaks some indigenous languages amounts to 7,364,645 people (6.1% of the total population). In proportion, although the number of indigenous language speakers has increased, this population group has de-

creased – it is being lost – compared to 2010 when it constituted 6.6% of the total population (6,913,362 inhabitants).

III.2. Focus: Mexico City (CDMX)

Mexico City is the country's capital and the seat of the Union Powers. Its population is 99% urban. In 2020, its population numbered 9,209,944 inhabitants, which represents 7.3% of the country's total population. Although it represents 0.1% of the national territory, being the smallest entity in the country, CDMX is the second most populated federal entity behind the State of Mexico which has just over 16.2 million inhabitants.

Greater Mexico City refers to the conurbation around Mexico City, officially called the Metropolitan Area of the Valley of Mexico, which includes Mexico City itself and 60 adjacent municipalities in the State of Mexico and Hidalgo. If the entire metropolitan area of the Valley of Mexico is considered its largest city, the metropolitan area of Mexico City reaches 21,804,515 inhabitants, making it the largest metropolitan area in North America, the fifth metropolitan area in the world (behind Tokyo, Delhi, Shanghai, and São Paulo), the second largest urban agglomeration in the Western Hemisphere (behind São Paulo) and the largest Spanish-speaking city in the world.

The Mexican capital is the largest urban place and the main political, economic, social, academic, financial, commercial, tourist, cultural, communication and entertainment center in the country. The city is also one of the central regions of Latin America, with GDP growth of around $ 200 billion (10% of the regional total). The main sectors of the economy are financial services, real estate, commerce, services, and manufacturing industry.

Classified as a global city, it is also one of the most important financial and cultural centers in the world, with one of the most dynamic economies internationally. Due to the size of its GDP (USD +3 billion), it contributes 17% of the total national GDP.

If it were an independent country, Mexico City would have been the fifth largest economy in Latin America in 2013. In 2019, its

Human Development Index was 0.837 (ranked very high), the country's top entity for Human Development Index.

Regarding the socio-economic profile, the largest percentage of the inhabitants of CDMX have completed higher education studies, and 64% of the population is economically active (97.8% of which is employed). We therefore understand that the migratory profile of those who move from Mexico City to other geographies in the world is high and qualified.

III.3. General overview of Mexican migration

With official data from the 2020 census carried out by INEGI – National Body for Statistics, Geography and Information Technology, Mexican migration has these characteristics:

- Causes of Mexican migration (Family 45.8%, Work 28.8%, Education 6.7%, Insecurity and Violence 4%, Other reasons 14.7%)
- Destinations (80% local, 15% national, 5% international)
- International emigration to the United States, by federative entity (Guanajuato, with 98%, is the state with the most emigrants to the USA; CDMX is the entity with the lowest percentage of emigration to the USA with 37%)
- Reasons for international emigration (Work 67%, Family 13%, Studies 11%, Violence 1%)
- Net migration balance (Baja California Sur 5.8%, CDMX -2.7%). The result of immigration and emigration to a given territory is the net migration balance, i.e., the difference between the number of immigrants and the number of emigrants in each geographical area and in each period. This balance can be positive or negative, i.e., in the first case a net population gain for the region under consideration, or a net population loss in the second case.

III.4. The Mexico-United States migration relationship

As we have seen, the dependency theory is based on wage differentials between exporting and job-receiving countries, which in the case of the Mexico-United States migration system currently presents a seven-to-one ratio for unskilled labor.

Although it has rarely been noticed, the reality is that the direct recruitment of day laborers on ranches and farms in the American Southeast is behind the massive migration from Mexico to the United States. Once migration began due to recruitment actions in Mexico during the 19th and early 20th centuries, the flow became self-sufficient thanks to the forces of the new migratory economy model. The feelings of relative deprivation discussed in section II.2 were reinforced by the increasing capitalist penetration into the Mexican countryside, which spread new consumer desires and expectations in line with US standards in the population.

The subsequent process of structural equilibrium reached its climax with the signing of the North American Free Trade Agreement (NAFTA) in 1994, which effectively reduced the autonomy of the Mexican state in the implementation of national economic initiatives or in protecting national entrepreneurship, making the Mexican fields a huge reserve of labor for industry and agriculture in the United States.

In essence, migration has resolved the inevitable contradiction between the weakening of local autonomy and the growing diffusion of new foreign consumption expectations in weaker nations, without the parallel diffusion of economic resources to access that consumption.

The story of how the increase in US border control did not stop the flow of Mexican labor, but ended its cyclical character, was told by Massey in 2002. The parallel story of how NAFTA in somehow shut down Mexican industry and severely weakened agricultural production was reported in detail by Delgado Wise and Márquez in 2006. This took place due to cheap Mexican food imports and high-intensity mechanized farming capital. The end of employment in various sectors of the Mexican economy and the severe reduction of productive investment opportunities in the field have stimulated permanent family migration north, reinforcing the effects of a militarized border.

These same conditions lead families to migrate north, facing desert and death if necessary. Once established across the border, there is little reason for these families to return and thus the alleged positive effects of migration on development are dispelled.

Therefore, I repeat that cyclical migrations of workers can have positive effects on development, especially at the community level. Permanent family migration does not have them, and instead implies that the places of origin are uninhabited. According to the evidence, this is what unfortunately happened in Mexico.

IV. The role of qualified professional migration: The Case Of The Global Network Of Mexican Professionals (RedGlobalMX)

The Global Network of Mexican Professionals represents a strategic ally and international best practice for Mexico, as it demonstrates an innovative vision that recognizes the role of professional migration as an actor of international cooperation and as an agent of empowerment, economic growth, and triangular and south-south cooperation.

RedGlobalMX was created in 2005, and for 17 years it has stood out as a model that transforms the phenomenon of 'brain drain' into a dynamic mechanism of 'circularity of knowledge', with mutual and tangible benefits for Mexico and the countries of residence. To date, there are 62 local chapters of the Network in more than 30 countries around the world.

The Europe region of RedglobalMX has existed since 2009. To date, there are 22 chapters in 19 countries of the region, structured into thematic commissions with specific work programs. The Europe region holds periodic elections to vote for a regional coordinator every two years through open elections. Each local chapter elects its own president and board of directors. The Europe Region, and RedGlobalMX in general, maintains a fluid relationship with the Institute for Mexicans Abroad of the Ministry of Foreign Affairs, with the network of Mexican Embassies and Consulates, and with local institutions in the host countries.

In Europe, RedGobalMX contributes to deepen and strengthen Mexico's bilateral relations; contributes to giving continuity to diplomatic and consular activity and to cultural promotion with a professional image; identifies strategic areas of opportunity with a sectoral and comparative vision; promotes business creation, economic exchanges and business missions; promotes academic cooperation and scientific and research exchange; contributes to the transfer of technology and to the enhancement of the creative and cultural industry; contributes to the empowerment and professional development of migrant women and facilitates the creation of strategic alliances with key players and comparative advantage for Mexico.

I am proud to have been the founder President of the Italian Chapter between 2016 and 2019, and Regional Coordinator for Europe in 2020.

Conclusions

- **Renewed, broader and more humane vision**: It is necessary to overcome the paradigm that identifies migration as a loss for the country of origin or as a phenomenon that arises solely from poverty and lack of opportunities, and consequently seen as a burden or discomfort for the country of destination.
- **Globalized and interconnected world:** Today, in a globalized world with highly interconnected economies and with the rise of the digital industry that permanently stimulates physical and virtual mobility, migration is a phenomenon that responds to multiple causes and has different typologies. Migration must be understood in a human and multidisciplinary way.
- **Migration, multidimensional phenomenon:** The partnerships and strategies that are generated to serve the global diaspora must differentiate the types of migration, the different causes that generate their mobility, the different challenges and needs that each one faces in their own regional or local context, and above all, one must be able to recognize the value and opportunities that each type of migration offers based on its characteristics, interests, and particular profile.
- **Migration, source of opportunities and cooperation:** Today, migration is no longer random but a structural component of any country's social life, which must be recognized in its economic, working, cultural and social value. The new strategies would be enriched with a global vision and a dual approach if they are able to contribute to the effective integration of the diaspora in the host country and to the activation of channels of collaboration,

exchange and proximity with the different institutions and actors in the countries of origin.

- **Migration governance and global citizenship:** The new migration governance must be based on personal dignity, human rights, solidarity, compassion, cooperation, and coexistence in fraternity (a human family approach). Dual citizenship should become an element of internationalization of the economy and national development.
- **Integrating skilled migration** also implies promoting their participation in social, cultural, and political life in the host country. School, family, entrepreneurial strategies, and national development plans should promote an 'us' – not 'us and them' – thinking.
- **Enhancement of migration with a view to developing human capital** aimed at economic growth, competitiveness, cultural integration, and internationalization. Only in this way will it be possible to generate a perception of 'round trip travel', that is, migration seen in the light of the mutual benefits for the economies and societies of all countries, with a vision of human brotherhood, solidarity, and international development, and not just in terms of remittances.

References

Castles S. – Delgado Wise R. (eds.), *Migración y Desarrollo: Perspectivas desde el Sur*, Miguel Angel Porrúa, 2007.

Kapur D. – Mchale D., *The Global Migration of Talent: What Does It Mean for Developing Countries?*, Center for Global Development, 2005.

Lacomba J., *Migraciones y desarrollo en Marruecos*, Instituto Universitario de Desarrollo y Cooperación, Editorial Catarata, 2004.

Loreto-Echeverria G. – Pérez-Rodríguez M.A "Migrations in contemporary society and its correlation with development", *RETOS Magazine of Science, Management and Development* 9, 17, 2019: 145-159 (https://doi.org/10.17163/ret.n17.2019.09).

Massey D. S. – Arango J. – Graeme H. – Kouaouci A. – Pellegrino A. – Taylor J.E., *Worlds in Motion: Understanding International Migration at the End of the Millennium*, Clarendon Press, 1998.

Portes A., "Migration and Development: conceptual review of evidence", *JOUR*, 2006.

Lecture n. 7

CULTURE
A Catholic Approach to Feminisms in Mexico City

*Cosmopolitan Peacebuilding as a
Guarantee of Women's Rights in Mexico City*

Prof. Julieta Becerril Romero – School of Law,
Anahuac University – Mexico City

In Mexico currently die 10 women per day as a result of femicide. This number is obtained from the official figures of the Mexican state, 2783 women victims of intentional murders and 940 alleged crimes of femicide for a total of 3,723 (SESNSP 2021). This social phenomenon rooted in socio-cultural patterns affects the life of women in Mexico. This is known as gender-based violence, in this case violence against women, specifically understood as "Any action or omission, based on gender, that causes damage or psychological suffering, physical, patrimonial, economic, sexual or death both in the private or public sphere that at its maximum expression materializes as femicidal violence" (LGAVLV 2021, article 5 FIV). This specific kind of violence is also defined in the law as "the extreme way of gender-based violence against women, product of the violation of their human rights in the public and private spheres, made by the set of misogynistic behaviors that can lead to social and state impunity and can culminate in homicide and other forms of violent death of women. In cases of femicide, the sanctions provided for in article 325 of the Federal Criminal Code will be applied" (LGAVLV 2021, article 21).

Mexico City is the capital of the country and recently has been object of the activation, for the second time, of the mechanism of gender alert (CONAVIM, 2019) precisely for the violence women endure, just for being women, in this territory. According to the statistics of the analysis with a gender perspective carried out by the Executive Secretariat of the National Public Security System (SESNSP, 2021), Mexico City has 11 of the 100 localities of the whole country with the highest number of investigations for femicide and in this localities violence has increased. From 2018 to 2019 the number grew from 38 to 63 investigations, which translates to a 60% increase. From 2018 to 2019, Mexico City went from concentrating 7.6% of femicides in the country, to 12% of them. In accordance with the foregoing, Mexico City is one of the three states of the entire republic, in which 35% of the cases of femicide are concentrated throughout the country, along with Veracruz and State of Mexico.

Now, from the international perspective, the Mexican State, as part of various international instruments, has assumed obligations related to this issue. From the perspective of International Human Rights Law, obligations to respect and guarantee human rights in general and specifically on women's rights have been assumed: obligations related to the prevention, punishment and eradication of violence against women. These obligations have been implemented in the Mexican legal system for their fulfillment and the problem persists and even according to the *numeralia* continues to increase.

Derived from the Inter-American Convention dedicated to this issue, the Belem Do Pará Convention, the States of said regional human rights protection system, including Mexico, adopted a series of obligations for the arrest, punishment and eradication of violence against women. Article 12 of said convention establishes the binding nature of Article 7 and the possibility of resorting to the system of individual petitions before the Inter-American Commission on Human Rights. Article 7 precisely, indicates all the obligations of the States Parties to deal with the social problem of violence against women specified in the content of the international convention.

Various doctrinaires have analyzed the problem, that from the legal point of view, is circumscribed to the field of the right to equality, since it is a problem that derives from a structural inequality that constitutes discrimination on the basis of gender, and that as such, it results in differential treatment that affects access to women's rights. (Belem Do Pará, 1994) This imbalance is manifested as one of the forms of gender violence, which, when taken to the extreme, is perpetrated as murder for gender reasons, typified in Mexico as femicide.

According to Article 1 of the Belem Do Pará Convention, violence against women is then understood to be "any action or conduct, based on gender, that causes death, damage or physical, sexual or psychological suffering to women, both in the sphere of public as well as private". Article 2 specifies what shall be understood as violence, including physical, sexual and psychological. This has been implemented at the national level in the General Law of Access for Women to a life free of violence. Derived from the Case of González et al. V. Mexico, before the Inter-American Court of Human Rights, Mexico was condemned to implement international regulations and take measures specifically for the phenomenon of femicide.

From the above, it is necessary to look at the Mexican state actions in the face of the problem in order to comply with its international obligations *vis-à-vis* the inter-American human rights system and to be able to determine if what is necessary is being fulfilled to attack the root of the problem and move towards a substantive equality and the construction of a sustainable peace that achieves the reconstruction of the social fabric and reconciliation between men and women from a personal perspective that allows integration of the Mexican society.

Hence, the right to equality takes on special relevance, since it is at the heart of the social issue. The right to equality includes both the principle of equality, the foundation and basis of the universality of human rights and legal security, as well as the principle of non-discrimination. This equality, in the strict sense, unfolds in two dimensions, the formal and the material / substantive.

The theories focus on the need to delve into the concept of substantive equality, since the formal one is the one that has been most developed, including this right in legal texts, which does not translate into a materialization in factual reality. Hence the importance of study to achieve real substantive equality.

One of the main factors lies in the direct, structural and cultural violence that exists and derives from social inequalities that generate an imbalance in the exercise of human rights and access to opportunities in equal circumstances. Imbalance, that manifests as unequal pay for example. Hence, the look at substantive equality rather than simple formal equality between men and women is crucial for the analysis of this problem. "Substantive equality refers to the fact that laws and policies must guarantee that women have the same opportunities for men in different social and personal spheres, and that there is a conducive environment for this to be achieved; that is, all obstacles must be eliminated so that equality is achieved in fact" (INAH 2016: 7).

When we speak of substantive equality, we can delve into the elements that, according to various doctrines, they must incorporate. There is debate about it, about what substantive equality means and should imply. Rosenfeld's vision argues that substantive equality refers to a 'fair' equality of opportunity, which seeks to transcend formal equality and equalize the 'starting point' of people so that their advancement is based on their merits. (Rosenfeld 1986) Lira, for its part, defines substantive equality as one that combines equal opportunities with equal results. (Lira, 2019) While Sandra Fredman, on the other side of the spectrum, classifies this vision as insufficient to address inequalities and proposes a four-dimensional approach Compensating for inequalities, counteracting prejudice / stereotype, promoting political participation and recognizing difference while eliminating detriment (Fredman 2016).

As a reaction to the situation of violence against women in Mexico in 2019 the feminist movement accentuated within the National Autonomous University of Mexico which took violence against women as a banner of struggle and was installed through strikes in different careers with two crucial moments the death of Lesvy Berlin and Miranda Mendoza. This even outgrew the University after the rape of a woman by policemen of Mexico City (Soto 2021).

This University movement gained strength in the streets having as a point of convergence the request for the generation of public policies to fight gender violence and stop femicide. (Soto, 2021). Within the broader context of fourth-wave feminism, these collectives have successfully broken the silence on the seriousness of the problem of violence against women in Mexico, helping to shape public opinion and the political and media agenda (Cerva 2020). According to Lucía Álvarez, the result was a 'new type' of movement that has a peculiar protagonist, it is diversified and, in many ways, different from previous feminist movements since it is lacking of specific and unified leadership, and has been deployed with its very 'own' language, direct and confrontational, even re-sorting to the use of violence as a means of "communicating and shaking". This movement has managed to impact public opinion, among other significant achievements like securing the attention of the authorities and triggering institutional and normative changes. (Álvarez 2020: 167) This violent protests are explained by Cerva, who analyses the way in which these mobilizations were intensified and amplified by hostile reactions in the public sphere and from a social media backlash. It argues that the energy and focus of contemporary Mexican feminist activism comes from a dual indignation: rage due to the epidemic of violence against women is intensified by further institutional violence in the form of hostile, revictimizing, anti-feminist public discourses (Cerva 2020).

As we can see, the latest feminist movements have resorted to violence as a tool of communication and impact to achieve the objectives. Before this scenario, I believe it is important to consider the role of an additional legal framework that has been developed in the international sphere as another branch of studies on conflict resolution and peacebuilding within which, the differentiated approach that women bring to international peacebuilding, has been made visible (UN Security Council S/RES/1325 2000).

The use of this additional perspective, is presented as a proposal to complement the international legal framework in the field of international human rights law. Since, as we saw, this framework only establishes mechanisms and obligations for the prevention, attention and punishment of the specific phenomenon, but it does not consider addressing the social consequences of it. I am referring to the breakdown of the social fabric and family disintegration to give some examples.

Peacebuilding is a doctrinal concept that was born in the field of international relations around 1990 in areas of armed conflict where it was sought to generate neutral spaces for peace from below, the concept has been developing, but its central factor is the importance of local actors to prevent, manage, transform and reconcile conflicts.

Precisely from the foregoing, it is necessary to make an analysis of the legal framework that Mexico has, to achieve these objectives and comply with international obligations on human rights. Specifically, what is related to the respect and guarantee of the right to a life free of violence for women in Mexico City in the light of peace-building tools.

Peace is a necessary value and principle that constitutes an essential element for the full experience and development of human rights that is also a human right of it's own and that directly violated in cases where there is violence. Peace has been classified into two different kinds, negative Peace defined as the absence of war and the positive Peace, which is not the absence of conflict because it is understood that conflict is part of human nature, it is the actual means towards sustainable and endurable peace.

This conflict in the field of interpersonal relationships is manifested in one of its facets in gender-based violence between the relationships of men and women. This violence affects to a greater extent women who make up a group in vulnerable situations and who have traditionally been discriminated against. From this differentiated trade for reasons neither objective nor reasonable, it is necessary to delve into the search for substantive equality so that it effectively materializes in access to opportunities. From the above, it is interesting to investigate the implementation of peacebuilding processes at the local level with the active participation of women who are especially affected by the problem, as can be seen from the number of femicides in the country.

However, the implementation of this international regulation at the national level is something that the authors speak of as cosmopolite conflict resolution for the construction of positive and sustainable peace. Ramsbotham explains that the use of the term 'cosmopolitan conflict resolution' indicates the need for an approach that is not situated within any state, society or established space of power, but rather promotes constructive means to manage conflicts both locally and globally. For the sake of humanity (Ramsbothan 2011).

Ulrich Beck who was a sociologist, addressed this theme of cosmopolitanism in contrast to the traditional concept of nation-state politics. Thus proposing the need for a cosmopolitan look in the political and social sphere in which otherness is recognized. The otherness of those who have different cultures, of the future, of nature, of the object, of rationalities. Cosmopolitanization as a product of modernization, creates specific situations, specific relationships, which mean that the other, the global other, the distant other, or even the national other, is both included and excluded (and there are different modalities of inclusion and exclusion) (Wieviorka 2015)

Therefore, if we acknowledge this situation, we can create new legal mechanisms to address femicide. By adding a peacebuilding perspective to the gender perspective and the human rights approach new options to prevent, manage, transform and reconcile conflicts arise. Cosmopolite peacebuilding according to Mary Kaldor depending on the conflict analysis, peace can be restored and maintained if such particularistic identity fissures can be overcome, and to do so, cosmopolitan attitudes are required, to understand which post-conflict reconstruction projects must be created and fostered. This sort of attitudes include for example: nonviolent communication, tolerance and a multicultural approach (Kaldor 2003).

This is also related to Global governance which is a non-hierarchical process that facilitates the combination of ideas, efforts and strategies of institutions and state and non-state actors around the solution of global problems. Although it includes international law and international organizations, global governance goes further in that, since it is not regulated by rules or doctrines; on the contrary, it flows naturally with a view to proposing solutions to real problems. This concept was defined in the 1995 report of the Commission on Global Governance, entitled Our global neighborhood, global governance "comprises the sum in which individuals and institutions, public or private, manage to manage common affairs".

So, the proposal is to start developing new legal mechanisms and public policies which include women as key actors to directly participate in building peace and creating solutions according to their different needs, truths, letting them actively collaborate and contribute to the reconciliation process towards a full exercise and coverage of their rights.

Mexico is part of this international regulation issued by the United Nations and just recently has been implementing it through the Network of Peacebuilders Women (MUCPAZ 2020) we will have to work hard as a country to stablish transitional and restorative justice that help heal the damages, impunity and inequality have done to Mexican women. We will soon see the results that might come out from this approach.

In conclusion, it is necessary to delve more into the relationship between the concepts of peace and substantive equality, so that we can develop new juridical tools and mechanisms that become useful in this social situations with a more integral approach that allows access to justice in this matters.

This overview of feminisms in Mexico City was intended to portrait the situation that us women live on daily basis and arise the analysis of this social and cultural issue through the catholic lenses. The question then remaining is, what is the role that as Catholics, both men and women, are called to play before this situation?

As Joseph Ratzinger wrote about cultural encounters, it is necessary to search for a dialogue between culture and faith, we need to focus on the intercultural dialogue of core values to find truth. (Ratzinger, 2005) Taking as a starting point that there is not only one feminism, but many. I believe that one of the subjects pending, is to contribute to the analysis of a feminism that represents the point of view of catholic women. Through the construction of this article, I found some academic approaches referring to a feminism founded on the personalist philosophy named "Personalist feminism." (Urban 2022; Maloney 2015).

Therefore, to find real solutions to this social problem, us Catholics are called to action through an open dialogue that weaves different visions with the core value of human dignity of each person involved at the center. Dialogue, that helps to build a healthy community in which men and women can establish fair and peaceful relationships in which it is possible for them, to love more and better.

References

ÁLVAREZ E. L., The Feminist Movement in Mexico in the 21st Century: Youth, Radicality and Violence, Mexico, 2020.
CERVA CERNA D., The Feminist Protest in Mexico. Misogyny in Institutional Discourse and Socialdigital Networks, Mexico 2020, Available at: http://www.revistas.unam.mx/index.php/rmcpys/article/view/76434/67796
CONAVIM, Informe del Grupo de Trabajo conformado para atender la solicitud de alerta de violencia de género contra las mujeres en las demarcaciones territoriales de Gustavo A. Madero, Azcapotzalco, Iztapalapa, Tlalpan, Xochimilco, Álvaro Obregón, Benito Juárez, Cuauhtémoc y Venustiano Carranza de la Ciudad de México, Mexico, 2019.
FREDMAN S., "Substantive equality revisited", *International Journal of Constitutional Law*, 14(3), Oxford Academy, 2016: 712-738, Available at: t.ly/29E7
KALDOR M., "A Cosmopolitan Response to New Wars", *Peace Review*, 8, 1996: 505–14;
——, "Cosmopolitanism and Organised Violence", *JOUR*, 2000.
——, *Global Civil Society: An Answer to War*, Polity Press, 2003. Available at: file:///Users/julietabecerril/Downloads/Goetze_Bliesemann_Cosmopolitanism.pdf
LGAVLV, Ley General de Acceso a la mujer a una vida libre de violencia, artículo 5 FIV, Mexico, 2021.
LIRA A., "¿Cómo Lograr La Igualdad Sustantiva?", *De La Teoría A La Práctica: Una Propuesta Transversal Desde Una Agenda Global*, México, 2019: 1-16. Available at: t.ly/YCar
MALONEY A., "The feminine Genius and culture", *eJournal of Personalist Feminism* Vol. 2, 2015, University of St. Thomas. Available at: https://www.stthomas.edu/sienasymposium/publications/ejournal/volume-two.html
MUCPAZ, *Red de Mujeres Constructoras de paz*, Inmujeres, Mexico, 2020. Available at: https://www.gob.mx/cms/uploads/attachment/file/557727/mucpaz.pdf
NATIONAL INSTITUTE OF ANTHROPOLOGY AND HISTORY (INAH),

Basic Manual of Gender Equity, Mexico, 2016, Page 7, Available at: t.ly/cI4m

Ramsbotham O. *et al*, "Resolución de conflictos. La prevención, gestión, transformación de conflictos letales.", 2011: 390; 391.

Ratzinger J., "Truth and Tolerance: Christian belief and world religions", 2005: 50-71. Available at: https://portalconservador.com/livros/Joseph-Ratzinger-Fe-Verdad-y-Tolerancia.pdf

Rosenfeld M., "Substantive Equality and Equal Opportunity: A Jurisprudential Appraisal", *California Law Review*, 74, 5, *EUA*, 1986: 1687-1712. Available at: https://www.jstor.org/stable/3480455?refreqid=excelsior%3A72928b9714437087f-0dcb205d73fb72b&seq=1

Secretariado Ejecutivo del Sistema Nacional de Seguridad Pública (SESNSP), *Información sobre violencia contra las mujeres. Incidencia delictiva y llamadas de emergencia 9-1-1*, 2021.

Soto Villagrán P., "Algunas reflexiones sobre el movimiento feminista en México", 2021. Available at: https://mx.boell.org/es/2021/04/09/algunas-reflexiones-sobre-el-movimiento-feminista-en-mexico

UN Security Council S/RES/1325, "Resolution on women and peace and security", 2000. Available at: https://peacemaker.un.org/node/105

URBAN, Pietr, "Care Ethics and the Feminist Personalism of Edith Stein", 2022. Available at: https://mdpi-res.com/d_attachment/philosophies/philosophies-07-00060/article_deploy/philosophies-07-00060.pdf?version=1654070911

Wieviorka M., "The Cosmopolitanization of the World. Conversation with Ulrich Beck", 2015. available at: http://www.scielo.org.mx/scielo.php?script=sci_arttext&pid=S0185-19182015000200353

https://www.stthomas.edu/sienasymposium/publications/ejournal/volume-two.html

Lecture n. 8

CHRISTIANITY
The Miracle of Guadalupe: The Catholic Tradition and Its Influx on the Society

Prof. Mario Ángel Flores Ramos –
Rector Emeritus of the Pontifical University of Mexico – Mexico City

> Where am I? Where do I see myself?
> By chance that way where the elders left off said,
> our ancestors, our grandparents:
> In the land of flowers, in the land of corn,
> of our flesh, of our nourishment;
> Perhaps in the heavenly land?
>
> (Juan Diego in the encounter
> with Our Lady of Guadalupe)

Historical Facts

In the sixteenth century, in April of 1519, precisely five hundred and three years ago, Spanish captain Hernán Cortés landed on the coast of the interior of Mexico, found a highly advanced civilization and an empire called 'Mexica' dominating the entire Mesoamerican area: the present Mexico, Guatemala and Honduras of which the Aztecs were the rulers headed by Emperor Moctezuma II (Bulard 2004). They were settled in about 1300 on an island in Lake Texcoco and had built their capital Tenochtitlán, where modern Mexico City is today. Little by little they were conquering that vast territory, with an iron fist and demanding from all other peoples, excessive tribute and taxes, as always happens with conquering peoples.

Their highly organized religion centered on human sacrifice offered to the Sun god for continued existence. For the Aztecs, the present world is not the first, there have been four others all ended in disaster, one by earthquakes, another by lava rain, the third, by a terrible hurricane and the fourth by a universal flood.

The present one would therefore be the 'Fifth Sun,' which came into being thanks to Aztec ancestors who sacrificed themselves by throwing themselves into fire to bring forth the sun and moon of this fifth world.

It is said that in 1487, to inaugurate the main temple in the capital city of Tenochtitlán, 20,000 captives were sacrificed in four days of festivities, preparing them with hallucinogenic substances, the priest opened their ribs with a knife and tore out their still-beating hearts, which were offered to the deities, being the main ones, Ometeotl (the father-mother god, a duality god, god of creation), Tonanzin (the mother of the gods) Huitzilopochtli (the god of war), Tlaloc (the god of rain) Coatlicue (the goddess of the earth), Mictlantecuhtli (the god of death).

There is a special character, Quetzalcoltl (the god of wind and wisdom), known as the feathered serpent; in fact, Quetzal is a famous Bird and Coatl means the serpent. He is a recognized deity for all ancient peoples down to the Aztecs, the enemy of war and destruction, wise and creative, the peacemaker. Legendary mythology confirms that he disappeared by the sea with the promise of returning once again by the sea with new strength and glory. Right when the Spanish army arrived from the sea with horses, never before known in these lands and with battle gear and battle armor, the emperor and the wise men thought, at first, of the return de Quetzalcoatl.

Two worlds meet

In 1519 when the Spaniards overlooked the valley that is home to the capital city of Tenochtitlán, they were astounded. Various elevated roads connected the island to the western, northern and southern shores of the lake. The city's population is thought to have reached 250,000. The entire Valley of Mexico counted with about one and a half million inhabitants, being at that time one of the largest and most populated valleys in the world.

Hernán Cortés begins to approach the capital of the Mexica. As he meets other peoples on the way, he realizes that they are not at all satisfied with the Aztecs for the onerous tributes imposed on them by Moctezuma. With the help of Malinche, an indigenous slave who becomes his cohabitant and knows the different indigenous languages and now Spanish, Hernán Cortés makes them his allies and thus enters the heart of the empire without using weapons. On the other hand, at first, Cortés is welcomed peacefully by Moctezuma. In the first days there is cordiality and dialogue between them. The relations begin to deteriorate when Cortés enters the sacred enclosure, at the high point of the pyramid, and begins to destroy the statues of the Aztec deities declaring them works of the devil.

The indigenous people revolt and Cortés, in fear, imprisons the emperor. The Spaniards once again enter the sacred enclosure to plant a cross, thus triggering a new uprising in which the emperor is killed. The Aztec nobles unite and elect Cuitláhuac, a young warrior who organizes the first resistance against the Spaniards, causing them to flee the city and leaving countless dead and prisoners, as the new emperor. That night is remembered by the Spanish as the "noche triste," or 'sad night'.

In the liberated capital, in the following days, Spanish and Tlaxcaltec prisoners are offered in thanksgiving to the Sun god by immolating them with the 'flowery death'. But divine protection seemed to recede when smallpox broke out: a new disease brought by the invaders, which quickly halved the population.

In December 1520, Hernán Cortés besieges the capital with help from neighboring peoples opposed to the Aztecs, succeeds in blocking every avenue of exit and entry, but its inhabitants, though prostrated by disease and starvation, hold out until August 13, 1521. The high and proud city was completely razed to the ground (Woods 2000). On its ruins would be born Mexico City, the capital of New Spain. Right on the Major Temple, the great pyramid that was destroyed, will be grafted the current Cathedral (The Dumo), the largest and most majestic temple in all of Spanish America (Carrasco 1999).

The ruling class is destroyed, the priests are killed, the old order is annulled, the territory is divided and the natives subdued. There are many historians who claim that the conquest of the Mexica empire was the bloodiest and most devastating of those accomplished by the Spanish in the Americas.

According to Aztec belief, the defeat also involved the deities. In the famous 1525 dialogue between early Franciscan missionaries and Aztec wise men, the latter replied, "You say we do not know the Lord of the Far and Near, you want us to destroy our rule of life handed down to us by our ancestors. Where can we still go? We are simple people, we are mortal, so let us die, let us perish, for our gods are already dead".[1]

It is fair to mention that even among the Spanish clergy there were those who denounced outright, all the atrocities, and there were many defenders of the natives, in the forefront the Dominican friar Bartolomeo de las Casas, and many others like Fray Toribio of Benavente called for the natives Motolinía, that is, 'the poor man' because of his closeness and simplicity. It was in that context that Francisco de Vitoria, a great academic from Salamanca, began to develop 'the Law of Peoples', which today we call human rights, as the great contribution of Christian thought to social justice.

We would need a chapter of our own to talk about the early Franciscan missionaries and his genuine work of evangelization.

The event of Guadalupe in 1531

After ten years of the conquest and destruction of the Aztec empire, the most significant civilization in that world, after the violent disappearance of its leaders and with them its religion with its gods, there was a sense of defeat, great sadness and despondency in the souls of the indigenous people. Although the relationship between the two peoples was beginning, the task of the first evangelizers was not at all easy.

What happens in December 1531 in Mexico? A singular event: near Mexico City Our Lady appeared to a poor Indian named Juan Diego. The 'Lady' told Juan Diego that she was 'The Perfect Ever Virgin Mary, the Mother of the very true and only God for

---

[1] Dialogue of the twelve apostles: ¿A dónde habremos todavía de ir? Somos gente sencilla, somos perecederos, somos mortales; dejadnos, pues, morir; dejadnos perecer, pues nuestros dioses ya están muertos. Anonymous of Tlatelolco, Canticle of 1523, Mexico.

whom we all have life'. With this she began a new history that would also slowly be the beginning of a new people.

The Guadalupian event was a case of miraculous and providential' inculturation: To meditate on it and deepen it today is to understand the importance of Mary in the evangelization of Mexico and elsewhere, presenting herself as a teacher of humanity and faith, announcer and servant of the Word, bearer of Christ and his Gospel, which must shine in all its splendor, like her miraculous image imprinted on the tilma, that is, the cloak, of the Mexican seer Juan Diego, whom John Paul II proclaimed blessed in 1990 and a saint in 2002.

What happened in 1531, both in terms of the message and the presence of the Virgin Mary, does not correspond with the theology of that time nor with the pictorial technique of the time. But, above all, it happened at the most opportune time for the indigenous peoples who needed to rebuild its reality by regaining confidence. This is why it can be called providential, indeed, truly a supernatural event.

In the pastoral letter of the Mexican Bishops' Conference of 2010, to commemorate the two hundredth anniversary of the beginning of Mexican independence, we read, "the apparition of the Virgin Mary of Guadalupe is a founding event of our national identity", and also "its historical development coincides with the development of the nation".[2]

The oldest reports on the apparitions of the Madonna of Guadalupe and her image on Juan Diego´s tilma are two documents in the Náhuatl language from the first half of the 16th century: l´Inin huey tlamahuizoltzin, i.e., 'This is the great wonder', attributed to Spanish priest Juan González, interpreter of the first bishop of Mexico City, Juan de Zumarraga OFM, written between 1541 and 1545, when Juan Diego and the bishop himself were still alive; and then, the most important Nican Mopohua, 'here is told', attributed to Aztec nobleman Antonio Valeriano, a

---

[2] See: Mexican Episcopal Conference, Pastoral Letter. Commemorate our history from the faith, to commit ourselves today with our country. Mexico, 2010, n. 11.

student at the Franciscan college of Santa Croce de Tlaltelolco, written between 1545 and 1555. The Nican Mopohua contains the most extensive, richest and most colorful narrative with the native's own sensibility.[3] It is good to remember that all these events were first disseminated among the indigenous people in his languages and writings, it will be more than a century later when the first translations to Spanish will be held (Vasquez 1988).[4] Also in the 18th century Lorenzo Boturini, an Italian historian came to Mexico with the desire to learn more about this tradition of Guadalupe and was surprised to realize that there were not many documents around, instead the oral tradition, throughout the country and in all circles was very solid. It was Boturini who was the first to form a very well-organized bible library of documents on indigenous culture in general and the Guadalupan tradition in particular, although due to many misunderstandings, he had many enemies and failed to scribe a text as was his intention and even the documents gathered in his bible library are somewhat scattered.

Before he was baptized, Juan Diego, the seer, was called Cuauhtlatoazin, a fascinating Aztec name meaning 'he who speaks like an eagle' or 'talking eagle'. He was a man of the people, simple, married and a peasant. Baptized in 1524 at the age of fifty with his wife; he was widowed four years later, and continued dedicated to his work and to listening to the catechesis organized by the missionaries for neo-converts at the school in Tlalteloco, near Mexico City (Léon Portilla 1988).

From December 9 to 12, 1531, there were the four apparitions of the Virgin Mary in the hill of Tepeyac. We can detach the main elements, which are in a great symphony with the Gospel and the culture of the original peoples:

---

[3] This is one of the most significant texts on the development of Nahuatl literature: Ángel María Garibay, Historia de la literatura Náhuatl. Mexico 1987 (Reprint), 236.
[4] A work in Italian on the subject: C. Perfetti, *Guadalupe. La tilma della morenita*, Edizione Paoline, 1988.

1. Our Lady is manifested in the midst of flowers and songs, celestial symbols for indigenous religiosity, and she speaks in nahuatl the language of Juan Diego and obviously of the Aztecs.
2. She presents herself as the perfect ever Virgin, Mother of the very true God for whom one lives. She describes herself to this true God by different names of indigenous religiosity, but with an altogether new meaning: creator of men (Teyocoyani), Lord of all that surrounds and envelops us (Tloque Nahuaque), the master of heaven and earth (Ilhuicahua Tlatipaque).
3. She makes the request to build in that place a small holy house, that is, a temple, to show the true God: 'I will give him to the nations through all my personal love,' Mary said. She presents herself as Mother of all who call upon her, touching with great sensitivity the hearts of those with a sense of abandonment because of the defeat and destruction of her symbolic and religious world.
4. He makes the invitation to be born again with valor and confidence: 'Let not your face, your heart be troubled; do not fear for this or any other infirmity, or other critical and painful things. Am I not here beside you, I who have the honor of being your mother? Are you not, perhaps, under my protection... Are you not, perhaps, in the hollow of my cloak, in the cross of my arms? What else do you need?' These words preserved in the Nican Mopohua tale remain in the hearts of all Mexicans throughout the centuries.
5. He makes Juan Diego his messenger before the ecclesiastical authority and bearer of his confirmation, his tilma, where his image will be miraculously printed in front of the bishop, uniting all two peoples in a new reality of mixed race and culture. This event is precisely the most impressive and extraordinary fact. It remains to this day in the sight of all in his Basilica where the faithful people gather.
6. In fact, the little house, the temple he asked for, not only refers to a sacred building, but more so to the building of a new people formed by the indigenous peoples and those Europeans now present in these lands. For the indigenous people, erecting a temple meant building a civilization, and she says this beautifully. She calls the temple 'sacred little house', because the temple, the civilization that the Virgin wants is a family where everyone gathers around the love of God: the Church.

7. The oral and written message is simple and with great sensitivity to the situation of the people who have lost everything; but the message in the image is profuse and profound. An image that has much to say to indigenous culture and much also for the Christian culture of the Europeans who have arrived in the new land. To the indigenous people it is clear that she is a woman preparing to give birth to a deified child, with the sun behind her. For the European gaze there is no doubt that we are before the woman of the apocalypse, wrapped with a mantle of stars and the moon under her feet, which leads us naturally to the contemplation of the Virgin Mary.

According to the narrative of Nican Mopohua, the name Madona of Guadalupe is given by Her in the dialogue with Bernardino, uncle of Juan Diego: I am the Perfect Virgin Holy Mary of Guadalupe. The term Guadalupe is known to the Spanish, for in Spain there is a river called Guadalupe that runs through Estremadura and there is a population and a shrine dedicated to the Virgin Mary by that name (Crémoux 2001: 10-12). Well, the name is of Arabic origin and means river of wolves, also, hidden river, that which carries and leads the water: In the message of Guadalupe in Tepeyac it means that she is not the water but leads us to Jesus Christ, the living Water. All this has a profound meaning of inculturation, so John Paul II called her 'The Star of Evangelization'.[5]

Development over the centuries

The tradition around Guadalupe, both in popular religiosity as well as in culture in general, was slowly but surely growing in a sustained form. We can recall that example Jesus gives us to show the dynamic of the kingdom of heaven, as the mustard seed, the smallest, but in so much it grows, will be the largest shrub.

The New Hispanic society characterized by many social strata, had something in common, religiosity and language. The Virgin of Guadalupe was present in the great celebrations and festivals as a reason for gathering and also in the great disasters as a support

---

[5] John Paul II, First trip to Mexico, 1979.

of hope, whether in pandemics, floods, earthquakes. There are so many personal and communal accounts, of miracles performed, to be unending.

Towards the end of the 18th century and the beginning of the 19th, there was a great movement, especially among the children of Spaniards born in New Spain and, of course, among the mestizos, who sought independence from the Spanish crown, the common characteristic was the identification with the Guadalupian tradition, as the proper and distinctive of the New World. The most symbolic moment of the beginning of the independence movement was the night of September 15, 1810, when Fr. Miguel Hidalgo, recognized as the Father of the Fatherland, took from the parish of Dolores, a small population in the center of the country, the image of the Virgin of Guadalupe as the flag of battle before the crowd that began the insurgent movement. It is thus considered the first flag of independent Mexico.

Throughout the centuries it has been a symbol that does not need to promote itself to make itself known, because it is found in all environments as a spontaneous expression of popular religiosity. It has not been erased even by the anti-clerical movements and the rabid religious persecution in the 1920s. We can recall that desperate action of the anticlerical government that in 1921, sent a floral tribute under the image of Our Lady of Guadalupe, with a bomb inside, a bomb that went off destroying the altar and everything around it, but the miraculous image suffered nothing, absolutely nothing.

Guadalupe Today

Today's shrine is a modern and large basilica for ten million people, with a large square in front with capacity for more than forty thousand where about twelve million a year go on pilgrimage being thus one of the most visited religious places in the world. Around the annual feast, December 12, there are millions who overlook the Basilica and there are many young people who arrive on pilgrimage, on foot, on bicycles, in minibuses, organized in groups, in runs of one hundred or two hundred kilometers.

More beyond this place, where the image is located in the little sagrada house, Our Lady of Guadalupe is present everywhere, in homes, offices, factories, workshops, neighborhoods and streets, in social demonstrations and in struggles for justice. It is a sign of identity and cultural trust.

Precisely as a cultural and religious sign, Our Lady is taken everywhere, where Mexicans have arrived, far from her homeland and families, beginning in America, The United States, where there are more than thirty million Mexican migrants.

Our Lady of Guadalupe is a clear path to Jesus Christ, the Gospel and the Church, although some of her faithful are not formally part of the Church, for all, she is a symbol and expression of Her motherly love and the universal love of God, shown for Jesus Christ.

The immediate future

The reality of Mexico City and even the country in our days is very much changing culturally in its development. A highly populated, dynamic modern city, with great cultural diversity and no doubt marked for secularism, that is, the gradual disappearance of the religious sense of life, or well the appearance of new religious forms.

The most current studies on the religious reality in Latin America have put the theme of the growth of the Pentecostals and Evangelicals with the consequent decrease of Catholics. Brazil and Central America are the regions with the most incidence. Also one can see with great concern what is happening in Chile for the growth of unbelief or secularization.

The situation in Mexico and Mexico City, in particular, seems, so far, to be slower in its change, both in the of the weakness of religiosity and the abandonment of Catholicism. Our Lady of Guadalupe has something to do, but the change in the modern world is irreversible and we are not out of the phenomenon of cultural globalization.

In the immediate future, Mexico City, its culture, the Catholic Church, have a great challenge to preserve its historical and cultural roots, its deep convictions, without renouncing all the positive that there is in the changing contemporary world.

Appendix: The model image of inculturation

The Virgin of Guadalupe, with her miraculous image that she imprinted on Juan Diego's tilma, left a concrete physique link that, prodigiously, has never altered.

Packed with agave fiber, an easily perishable organic material, the tilma has been preserved for about five hundred years until today, although fibers of this material do not last more than eight years in a humid and potassium nitrate-rich environment such as the Tepeyac.[6]

The image of the Virgin on the tilma of Juan Diego manifests itself as a synthesis de the religious sensibility of all two peoples, the original peoples and the European peoples, thus opening a way of dialogue and encounter that remains to this day in the 'little sacred house' that is, in the Church where all gather as true brothers around Mary and Jesus.

It was the bishop who asked the Indian Juan Diego for a sign to fulfill the will of the Virgin of Guadalupe, then the blessed image on the tilma is the sign that Mary handed down for the bishop except the faithful layman, the simple man full of trust. The image is handed over to the bishop as the pastor of the Church, but she reveals herself to all and remains for all, through the mediation of Juan Diego, as the spiritual and loving mother of the Church.

Today we are once more in the return of a culture of the image with the new technologies. Our Lady of Guadalupe is more relevant than ever if we attend to her meaning imprinted in her image that makes her so close to everyone.

The Virgin of Guadalupe has been considered for theological reflection of our times as an icon of perfect inculturation, both for John Paul II, Benedict XVI and Pope Francis: "At the dramatic

---

[6] Analysis of some fibers from the cloak of Juan Diego or icon of Our Lady of Guadalupe, carried out by the Institute of Biology of the UNAM, Institute of Biology, UNAM, Mexico 1946 (Oficio 242, file 812.2/2).

time of the conquest, Our Lady of Guadalupe transmitted the true faith to the indigenous people, speaking their own language and clothed in their own garments, without violence or imposition", showing the loving face of the true God by whom we have life.[7]

There are many signs of her true inculturation, a model for all times for evangelization:

> "a. He shows a great and sincere love for the natives to the point of identifying with them;
> b. embraces what was good, right, and wise in Aztec culture;
> c. adapts to the Aztec culture, purifying the aspects deformed by sin;
> d. perfects what was good in Aztec culture with the Christian message;
> e. reaches a harmonious synthesis between Aztec culture and the Gospel message.
> The Guadalupan event as a whole, i.e., message, image of Our Lady of Guadalupe, Nican Mopohua, temple, Juan Diego, devotion of the people, is a perfectly successful model of indigenous theology, which continues to act today in the Christian life of God's people" (Larios Valencia – Flores Ramos 2016: 76).

---

[7] Pope Francis, *Homily during the Lac Ste. Anne Pilgrimage*, July 26, 2022

References

Carrasco D., *City of sacrifice: The Aztec Empire end the Role of Violence in Civilization*, Beacon Press, 1999.
Crémoux F., *Pèlegrinages et miracles à Guadalupe au XVIe siècle*, Casa de Velázquez, 2001.
Garibay Á., *Historia de la literatura Náhuatl*, 1987.
Burland A., *Montezuma, Il Signore degli Aztechi*, Einauidi, 2004.
Larios Valencia J. O. – Flores Ramos M. Á., *Our Lady of Guadalupe. La morenita: Icon of enculturation and mission*, 2016.
Portilla M. L., *Testimonios de la antigua palabra*. Comisión Nacional Conmemorativa del V Centenario del Encuentro de Dos Mundos, México.
Vázquez P. F., *The Apparition of Santa María de Guadalupe*, Editorial Jus, 1981.
Woods M., *Conquistadors*, University of California Press Berkeley and Los Angeles, 2000.

Lecture n. 9

RELIGIONS
Popular Religiosity in Mexico: An Approximation

Prof. Rodrigo Guerra López –
General Secretary
of the Pontifical Commission
for Latin America – Vatican City

Introduction

In the following lines I try to show some essential elements useful to get closer to the phenomenon of contemporary popular religiosity, particularly in Mexico. I renounce any type of exhaustiveness and offer the following considerations merely as an approximation. An important bibliography on popular religiosity in Mexico has been published through the years (González Reyes – Pachecho 2019; Hernández 2019; Sánchez Hernández 2008). I invite the reader to take it in account to get a wider understanding of this topic.

1. Religion in Mexico

In the first place, the population census of Mexico carried out in 2020, offers data to recognize the changes and new patterns of religious composition in Mexico. To begin with, every ten years we see that in Mexico, although the Catholic faith continues to be preponderant, there is a gradual deterioration of those who recognize themselves as 'Catholics'.

Secondly, the Evangelical-Christian churches are growing, slowly but steadily, while we see how new churches emerge in this area, demanding particular recognition, either because they belong to autonomous denominations, because they promote different doctrinal or liturgical cultures, or because the practitioners define themselves as 'Christian', 'Evangelical' or 'Pentecostal'.

Third, we can see how secularization, understood as the loss of relevance of religion in social life, seems to be advancing hand in hand with the increase of Mexicans not affiliated with any religion. However, at the same time we perceive that these are not for the most part atheists, but rather believers without a church.

Ciudad de México

And fourthly, there is the emergence of other religions: some that have been present since time immemorial but were unknown by the censuses (such as religions with ethnic roots); others that are new presences (such as Buddhism, Islam, and others of oriental origin); some that are not registered as religious associations, because they do not have that structure, but do have followers and adherents (such as religions with Afro roots, as well as New Age and esoteric spiritualities); some more that are popular cults (for example, the practitioners of 'Santa Muerte' and 'Niño Fidencio'), which are fractured from popular Catholicism, and still others which have their own growth (for example, spiritualists).

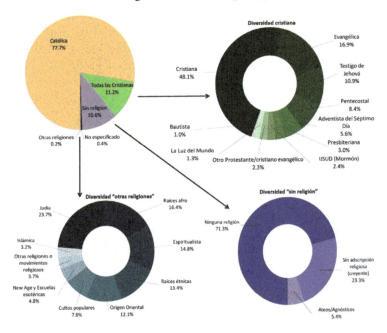

Renée de la Torre and Cristina Gutiérrez, commenting on the results of the census, affirm:

> In these years, the Catholic Church has gone through one of its most critical stages; partly due to the priestly pederasty scandals and the

systematic concealment strategies of abuses by the hierarchy, but also because of its rigid clerical structure that does not compete with the organizations of the evangelical religions that are open to a greater participation of their members, and where ministerial careers are much shorter. Despite this, the numbers of religious affiliation do not decline with the same intensity. This leads us to think that the weight of Catholicism is not only in the hierarchy but, above all, in the experiences linked to traditions and family gatherings, with village festivals, and especially with the daily faith professed to the Virgin and to the saints (De La Torre – Gutiérrez 2021).

This last comment seems to point precisely to what we call 'popular piety' within the Church.

2. From popular religiosity to the spirituality of the people

The II General Conference of the Latin American Bishops, held in Medellín in 1968, noted that popular religiosity is "the fruit of the evangelization carried out at the time of the Conquest" (VI, 2) and that it is a "religiosity of vows and promises, of pilgrimages and countless devotions, based on the reception of the sacraments, especially baptism and first communion" (VI, 2). The Conference finds in these religious expressions an "enormous reserve of authentically Christian virtues, especially regarding charity" (VI, 2).

All this does not mean that the bishops in Medellin do not see many risks and limits in these expressions of faith. The Conference points out, for example, that they are easily influenced by "magical practices and superstitions" (VI, 4), that "participation in official cultic life is almost non-existent" (VI, 2), and that "the existence of faith behind any apparently religious expression is not to be easily assumed Christian" (VI, 6).

In short, although the Medellín document has a positive view of this kind of religiosity, it considers it still very incomplete, and rather as a starting point for a more authentic religiosity. These religious manifestations are just "babblings of an authentic religiosity, expressed with the cultural elements that are available" (VI,

4). In them, "'seeds of the Word' that constitute or can constitute an 'evangelical preparation' are found" (VI, 5).

Years later, Pope Saint Paul VI recognizes in *Evangelii nuntiandi*, n. 48, that the expressions of popular religiosity were "for a long time considered less pure and sometimes despised", but that today they are being revalued. Although he positively values popular religiosity, he does not fail to point out its risks: falling into superstition, not producing "true adherence to faith" and engendering sectarian attitudes. When it comes to marking positive values, he gladly expands on the evangelical riches that popular piety possesses: "Patience, sense of the cross in daily life, detachment, acceptance of others, devotion". One can even perceive a certain admiration towards those who live with "this thirst for God that only the poor and simple can know", when he recognizes that many of the interior attitudes that popular piety engenders in them "can rarely be observed to the same degree in those who do not have that religiosity". He also recognizes in these faithful a special knowledge of "the paternity, the providence and the loving and constant presence" of God in their lives.

In 1979, the III General Conference of the Latin American Bishops, gathered in Puebla, explains that popular religiosity is in the context of the pastoral option proposed by the bishops to evangelize culture. The second chapter of the second part – entitled "What is evangelization?" – begins by specifying what is meant by evangelization. It then deals with the evangelization of culture and points out that, in order to achieve it, "it is of primary importance to attend to the religion of our peoples, not only assuming it as an object of evangelization, but also, because it is already evangelized, as an actively evangelizing force" (DP 396). Then, it develops the topic "Evangelization and popular religiosity" (DP 444-469). From this perspective, the religious manifestations of the people not only have the riches of being seeds of the Word, but also have the strength of being fruits of the gospel planted five centuries ago in our continent.

As we have already pointed out, these expressions are an "actively evangelizing force" (DP 396), through which the people evangelizes itself: "Popular religiosity is not only the object of evangelization but, insofar as it contains the incarnate Word of God, it's also an active way in which the people continually evangelizes itself". (DP450)

In the V General Conference of the Latin American Episcopate, held in Aparecida in 2007, the bishops affirm: "At different moments of the daily struggle, many resort to some small sign of God's love: a crucifix, a rosary, a candle that is lit to accompany a child in his illness, an Our Father whispered through tears, an endearing look at a beloved image of Mary, a smile directed to Heaven amid simple joy" (DA 261).

Along the lines of Puebla, Aparecida recognizes the evangelizing potential of popular piety. This is a spirituality "embodied in the culture of the simple" (DA 263). The bishops are aware that "cultural traditions are no longer transmitted from one generation to another with the same fluidity as in the past" (DA 39); but, even weakened, this process is still happening to some degree in Latin America. In these processes, popular spirituality is not secondary. On the contrary, thanks to it, the "Christian people evangelizes itself" (DA 264). "Popular piety is a legitimate way of living the faith, a way of feeling part of the Church, and a way of being missionaries" (DA 264).

The bishops point out the risk that the Church runs by despising popular piety, or by "considering it a secondary way of Christian life" (DA 263). This spirituality is "an expression of supernatural wisdom" (DA 263), lived by people who have very little of what is known as religious instruction, and still "it is not less spiritual for that reason, but it is so in another way" (DA 263). Because "the wisdom of love does not depend directly on the enlightenment of the mind but on the internal action of grace" (DA 263).

Finally, Pope Francis, referring to popular piety, in *Evangelii gaudium*, explains that "to understand this reality, it is necessary to approach it with the gaze of the Good Shepherd, who does not seek to judge but to love. Only from the affective connaturality that love gives can we appreciate the theological life present in the piety of Christian peoples, especially in their poor. I think of the firm faith of those mothers at the foot of the sick child's bed who cling to a rosary even though they do not know how to weave to-

gether the propositions of the Creed, or in so much hope poured into a candle that is lit in a humble home to ask for help to Mary, or in those looks of endearing love to the crucified Christ. Whoever loves the holy faithful People of God cannot see these actions only as a natural search for divinity. They are the manifestation of a theological life animated by the action of the Holy Spirit who has been poured into our hearts (cf. Rm 5,5)" (EG, 125).
And further on, he will add:

> The expressions of popular piety have much to teach us and, for those who know how to read them, they are a theological place to which we must pay attention, particularly when thinking about the new evangelization (EG, 126).

3. Popular piety defies the processes of secularization.

In conventional theories on secularization, as societies gradually become more technical and complex, they tend to displace the existential centrality of religiosity. Marxism as social theory, in fact, is built on the assumption of increasing secularization. In European societies, secularization happened to a large extent. Huge social sectors that were once Christians abandoned faith and chose to organize their personal and community life based on factors unrelated to the religious dimension of existence.

However, in Latin America, popular piety is not only a social practice but also one of the most decisive dimensions in the constitution of community consciousness. In other words, the warning of the community as a community in the peoples of Latin America has in the faith lived by the people, with the signs and languages of the people, one of its most characteristic factors.

The pastoral failure in Latin America of the theologies of the death of God and of the theology of liberation's versions with the greatest Marxist influence occurred precisely because of the lack of positive appreciation of popular piety. Quite the contrary, pastoral praxis that remains open and allows itself to be accompanied by popular piety, tends to symbolically recover some of the most important truths of the faith and undoubtedly motivates to struggle for justice and liberation of the people.

4. The Guadalupan Event and the Postmodern Moment

The Guadalupan Event is, in this respect, an emblematic case. In 1521, the conquest devastated the indigenous communities of the Mexican highlands. Ten years later, everything was desolation. The 'sad songs' that various poets wrote after the conquest are a sign of a civilizational, cosmic and theological collapse (Garibay 1974; León-Portilla 1959). However, starting in 1531, an empirically verifiable sociological process, based on the reorientation of the religious dimension of the life of conquerors and conquered, facilitated the reconstruction of the social fabric and encouraged miscegenation (Alarcón 2013).

On December 9, 1531, the apparitions of Our Lady of Guadalupe took place. Conversions multiplied. The bishops meeting in Puebla in 1979 would point out: "The Gospel incarnated in our peoples brings them together in a cultural historical originality that we call Latin America. That identity is very luminously symbolized in the mixed-race face of María de Guadalupe that rises up at the beginning of evangelization" (DP 446).

Thanks to Our Lady of Guadalupe, those who are peripheral were able to find a motherhood that welcomes them, that is, a Mother of the oppressed who liberates the poor and becomes solidary with them. The devotion to our Lady of Guadalupe is spread all over the Continent, however it is clear there are many other images of our Lady relevant to the different nations. That is why, it seems to me, the Guadalupe event should not be understood as an hegemonic devotion, a (Mexican) nationalistic call or a substitute of other representations of Our Lady in Latin America. On the contrary, Guadalupe somehow opened the regional scenario to all these invocations and helped us all to discover the novelty of Christian faith under the light of the marian motherhood.

Somehow, Our Lady of Guadalupe is a synthesis of some of our dearest intuitions in Latin America to renew personal faith and even the Church. Her message to Saint Juan Diego, is a good example of feminine mercy and tenderness, preferential option for the poor, vindication of the dignity of the prehispanic natives, inculturated evangelization, sinodality – saint Juan Diego evangelizes bishop Zumarraga –, and reconciliation among peoples.

In the present postmodern Latin American moment, full of wounds and violence, full of uncertainties and not always successful searches, the Tepeyac event, and the marian way of understanding Christian faith can re-integrate what seems dispersed or even antagonistic. Even more, learning from the message of Our Lady of Guadalupe can illuminate our context for discovering new fraternal ways of living diversity and keeping essential unity. These last words are not a mere pious expression or a wishful thinking. Living diversity and keeping – simultaneously – unity is somehow the core of the Latin-American baroque culture that exists not only as a particular architectural, pictorial or musical trend of the past but as singular cultural 'substratum' in Latin American people, even today. This 'substratum' embraces differences but always in the atmosphere created by a sapiential point of reference (Morandé 1987; Echeverría 1998).

The Guadalupan event *qua* event, is an undeserved and gratuitous irruption of a merciful initiative. It summons hearts in a mysterious and effective way. Preparing the way for the Guadalupe Jubilee of 2031, can help us today to find more pertinent methods and languages for the evangelization of the new youth cultures, urban and non-urban. To the extent that Guadalupe manifests the maternal face of God, postmodern sensibilities can find a greater affinity with Her, so that her Son can make all things new in times of change of epoch.

References

Alarcón P., *El amor de Jesús vivo en la Virgen de Guadalupe*, Palibrio 2013.

De la Torre R. –Gutiérrez C., "México: menos católico, más diverso y menos religioso que hace una década", *Nexos*, 2021. Accessed at: https://www.nexos.com.mx/?p=54644

Echeverría B., *La modernidad de lo barroco*, Era, 1998.

Garibay A.M., *La literatura de los aztecas*, Ed. Joaquín Mortiz, 1974.

González Reyes G. – Pachecho M. (eds.), *La religiosidad popular en México: una visión desde la historia*, UIC, 2019.

Hernández S., "La religiosidad popular en la construcción identitaria: lucha, legitimación y poder de grupos marginados", *Vínculos. Sociología, análisis y opinion* 15, 2019: 155-178.

León-Portilla M., *Visión de los vencidos*, UNAM 1959.

Morandé P., *Cultura y modernización en América Latina*, Encuentro, 1987.

Sánchez Hernández G., "Religiosidad popular católica en el Distrito Federal: nuevas formas de relación con lo mágico, lo religioso y el *new age*", *Itinerarios* 8, 2008: 255-267.

Part Two

Workshops

Workshop n. 1

LAW
From Tenochtitlan to CDMX: Legal Criteria for the Administration of a City

Gianmaria Alessandro Ruscitti

Introduction

The construction of a correct legal analysis of Mexico City cannot in any case disregard the necessary historical, social and economic insights, which invariably intersect the destiny of the entire country, since its pre-Columbian origins.

Indeed, the current metropolis, which plays a decisive role in the life of the Mexican Federation, can be depicted as a mirror of many contradictions, colors and nuances.

An initial distinction of a constitutional nature is appropriate, so as to make the complexity of the legal system of reference more evident. The United Mexican States is a Federal Republic made up of thirty-one individual states, to which is added a very peculiar entity – from the administrative point of view – which is Mexico City. This last, coinciding with the administrative territory delineated in the original Federal District, due to the rapid growth of the population and the economy, has largely expanded outside of the territorial borders, making it necessary to attempt an organic regulation of the services, which has led to the birth of the Metropolitan Zone of the Valley of Mexico, which at the present time groups together, besides the original nucleus of 16 *alcadías* of Mexico City, 59 *municipios* of the State of Mexico and 1 *municipio* of the State of Hidalgo.

The current population in the administrative area of Mexico City alone is, according to the most recent surveys[1] 8,918,653 million,

---

[1] Anuario estadístico y geográfico por entidad federativa 2020 / Instituto Nacional de Estadística y Geografía. México: INEGI, c2021.

while the total number of residents in the metropolitan area is realistically over 21,919,000 million, making it larger than all five of the next largest cities of the country combined (México: INEGI, c2021). The territorial size of the conurbation reaches 7866 square kilometers and is one of the largest metropolitan areas on the planet.

This immediately makes clear the absolute importance not only politically, but also economically, socially and culturally of the city, both for the Federal Republic and globally.

Also noteworthy is the literacy rate, which is over 97.7%, compared to the general Mexican average of 93.6%, and the high percentage of university students and graduates, which is far higher in percentage terms than in the rest of the country (México: INEGI, c2021).

The federal capital is also the nation's economic engine (OECD 2020), with an economic and productive growth that generally sets it apart from the rest of the country,[2] placing it in that peculiar category of planetary mega-cities.

However, this considerable concentration of governmental structures and large centers of economic influence make it exceptionally vulnerable to distorting phenomena, typical of megalopolis, such as corruption and the infiltration of illicit interests into the bureaucratic apparatus, as the implementation of control and transparency tools appears increasingly vital in the proper governance of the city.

Finally, we cannot fail to give ample space to the new Political Constitution of Mexico City, which represents the best legal instrument to understand the present situation of the metropolis, its problems, its challenges, and the enormous will of the citizenship to build an inclusive and sustainable city.

The historical reconstruction, the legal analysis and the study of the social element move, in this short chapter, necessarily in unison, so as to be able to fully understand the facets of a contem-

---

[2] GDP per capita in Mexico City was more than six times higher than in Chiapas in 2018. OECD Regions and Cities at a Glance 2020, OECD Publishing, Paris.

porary megalopolis with very deep roots, whose complex system of government may represent a challenge for the future of the United Mexican States and determine the global role of the city in the next years.

1. Mexico City: historical profiles

The capital of Mexico is geographically located in the Central Plateau of Mexico, within a vast lake area better known as the Valley of Mexico and stands on the ruins of the ancient city of Tenochtitlán.[3]
The latter was founded in the first half of the 14th century A.D. by the Aztec people, as the great capital of the empire, on the two main islands of Lake Texcoco, which has now disappeared. The ancient imperial city, as can be seen from the great ruins and valuable artistic and archaeological discoveries made over the past centuries, encompasses countless cultural contaminations. The Aztec people had conquered the other kingdoms that dominated much of present-day Mexico, acquiring their beliefs and traditions, especially in the case of the Toltecs and the Mayan culture, which, in the Yucatan peninsula, had developed with enormous progress in various fields.
It is essential to understand that pre-Columbian Mexico, far from being populated by a homogeneous ethnic group, was instead comparable to a fragmented mosaic of cultures, many of which had irremediably disappeared or been annihilated even before the arrival of the Europeans, and others that still barely survive today.

---

[3] "Around the 15th century, there lived the Mexica, a people considered as insignificant by the neighbours, so much that they had to live in an abandoned island in the middle of the lake of Texcoco. In 1376, the Mexica's emperors began to rise, and the City of Tenochtitlán (that little city in the abandoned island on the lake) began expanding. As a result of 2000 years of life in Mesoamerica, during the reigns of Montezuma I and Montezuma II, and thanks to their great skills as military and social leaders, the Mexica (also known as Aztec) empire grew so much as to arrive to the lands that today constitute Guatemal". See García P. V., "*The Spanish Conquest of Mexico in 1521: After 500 Years*", presented at Scuola Sinderesi, 16 october 2021, Pontificia Università Gregoriana, Rome. See also: De Rojas 2017.

Today's Mexico City is built on the foundations of the vast Aztec empire, which in turn was the bearer of an even older pre-existing culture, which by no means can be considered extinct (Mundy 2021), but which survives, under the surface, in the Mexican population and its traditions.
In 1521 the Aztec empire fell to Hernan Cortez and the last emperor of Tenochtitlán, Montezuma, was killed in a palace conspiracy by his brother Cuitlahuac, thus ending the history of the ancient kingdom and opening the door to exploration, colonization and the birth of modern Mexico.
The decision to build a new city on the ruins of the previous settlement clearly shows the will to demonstrate the full domination of the new order over the previous one, generating, however, if only indirectly, a historical continuity of power and absorption of culture in a hybridization that characterizes, essentially, every feature of modern Mexico, and of which Mexico City is the greatest expression.
Indeed, many cultural-historical and even religious traditions that characterize modern Mexican culture demonstrate the fusion of the pre-existing identity and the European culture brought by the Spanish.
The fact that the absolute majority of today's Mexican population is the result of a constant overlap between the Spanish colonisers and the natives (Garavaglia – Grosso 1994) is not irrelevant, since the limited persistence of isolated ethnic groups (Vargas Becerra – Flores Dávila 2002; Sandoval Forero 2002), both Indigenous and Europeans, has in no way prevented the creation of an original Mexican culture, which demonstrates its uniqueness both socially and legally.
This full harmonisation between the two histories is also very evident on a religious level, where the destruction of the city's most important idols and temples by the first bishop of Mexico City, Juan de Zumarraga, was accompanied by the miraculous apparition of the Virgin of Guadalupe, who was able to enrapture the hearts of the natives and, with her appearance, unite conquerors and conquered, whose traditions, dances and celebrations survived, albeit changed, in the new culture that was being generated.

Where there were pagan temples, churches were built[4] and where there were idols, saints took their place. This general construction of the new Mexican society, is largely reflected in the urban fabric of Mexico City itself.

Before it was consecrated as a state capital in 1824, the city maintained its role as a centre of Spanish colonisation and a fundamental administrative heart for almost three centuries, thanks to its strategic geographical location, which made it essential for trade, which in turn ensured its rapid growth and expansion.

1.1 Colonial capital

The original juridical structure imposed by the first colonisers[5] saw the construction at first, under Cortez, of a Captaincy General of the new Spain, which then evolved into a continental *Audiencia*, a typical body of an executive-judicial nature, endowed with great powers. Subsequently, starting in 1529, Mexico was constituted a Viceroyalty, and subjected to the political government of Antonio de Mendoza, directly invested by the Spanish King Charles V, with headquarters in the newborn city of Mexico.

The most important regulation during the first viceroyships was the attempt, through the New Laws in 1542 (Caballos 2009: 95-109),[6] to determine the legal position of the Indigenous, who at that time represented the absolute majority of the inhabitants of the area.

---

[4] The large Cathedral, whose construction began in 1573, took the place of the first church in Mexico, built in 1525, which had been erected on the ruins of the Huitzilpochtli temple. The Church of St Francis itself was partly built with the materials left over from the destruction of the aforementioned temple. See also: Holler 2007: 107-120.

[5] The initial political structure was borrowed from Spanish cities of the time: the Ayuntamiento or Cabildo. In December 1522, the first civil collegiate body (cabildo) of Mexico City was established, and in 1523 the first procurators were elected. The civil collegiate bodies were structured through two administrative positions: the alcalde or mayor and the 'regidor' or councillors. Both performed an administrative function at the municipal level, although the alcalde also served as local judges in criminal matters. See Rodríguez Kuri 2012: 70-71; Contreras Bustamante 2001.

[6] For a reconstruction of the juridical evolution of the working condition of the natives see also: Corral 2011: 129-169

The latter had seen their human and social condition devastated by their subjugation to the Spanish. For example, the pre-Columbian Mexican population was estimated to be around fifteen million, and by the beginning of 1600, just eighty years after the fall of Tenochtitlán, it had been reduced to less than a million and a half (McCaa 2000: 241-304). This was due, on the one hand, to the impossibility for the natives to develop adequate immune defenses against the diseases transmitted by the conquerors, while, on the other, they suffered inhuman exploitation, legally crystallized in the *encomienda*,[7] which allowed the free use of indigenous labour in the mines and fields.

Throughout the 16th century, a strong clash developed between the emerging landowning aristocracy, with the support of both a large part of the clergy, who had acquired vast income-generating territories through bequests and donations, and the Crown, against some Catholic missionary groups, who wanted the Indians to be recognised as free citizens, with all that this entailed in terms of rights and property.

The figure of Francisco de Vitoria,[8] a Dominican and jurist counted among the fathers of international law, who dealt extensively with the issue of land ownership and the freedom of the Indians, cannot be overlooked:

> *They lived, privately and publicly, in peaceful possession of their goods. Therefore, unless it is proved otherwise, they must be considered as true lords and masters, and cannot be dispossessed of their property (...) From all that has been said, the following conclusion can be deduced: that neither the sin of infidelity, nor other mortal sins prevent the Indians from being true lords and masters of their own property, either publicly*

---

[7] A legal institution established from 1503 onwards, which provided for the assignment of a territory to a soldier or officer to exploit its wealth and manage the local population by educating and converting them to Christianity. In practice, this resulted in a disguised form of slavery. For more details see Simpson 1950; Lockhart 1969: 411- 429.

[8] Born between 1483 and 1493, professor at the University of Salamanca, he was the author of numerous fundamental works such as De Indis (1532); De Iure Belli (1539); Relectiones theologicae (1557); Confessionario (1562); Summa Sacramentorum Ecclesiae (1560).

or privately, and that Christians cannot in this way appropriate their territories[9].

Although Philip II, under the positive influence of Catholic jurists[10], again prohibited slavery and forced labour of the Indians, reaffirming their full freedom, the condition of the natives was not improved. The royal edicts often remained mere theoretical provisions that were not accepted by the owners of the *haciendas*, mines and *obrajes*, for whom free labour was an irreplaceable source of wealth.[11]

In the meantime, the economy of Mexico City grew, as did its population,[12] while the territory of New Spain reached enormous proportions, including the Philippine Islands in the Pacific, which were also subject to the viceroy's rule for a limited period.

---

[9] Freely translated by De Vitoria F., *Relectio De Indis*, italian edition and translation by Lamacchia A., Levante Editori, Bari, 1996. Original text: "*Essi vivevano, privatamente e pubblicamente, in possesso pacifico delle loro cose. Pertanto, se non costa il contrario, devono essere considerati come veri padroni, e non si può spogliarli della loro proprietà (...) Da tutto quello che si è detto si desume questa conclusione: che né il peccato di infedeltà, né altre colpe mortali impediscono agli indios d'esser veri signori e padroni dei propri beni, tanto pubblicamente come privatamente, e che i cristiani non possono a tal titolo appropriarsi del territorio di quelli*".

[10] The Dominicans had also been very prominent in the adoption of the earlier *Leyas Nuevas*. See Getino 1945: 265-360.

[11] The contrast between the conservative interventions of the centralised clergy, aimed at protecting economic rents to the detriment of the indigenous population and at the side of the aristocracy, continues, as opposed to the missionary activity of the small number of priests who are directly deployed for the liberation and enfranchisement of all men (Schwaller 2000).

[12] The social fabric of the capital (and of the entire Spanish colony) in the 17th century acquired an unusual complexity: the indigenous population and the Spaniards were joined by an ever-increasing number of people of African descent, brought in as slaves to compensate for the enormous loss of labour caused by constant epidemics and inhuman exploitation. Thus, a system of differentiation of the population on a racial basis began to take shape, on which the legal status of every person in New Spain and the capital depended: Indians, Spaniards, Blacks, Creoles, Metis, Zambos, Moors (moriscos), Mulattos and Castizos formed a new society, with an increasing level of conflict and tension, which would contribute to the strong revolutionary drive of the following centuries. See Kandell – Bignami 1992: 195- 201.

1.2 The crisis of the Spanish Empire and independence

The loss of prestige of the Spanish Crown and the lack of economic renewal led, from the second half of the 17th century onwards, to an increasingly marked decline in Spain's global influence. This, however, was not immediately reflected in a loss of power in the American colonies, where the grip of viceroy administration remained firmly in place for some three centuries.

What is most evident, however, is that as Spanish economic progress declined, the area of Mexico, and Mexico City itself, gained more and more strength and, more importantly, became aware of the great wealth of its territory, and the diminishing need for the presence of European rulers. As early as the 18th century, a new ruling class, made up of Creoles[13] began to increase its influence, detaching itself from and opposing the dominant Spanish elite.

Furthermore, society experienced an initial phase of great expansion, which, thanks to trade and the conquest of new territories towards North America,[14] led to a considerable growth of all classes, with the exception of the Indians, who maintained a position of semi-slavery in the *haciendas* and mines, with the sole exception of the experiment of the *ejido*, a unit of collective administration of the territory (Vázquez Castillo 2004; Kourí 2015: 54-61; Haenn 2006: 136-146), strongly opposed, even in blood, by the large landowners.

It is difficult to understand why it was necessary to wait until the beginning of the 19th century to be able to speak of Mexican independence, and to consecrate Mexico City as the capital of a new nation. Certainly, it must be noted that the wealth generated locally, the presence of increasingly educated and cultured classes and the growing military strength of the local militias could have represented, even a century earlier, an opposition force to Spain that was difficult to overcome. What was certainly influential was the late formation of the idea of a Mexican nation, which had not

---

[13] The term 'creole' identifies the descendants of Europeans born on American soil. For more details see the interesting study on Creole identity by Villella (2016).
[14] An interesting insight can be found in Haas 2014.

yet been able to adequately form itself at a social level, and the absolute dependence on an administrative structure completely subservient, at the top level, to the Spanish Crown. Furthermore, the contribution of the clergy was decisive in guaranteeing a high level of social peace, due to their influence on the poorer and more discriminated classes, in favor of maintaining the *status quo*.

It should also be considered that Mexico City, before independence, had already achieved a position of absolute pre-eminence, not only in terms of trade and administration, but also because of the presence of monuments, churches and universities of prime importance, so much so that it was defined as "the most important centre in the northern hemisphere of the Isthmus of Panama" (Calderazzi 1963: 147-170).

Its location, well before the 19th century, allowed it to be categorized among the so-called natural capitals, whose prestige and history made it unsurpassed by other Mexican cities.

And again, it was the heart and highest ambition of the revolutionary movements, which are one of the building blocks of the entire Mexican identity.

At the gates of the future capital, the first irregular army of rebels clashed in 1811 (Henderson 2009) against General Calleja's army, which saw the victory of the Spanish and the defeat of the first revolution. However, what is decisive is that, under the leadership of Father Hidalgo (Timmons 1967: 574-575), a Creole priest from Penjamo, considered one of the fathers of modern Mexico, more than eighty thousand people, mostly from the poorer classes, rose up to demand the abolition of slavery, which in fact remained in large parts of the country, the cessation of the tributes to which the Indians were obliged by law, and independence from Spanish rule.

Despite the failure of the rebellion, and the cruel consequences of the popular uprising developed both ways, the unstoppable wheel of change had begun to turn.

Hidalgo's successor, the mestizo priest Morelos (Escudero 2008: 235-247), managed to collect the remains of the revolutionary movement and to build, out of the original fury, a first system of organised and constitutionalised opposition to the Crown. He was responsible for the drafting of the first Constitution on Mexican soil, in 1814, in the self-proclaimed republic of Apatzingan.[15] This Supreme Charter expressed not only the independence "*La América es libre, e independiente de toda otra nación*" (*America is free, and independent of any other nation*) and the recognition of popular sovereignty "*La soberanía dimana inmediatamente del pueblo*" (The *Sovereignty derives directly from the people*), but also the abolition of slavery and the intolerability of torture.[16]

Although Apatzingan's constitutional experience was exhausted in barely a year, snuffed out in blood by the shooting of Morelos by government forces, the seeds of revolution had spread throughout the country and the path to independence seemed inevitable.

In 1821, General Augustin Iturbide, with the support of the upper middle class and conservatives, took advantage of the serious crisis in the Spanish monarchy and conquered Mexico City with his army, declaring independence and appointing himself Emperor. Beheaded a few years later, a period of great instability began, which affected the whole region. In 1824 Mexico became a federal republic built on 19 states and based on a weak and often unenforced constitution. An initial attempt to enhance local autonomy was replaced by the construction of a highly centralised administrative system under General Sant'Anna, in which Mexico City was not only the seat of government and federal bodies, but also the absolute centre of the nation.

In this chaos, however, post-revolutionary weakness imposed not only a great loss of productivity and wealth on the population, but accentuated the interference of new European powers, which aimed to take over from the vanished Spanish crown. To all this was added the strong expansionism of the USA, which deprived Mexico of large territories in the north, greatly diminishing its international prestige.

Like the revolutions, the evolution of the country's constitutional structure continued, in particular through the 1857 Constitution,

---

[15] See in this regard De La Torre Villar 1978.
[16] *Elementos Constitucionales Circulados Por El Señor Rayón (4 De Septiembre De 1812)*, taken from the above text.

which led to the implementation of civil rights and the redistribution of Church land, as well as the loss of ecclesiastical privileges, and the decollectivisation of indigenous community structures in favour of the direct development of small-scale land ownership.

In 1867, the installation of Porfirio Diaz as dictator[17] led to a period of great expropriation of small property in favor of the few, with the denial of the most basic freedoms and widespread discrimination against the indigenous peoples. In addition, the administration of the state was further centralized, favoring the growth of the capital and the concentration of the economic and governmental apparatus.

The subsequent crises and revolutions culminated in the Constitution of 1917,[18] where democratic and reformist principles, together with the desire to develop a welfare state, finally found not only their dispositive crystallisation, but also a slow and steady practical application.

Although a period of conflict and unrest continued until the Second World War, in the following period Mexico and its capital saw a steady growth in democracy and economy, with the settling of old conflicts, the pacification between church and anticlerical movements, and a more equitable development of land ownership. However, as we shall see later, new challenges, such as international drug trafficking, corruption, and appeasement between the various ethnic groups, remain crucial in determining not only Mexico City's future as a global city, but the fate of the entire federal republic.

2. The constitutional system of Mexico City

With the conquest by Spanish troops, the ancient city of Tenochtitlán was subdivided, according to the typical Spanish structure of city government, into autonomous administrative areas called

---

[17] For an in-depth look at this important historical figure see: Garner 2014.
[18] Mexico, *Constitución Política de los Estados Unidos Mexicanos*, La Secretaría de Gobernación, 1917.

cabildos,[19] which can be assimilated, albeit with all the particularities of the case, to a form of municipal council. Originally, the city was organised into three *cabildos*, two dedicated to the administration of the areas populated by the natives, and a third, corresponding to the centre of the current capital, to the area inhabited by the Spaniards, and the seat of the main institutions of the emerging viceroyalty. The government structure answered directly to the *Audiencia* (Cunningham 1919), a territorial control body that, in turn, answered to the Spanish Crown and, for it, to the Viceroy. The *cabildo,* structured in the form of a council, was responsible for managing local affairs and was chosen through a mixed system of appointments and elections. Within the *cabildo* area, smaller homogeneous areas were also structured, not dissimilar to our metropolitan municipalities, called *barrios*, with directly elected autonomous councils and limited but relevant power in the fulfilment of community interests.

The relevance of the *cabildo* can be understood through the constitutional power-sharing system of compartmentalised sovereignty between the state and the citizen community (Annino 1988: 727-763), with an extremely relevant protection of the *derecho comunal de los pueblos.*

Furthermore, the distribution of local power between whites and natives, although asymmetrical, was extremely important and could well be described as complementary (Annino 1988: 727-763).

The local power structure basically allowed the Creole population to develop its own leadership that was increasingly influential on both the fate of the city and Mexico.

They were so decisive as structures that any attempt by the crown to reduce their relevance was balanced by the growth of autonomous political structures, mainly creole, such as brotherhoods, militias, orders and guilds (Annino 1988: 727-763).

---

[19] The 2017 Political Constitution of Mexico City, in Article 54, defines the current *cabildo* as *El consejo de alcaldes y alcaldesas se denominará Cabildo y funcionará como un órgano de planeación, coordinación, consulta, acuerdo y decisión del Gobierno de la Ciudad de México, y las personas titulares de las alcaldías.*

As colonial power expanded, Mexico City grew extremely rapidly, changing its ethnic composition and transforming itself from an administrative centre into an economic and commercial heart. In 1782, its administrative subdivision included eight major districts and thirty-two minor ones, subject to the political government of an *alcalde*, a figure similar to the mayor and endowed, until the 19th century, with not only administrative but also jurisdictional powers.

In 1824, the legal structure of the city was transformed, by an act of Congress and in accordance with the newly created Constitution, into a federal district, whose territory was delimited in a concentric area whose heart was established in *Plaza Mayor*. After a period of complex evolution, in which the city was first transformed into a department (Department of Mexico 1836) and again reconstituted into a federal district, with the typical prerogatives of a state (1857 Constitution), and after a reshaping of the boundaries with neighbouring states (States of Mexico and Morelos 1898), it was finally placed under the direct rule of the federal president in 1928[20].

2.1 The choice of district. The role in the federal state. Constitutional functions. The 2016 reform

The extreme importance of the city, and its wealth in terms of population and economy, led to the decision, as early as the mid-19th century, to entrust its management directly to the President of the Republic.

This did not exclude the creation of intermediate forms of representation, such as the *Asamblea de Representantes del Distrito Federal*[21], with specific competencies in regulations and ordinances, in order to better meet the local needs of the city. However, this was largely insufficient to guarantee adequate

---

[20] Mexico: Federal District, in Encyclopedia of Latin American History and Culture. 2021 https://www.encyclopedia.com/humanities/encyclopedias-almanacs-transcripts-and-maps/mexico-federal-district (24 november 2021).
[21] Introduced by the constitutional reform of Art. 73 para. VI of 1987.

representation of citizens' demands and the development of an autonomous political power in the Mexico City area, whose orientations were subordinate to the fulfilment of primary federal interests.

Against this backdrop, the need, after almost a century, to reform the legal system in its entirety led to the 2016 constitutional reform, which radically changed the governance of the capital and its legal framework.

In particular, the reformed Article 40[22] of the Mexican Political Constitution considers Mexico City as a constituent entity of the federation, and places it in a position comparable but not assimilated to the individual states.

Mexico City does not have the dignity of an autonomous state, as can be seen from the wording of Article 43[23], where the city is included in the list of states making up the federation, but is placed in a separate position from them.

Its constitutional position is outlined in Article 44:

> *La Ciudad de México es la entidad federativa sede de los Poderes de la Unión y Capital de los Estados Unidos Mexicanos; se compondrá del territorio que actualmente tiene y, en caso de que los poderes federales se trasladen a otro lugar, se erigirá en un Estado de la Unión con la denominación de Ciudad de México.*[24]

---

[22] *Es voluntad del pueblo mexicano constituirse en una República representativa, democrática, laica y federal, compuesta por Estados libres y soberanos en todo lo concerniente a su régimen interior, y por la Ciudad de México, unidos en una federación establecida según los principios de esta ley fundamental.* Last reform: DOF 30-11-2012, 29-01-2016

[23] *Artículo 43. Las partes integrantes de la Federación son los Estados de Aguascalientes, Baja California, Baja California Sur, Campeche, Coahuila de Zaragoza, Colima, Chiapas, Chihuahua, Durango, Guanajuato, Guerrero, Hidalgo, Jalisco, México, Michoacán de Ocampo, Morelos, Nayarit, Nuevo León, Oaxaca, Puebla, Querétaro, Quintana Roo, San Luis Potosí, Sinaloa, Sonora, Tabasco, Tamaulipas, Tlaxcala, Veracruz de Ignacio de la Llave, Yucatán y Zacatecas; as well as the City of Mexico.* Last reform 17-05-2021.

[24] Freely translated: "*Mexico City is the federative entity seat of the Powers of the Union and Capital of the United Mexican States; it will be composed of the territory it currently has and, in the event that the federal powers are transferred to another place, it will be established as a State of the Union with the name of Mexico City*".

The need to constitutionalise the role of the capital responds to an increasingly pressing need to define not only the division of competences and the administrative structure of the authority, but above all responds to the crisis of the state in relation to the emergence of mega-cities (Li *et al* 2019: 1382-1395).

The management of cities with a population of millions and economic and cultural relations on a global scale can in no way be equated with the ordinary legal structure of ordinary municipalities.

This has recently appeared in the Italian legal experience in the need to introduce Rome as the capital city of Italy into the constitution (Ruscitti – Perinu 2021). The global role of the latter requires a specific legal system capable of responding to its exceptional needs. The state is increasingly assuming a role of direct control over megacities, which are becoming similar to islands within the territory, as is clearly the case for the two main global cities, London and New York, which enjoy a dimension of their own, detached from the country to which they belong.

However, this crucial role hides a fundamental weakness (Kübler – Lefèvre 2018: 378-395), where it translates into a limitation of the democratic representation of the resident population, with the extreme difficulty of finding a balance in the governance of a city that is increasingly tending towards its own autonomy and the risk that it is, instead, unfairly deprived of the resources necessary for its overall development.

Mexico City, therefore, and the great reform of 2016, go in the explicit direction of reconciling the necessary federal control over the capital with the liberation of resources and the implementation of a democratic government capable of giving the city an increasingly international role.

It is now clear that the role of megacities is growing globally (Labbé – Sorensen 2020), and preventing a megacity like Mexico City from creating its own space would be a limitation to the growth of Mexico as a whole.

It cannot be ignored, however, how the Mexican revolutionary experience, as summarised albeit briefly in the first paragraphs, rigidly influences the relationship with the Capital, so much so as to regulate, in the same political Constitution, the hypothesis of transferring the seat of government to another place. An element which not only underlines the decisive role of the city, but which does not exclude the hypothesis of constitutional crises.

2.2 The Political Constitution of Mexico City

Although, as stated above, the Mexican capital does not attain the dignity of a state, it has an autonomous constitution, the result of the work of a constituent assembly, which was promulgated on February 5th, 2017 by the *pro tempore Jefe de gobierno*[25] of the city, and came into force on September 17th, 2018.

This constitutional choice is extremely innovative, since it is the result of a compromise between the various political forces united in a body partially invested by the people:

> *Asamblea Constituyente expresa la soberanía del pueblo y ejercerá en forma exclusiva todas las funciones del Poder Constituyente para la Ciudad de México, por ende, entre sus atribuciones se encontraban las de aprobar, expedir y ordenar la publicación de la Constitución Política de la Ciudad de México.*[26]

Indeed, the direct reference to popular sovereignty, on the one hand, and to constituent power, on the other, lead to the identification of an original power in the realisation of the new political-constitutional structure of the city.

In reality, this is only apparent, since the political Constitution of Mexico City (Const. CDMX) draws its legal legitimacy from

---

[25] Designation of the holder of the executive power of Mexico City, now determined in his functions by Article 32 - C of the 2017 Political Constitution.

[26] Statement by Miguel Ángel Mancera Espinosa, Jefe de Gobierno de la Ciudad de México, in preamble to the decree promulgating the Mexican Political Constitution, Gaceta Oficial De La Ciudad De México, 5 de Febrero de 2017.

Freely translated: "*Constituent Assembly expresses the sovereignty of the people and will exclusively exercise all the functions of the Constituent Power for Mexico City, therefore, among its attributions were those of approving, issuing and ordering the publication of the Political Constitution of Mexico City*".

Article 44 of the Constitución Política de los Estados Unidos Mexicanos and not from an extra-legal generating force[27]. Similarly, it should be noted that the composition of the constituent assembly of Mexico City is representative not only of the resident population, but also of the federal powers.[28]

It assumes a general value for the city, so much so as to be defined, in art. 71, as inviolable and not amendable by acts of force or violence and capable of maintaining its value even in the event of the institutional order being broken. This appears, once again, consistent with Mexican revolutionary history, but of little relevance from an exquisitely legal point of view, where constitutional sources, as we know, require for their effectiveness, if and when they can be considered original, popular support for the institutional structure established by the will of the people.

However, the case of the Political Constitution of Mexico City appears peculiar, correctly considering it as a source derived from the Mexican Federal Constitution (*ex* art. 44). In this case, the breakdown of the federal order and its institutional collapse could, under Art. 71 Const. CDMX, not directly overwhelm this legal source, which would have, in the will of the people, its own autonomous legitimacy (although, in practice, this seems extremely unlikely, since it does not seem realistic to be able to separate the destiny of the Mexican federal government from that of the capital, in cases of revolutionary events or foreign invasion).

Mexico City's form of government is established in its constitution as republican, democratic, representative, secular and popular,

---

[27] Art. 1 para 5 Const. Pol. CDMX: *Las autoridades de la Ciudad ejercen las facultades que les otorga la Constitución Política de los Estados Unidos Mexicanos, todas aquellas que ésta no concede expresamente a los funcionarios federales y las previstas en esta Constitución.*

[28] *La Asamblea Constituyente se caracterizó como institución legislativa por tres elementos. El primero es que su integración fue mixta, 60 legisladores fueron electos por voto ciudadano y 40 fueron designados por cuatro bloques: senadores de la república, diputados federales y representantes del Poder Ejecutivo federal y el jefe de Gobierno de la Ciudad de México. Esta composición se debe a que la Ciudad de México por reforma constitucional es la sede de los poderes de la Unión y una entidad federativa (no un estado con mayores facultades), por lo que los actores públicos que intervienen en su gobierno trascienden el ámbito local y tocan el federal* (Polina 2020).

based on the separation of powers, political pluralism and popular participation.

Territorially, its spatial dimension remains crystallised in the decrees of December 15th and 17th, 1898 of the Union Congress, and it is divided into autonomous territorial demarcations, with their own government, called *alcadias*.[29]

The latter relate to the central government of Mexico City on the basis of the principle of vertical subsidiarity and proximity, through the implementation of administrative decentralisation. They exercise a wide range of competences, some exclusively (art. 53, par. 3 a), others concurrently with the central authority (par. 3 b).

In addition, they are guaranteed the possibility of associating with each other and with neighbouring municipalities of other federal entities in order to better meet any cross-cutting interests.

However, it is clear that the provision of power and its implementation, especially in the context of *collaborative implementation*, is often extremely complex, especially where there are no predetermined instruments for consultation. The mere political will, in relation to administrative entities belonging to different federal areas, appears extremely limiting to the concrete possibility of launching integrated projects.

To allow Mexico City, or the individual *alcadias*, to determine autonomously *opting in* of neighbouring territories would be seriously destructive of the constitutional sovereignty of the adhering states. However, the territorial delimitation determined on criteria that date back more than a century appears largely inadequate and generates serious distortions in the management of services.

2.3 A Constitution for all

One of the distinguishing features of the new constitution is certainly its inclusive function, with a particular focus on the protection of human rights.

---

[29] Art. 53 Cost. Pol. CDMX: *Las alcaldías son órganos político administrativos que se integran por un alcalde o alcaldesa y un concejo, electos por votación universal, libre, secreta y directa para un periodo de tres años.*

First of all, the explicit reference to the pre-Columbian origin of the city is relevant to our discussion, so much so that the preamble expressly refers to the city of Tenochtitlan, quoting an expression of the Aztec ruler Tenoch in 1325: *En tanto que dure el mundo, no acabará, no perecerá la fama, la gloria de México Tenochtitlan.*[30] This not only has a historical and identity value, but also best expresses the continuity of Mexico City's role as a natural capital and global centre of culture.

The constitutional structure desired for the fundamental charter of the city is also well expressed in the presence, alongside the ordinary distribution of competences, normative and production sources, jurisdictional rules and administrative functions, typical of the statutes necessary for the functioning of the cities, in the choice to expressly include human rights, general legal principles in the social and economic sphere, and above all to value and recognise the rights of indigenous populations.

Article 2 of the Const. CDMX states that the city is intercultural, multilingual, pluriethnic and pluricultural, and that it recognises and protects the *pueblos* and *barrios*[31] historically present in the territory and the indigenous peoples. It also emphasizes that the city is not a place closed to its inhabitants, but is open to internal and foreign immigration, as well as to the reception of refugees, political exiles and those seeking protection.

The city, in its diversity, sets as its constitutional foundation the defence of human dignity, individual freedom and equal rights. To this end, the constitution implements a series of supreme social principles, some borrowed directly from the Western legal tradition, such as the pre-eminence of the public sphere in satisfying community interests over private property, to its own characteristic principles, however, such as harmony with nature[32]

---

[30] Freely translatable into: *As long as the world lasts, the fame and glory of Mexico Tenochtitlan will not end or perish.*

[31] For the importance of the barrios in the historical community of Mexico City, in addition to what has already been said in the historical part, we refer to the important texts by Lira (1995); Granados (2008); Gruzinski (2012); Macune – Zapata (1978).

[32] The entirety of Article 13, entitled *Ciudad habitable,* recognises as essential rights the

or the implementation of the protection of the status of victims of violence, to the point of establishing a true *Derecho a la Ciudad* (Art. 12),[33] which emphasises the collective belonging of the *res publica*.

It is in relation to minorities, however, that the Mexico City constitution assumes an exceptionally innovative role, breaking down centuries-old cultural prejudices and emphasising the dream of a truly inclusive and transversal body. In fact, it not only imposes formal equality of all human beings, but also mandates positive actions to eliminate racism and to protect and implement the cultures of the most discriminated social groups, such as Afro-descendants and indigenous people. Article 11, entitled *Ciudad incluyente (Inclusive city)*, guarantees a constitutionalisation of the rights of minorities, expressly and in detail recognised as *personas que debido a la desigualdad estructural enfrentan discriminación, exclusión, maltrato, abuso, violencia y mayores obstáculos para el pleno ejercicio de sus derechos y libertades fundamentals*.[34]

Furthermore, the CDMX political constitution devotes ample space to the political self-determination of indigenous peoples, their cultural enhancement and economic development, due to the massive historical suffering and discrimination they have endured. The indigenous peoples, considered an integral part of Mexico City, are guaranteed the possibility of organising themselves in their own institutions capable of exercising collective rights over community goods, as well as powers of representation and consultation.

---

protection of the natural environment and ecological balance, for present and future generations. It recognises the dignity of animals as sentient beings and the need to respect their life and integrity. It recognises the right of people to enjoy healthy and safe public spaces and to enjoy leisure time in a healthy environment.

[33] *The right to the city is a collective right that guarantees the full exercise of human rights, the social function of the city, its democratic management and ensures territorial justice, social inclusion and the equitable distribution of public goods with the participation of the citizenry.*

[34] *People who, due to structural inequality, face discrimination, exclusion, mistreatment, abuse, violence and increased obstacles to the full exercise of their rights and fundamental freedoms.*

Alongside the traditional western bipartition between private and public property, the right to social property, typical of the Mesoamerican tradition, is recognised. The latter (Vázquez 2013; 2018; Bojórquez-Luque 2011: 297-311; Madrid *et al* 2009: 179-196; Pérez Castañeda - MacKinlay 2015: 45-82) transcends the European conception of the social function of property, and evolves into a use of goods and land that is differentiated from both private and state use, especially in the economic-productive sphere, placing itself in an intermediate position, i.e. towards the interests of a specific community that has direct interaction (Pasara 1973: 211) with the *res*. It does not find a coherent normative classification, often remaining on the margins of contemporary legal discussion, including Mexican law. However, it seems that it can be linked to the indigenous experience of the *ejido*,[35] which has recently seen a notable growth in interest, and whose structures for sharing the territory may represent a possible innovation of community management of spaces, including urban ones.

2.4 Planning a Megalopolis: urbanization and healthy environment

The anthropic development of the Valley of Mexico, as discussed in detail in the historical section, can be traced back to the foundation of Tenochtitlan. Although the valley was already widely inhabited, thanks to the presence of fertile land and Lake Texcoco, it was only with the arrival of the Aztecs that the natural environment was subjected to and modified for human needs. Recent studies (Mundy 2021) estimate the native population living in the ancient capital at over one hundred and fifty thousand. In the period of greatest splendour, the Aztecs built large structures for water control and management (Torres-Alves – Morales Nápoles 2020: 107057), countless temples and palaces, since by the time the Spanish conquerors arrived, the city already had a well-structured urban layout.

The foundation of an initial Spanish core began to radically change the original layout, with the construction of European-style streets

---

[35] See: historical part, p. 6.; see also: Perramond 2008: 356-371.

and neighbourhoods characterised by narrow alleys and closely packed buildings. In addition, the rapid expansion of the population, after the initial decrease due to the depopulation of the natives, led to hydraulic changes that dried up Lake Texcoco (Alcocer – Williams 1996: 45-61) and its definitive disappearance. Nowadays, however, it should be noted that there are some projects aimed at partially restoring some of the areas to regenerate some of the biodiversity that once existed in the area (Cruickshank García 2003).

The urban development of the city has tended to be haphazard over the centuries, with neighbourhoods and government buildings being built according to the fashions, often European[36] force at the time, without any organic planning.

While this contributes to the presence of historic districts of great architectural and historical interest, it also generates a situation of considerable chaos, both in terms of transport and the integrated management of services.

It was not until 1976, following the reform of Article 115 of the Political Constitution of the United Mexican States, that urban planning was legally introduced, with the establishment of an Advisory Council of Mexico City to coordinate urban development and try to manage the city's increasingly rapid growth.

It must be considered that, since the 1950s, the population explosion had given rise to a series of satellite towns, populated by tens of thousands of people, often lacking the most basic services, even road connections.

Added to this was a phenomenon typical of those years, namely the construction of huge low-cost housing estates that devastated the existing urban structure.

More recently, late in the day, the Commission for Art in Pub-

---

[36] For example, under the government of Porfirio Diaz the city adopted the French architectural style, while under Miguel Aleman there were many houses inspired by the Normandy country style. In addition, the development of the various neighbourhoods was influenced by the social class to which they belonged, so the wealthy areas of San Rafael and Santa María developed in the English style, while the Roma district favoured the art-nouveau style. See Zabludovsky 1995.

lic Spaces (1994) was set up, with the aim of preventing further destruction of the city's architectural heritage, and the Urban Development Commission (2012), aimed at finding solutions to the housing crisis, which had exceeded a deficit of over one million people in the metropolitan area (Berlanga 2017: 146-161; Garcia Cortes 1972).

It is only with the current Constitution (2016 CDMX) that the Capital of Mexico has equipped itself with an integrated planning system and, above all, adopted a set of fundamental guiding principles in the future growth of the city.

In particular, the City recognizes the social function of land, whether it is in the form of public, social or private property. It recognizes the fundamental importance of ecological preservation, environmental protection and natural resources. Furthermore, it guarantees the maintenance and implementation of housing units in areas of cultural or ethnic interest, limiting forced population transfers (Art. 16 paragraph C no. 2 and 3).

The public interest is extended to the protection of the genetic heritage of native species (art. 16 paragraph A no. 2), and respect for *the vital cycles of nature* is constitutionalized as a principle of sustainable development and land consumption (Anaya – Altamirano – Rincon 2020: 603-639.).

To this end, Mexico City has a *Plan General de Desarrollo* and a *Programa General de Ordenamiento Territorial* aimed at identifying areas of unbuildability, environmental protection, water catchment, hydrogeological risk and natural, cultural and local protection.

Of particular relevance is the introduction in the Constitution as a fundamental right of the *Diseño Universal,* an extremely recent concept that can be translated as *Universal Design* (Connell *et al.* 1997), the aim of which is the realisation of every building or urban structure in such a way that it is accessible to every person (Story 2001), regardless of age or disability, thus creating the legal and theoretical basis for the realisation of a truly inclusive city.

This concept, therefore, goes far beyond the limited discussion of architectural barriers, but aims to provide an organic response, in the form of a principle, to the right of everyone to participate in

public life and to enjoy the same possibility of access and movement.
Its innovative nature of inclusion has led to the overcoming of the traditional architectural concept, transferring this principle to areas such as health care and education (Rose 2000: 45-49).

2.5 Protecting the system: tools for transparency, anti-corruption and democratic participation

Large global megacities suffer from a number of typical problems, which undermine the internal functioning of institutions and can lead to an inability to manage the *res publica* properly, with disastrous effects on the quality of life and economic growth of the territory.

Among the various issues that can be considered, four appear to be priorities in relation to Mexico City.

First and foremost, there are complex and organised criminal phenomena, which are able to access large financial resources and, at the same time, to generate a strong political influence on both the local population and the institutions, gaining the direct or indirect control of entire offices or public functions.

This undermines the very basic categories of modern democracy, limiting or suffocating the rule of law, preventing the development of appropriate forms of representation and taking sovereignty, or the effective exercise thereof, away from the population, which falls into the hands of criminal groups (Garay-Salamanca – Salcedo-Albaran 2012: 15).

The real risk that may develop, in the presence of increasingly powerful criminal structures, as in the case of the Italian mafia phenomena or in the case of Central and South American drug trafficking (Mazzitelli 2015: 299-324; Chalton 2014), is that we may witness a true Co-opted State Reconfiguration (CStR),[37] in

---

[37] GARAY SALAMANCA AND SALCEDO ALBARAN (2012) define the concept of CStR as "*the action of legal and illegal organisations that, through illegal practices, aim to methodically and from within modify the political regime and influence the creation, modification, interpretation and application of the rules of the game and public policies. These practices are undertaken*

which such groups not only manage to establish agreements with the state or institutions, even at local level, that make it up, but even go so far as to shape the public administration according to their own utility and convenience (Garay-Salamanca and Salcedo-Albaran 2012: 20). This causes the State Capture (StC), which occurs in the presence of massive economic criminal infiltration, to begin to change from within, with the consequence that the public apparatus stops pursuing its own social and general interests and begins to contribute to the legitimisation of criminal structures, which significantly increase their grip on the population and the territory. This mutation takes place not only through its own economic activities, such as corruption, but also through intimidating and violent methods, such as threats, kidnappings, murders and rituals of submission.

The influence of criminal organisations can extend beyond the institutional sphere and, thanks to their economic power and with the support of corrupt officials, achieve the subjugation of academia, the media, civil society and political parties, definitively paralysing the democratic mechanism (Garay-Salamanca and Salcedo-Albaran 2012: 35).

The institutional system is at its weakest where attempts and control measures appear to have failed, and criminal organisations are brought to the level of interlocutors, with whom to initiate agreements, aimed at pacifying the areas concerned and reducing petty crime or the war against the forces of law and order, in exchange for a form of connivance on crimes of wider relevance such as drug trafficking, public contracts and the management of billion-dollar services.

The situation in Mexico City cannot be ascribed either to the level of CStR or StC (Garay-Salamanca and Salcedo-Albaran 2012: 65), but it certainly raises concerns about the activities of certain criminal groups, whose presence and wealth, as well as violence,

---

with the intention of gaining considerable advantage and securing political, legal and social legitimacy for their long-term interests, even if these do not pursue social welfare".

force legitimate authorities to make constant and effective measures to defend governance and democracy.

Especially in the positive perspective of administrative decentralisation, where the new Constitution aims to implement instruments of horizontal and vertical subsidiarity, the danger of a general weakening of the system of protection of public interests cannot be excluded: the more democratic participation is broad and directly linked to the development of decision-making processes, the more the influence of powerful criminal groups becomes decisive at local level.

Not all the manifestations of democratic crisis that can be identified in Mexico City can be traced back to the presence of organised criminal groups alone, but the post-revolutionary structure typical of Mexican politics and society must always be considered, since some authors (Rivas 2012: 244-247) consider the current difficulties as a phase of the state-making process.

The second problem, therefore, is to adequately guarantee the development of a democratic process. The new Political Constitution of CDMX provides, in article 25, a series of instruments of direct democracy, aimed at allowing citizens to take part in the process of city government. These are, in particular, the *referendum, plebiscite, consulta popular, iniciativa ciudadana, consulta ciudadana y revocación de mandato*. The powers conferred directly on the population are exceptionally broad, recalling typical European institutions, such as the referendum and the popular legislative initiative, to typically North American institutions such as the revocation of the mandate of elected officials, and instruments of connection and expression of the will of the people such as citizen consultation.

With regard to representative democracy, the most traditional and effective form of translating popular sovereignty, the new Constitution introduces (art. 27) both the possibility of autonomous candidacies and the implementation of social bodies and parties, and places an instrument of regularity control in the hands of the *electoral authority*, which has the task of verifying the regularity of elections.

This authority, which immediately appears to take on a decisive role in the democratic life of the city, takes the administrative form of the *Organismos Autónomos*,[38] similar in part to the European Independent Authorities.

Characteristic elements are independence from political power, administrative autonomy, internal regulatory autonomy, and its own powers of control and decision-making.

It must be considered in this respect that, despite strict legislative provisions, citizens' trust in the electoral authority appears to be declining (Pérez-Verduzco 2020: 103-115), and this leads us to the need to address the two other fundamental problems facing the city: corruption and transparency.

Corruption is one of the main problems in the proper management of mega-cities, and Mexico City, like the entire country, suffers the effects (Morris 2013: 43-64; 2012: 29-43). In spite of the remarkable attempts of the highest institutions,[39] the situation remains particularly critical, with the Corruption Perception Index placing Mexico in the unfavourable position of 124/180 on a planetary scale, far from ideal situations.[40]

The great wealth of the capital and the concentration of speculative and financial interests make it exceptionally exposed to the phenomenon, as it is essential for the administration to implement control tools.

An entire chapter[41] of the 2016 Political Constitution is consequently dedicated to fighting corruption. Among the tools provided, the most important appear to be built on three levels. The

---

[38] Art. 46 Const. Pol CDMX: *Los organismos autónomos son de carácter especializado e imparcial; tienen personalidad jurídica y patrimonios propios; cuentan con plena autonomía técnica y de gestión, capacidad para decidir sobre el ejercicio de su presupuesto y para determinar su organización interna de conformidad con lo previsto en las leyes correspondientes.*

[39] Federal President Lopez Obrador himself has made the fight against corruption one of the main points of his government programme, involving international organisations and tightening up the relevant legislation, including using constitutional laws to increase the effectiveness and scope of law enforcement.

[40] However, the index seems to positively note the efforts made, especially at the federal level, to combat the phenomenon, reporting an improvement of six positions compared to the year 2019 according to the Corruption Perception Index.

[41] Chapter 1, Art. 61 et seq.

first provides for the establishment, within each public body of the Capital, of an autonomous supervisory body to prevent and investigate corrupt phenomena. Their independence is guaranteed by staff rotation and the support of the *Sistema Local Anticorrupción*, a body in charge of the city coordination of investigation and sanction activities, data collection and information. This forms the second level of counteraction, which connects the local city bodies with the federal ones, carrying out joint programs to defend the administration and contributing with the presentation of regulatory proposals to implement its effectiveness.

The third and final level provides for the establishment of an independent inspection body, *the Entidad de Fiscalización de la Ciudad de México,* which analyses the performance of individual administrations and local authorities, checking their financial management and identifying any distortions and responsibilities of public officials (Vera 2017: 87).

This three-level structure of control, prevention and sanction is flanked by a further independent body, in charge of transparency, called, according to Article 49 of the Constitution CDMX, *Instituto de Transparencia, Acceso a la Información Pública y Protección de Datos Personales*. This authority is set up to guarantee access to public administration information, ensure the protection of citizens' personal data and thus enable the *disclosure of* public activities.

What seems essential, however, is to guarantee, in addition to the correct identification of the general principles of transparency and good administration, the opening of direct channels of access, by means of IT tools and digital platforms, to allow citizens to constantly monitor the activities, at least the most relevant ones, of the administration.

In fact, the risk of the reform is that the excessive bureaucratisation of the system will not be matched by adequate implementation of citizens' rights, which could, in theory, remain the prerogative of the few and light years away from the means of the poorer classes of the population.

The smart city, or *ciudad digital*, cannot be understood as the exclusive connection of inhabitants to a fast and efficient internet network, but it must guarantee immediate and direct access to the public administration, its services, its documents, and give the possibility to present, without complications, instances and requests for access. Digital democracy cannot be born only from the presence of technological hubs, but from the concrete possibility of interaction between the governed and the governors, and the latter must find themselves, thanks to true transparency, operating in a glass house.[42]

Conclusions

The new political constitution of Mexico City represents the latest example of legal and social commitment to the radical improvement of a mega-city, to overcoming inequalities, and to the enhancement of culture, with a view to cultural growth and political representation.

Indeed, the Mexican capital has the full capacity to act as an accelerator for the entire federation, but it needs the right tools to be able to grow sustainably, and above all it needs to be protected from the corrupt and criminal phenomena that have so far seriously undermined its potential.[43]

In addition, urban development requires careful planning and regulation to ensure, on the one hand, the construction of the housing units necessary to guarantee minimum standards of essential services to residents,[44] and on the other hand, to protect the historical, cultural and ethnic peculiarities that characterise many neighbourhoods.

---

[42] On administrative transparency, see: Carloni 2009: 779-812.
[43] *The Valle de México does not generate enough agglomeration benefits relative to its size. GDP growth of late has mainly been driven by population growth. Annual per capita economic growth averaged 0.5 in the period 2003 - 2010. Labour productivity (GDP per worker) in the metropolitan area (per the OECD definition) is about average among the 33 Mexican metropolitan areas. Its performance is well below the potential of a vibrant agglomeration of this size in an emerging economy.* OECD, Executive Summary, in *OECD Territorial Reviews: Valle de México*, Mexico, OECD Publishing, Paris, 2015.
[44] *In some neighbourhoods, more than 40% of homes lack at least electricity, water or drainage* (OECD 2015).

The exceptional historical importance of the metropolis should not be a hinderance but an asset to give it further international relevance, just as the revolutionary culture should be channeled in the right effort towards positive change in the democratic and non-violent renewal of the city, in a truly egalitarian perspective, with a consequent reduction of inequalities.

The constitutional approach analysed above demonstrates the will of the citizens to build a new city and a new society, based on the latest and most advanced legal principles, with the implementation of rights and respect for diversity and the natural environment.

However, rules are not enough if we do not succeed in building or reforming, on the basis of the stated principles, the institutions that are called upon to implement the necessary projects, to stop and combat distorting phenomena and to plan development correctly.

The fear, despite the reform, that the persistence of a multi-level system of government, based on the coexistence of local, federal, state and community authorities, in the absence of a very strong commitment to consultation, will prevent the implementation of cross-cutting works and services, remains well-founded.

Just as the danger that the interests of a few will undermine the proper use of natural resources, especially water resources, by increasing land consumption and holding back innovative development, cannot be ruled out when strong constitutional rules are not implemented administratively and financially.

In any case, the 2016 Constitution, the result of a historical and social evolution of more than five hundred years, containing the best and most advanced rights, principles and instruments that European and American jurists have been able to elaborate in the last centuries, represents a global example, demonstrating how Mexico City is ready, in the near future, not only to face the important challenges that await it, but to claim its place among the great planetary mega-cities.

References

Alcocer J. – Williams W. D., "Historical and recent changes in Lake Texcoco, a saline lake in Mexico", *International Journal of Salt Lake Research* 5/1, 1996: 45-61.

Anaya, J. A. – Altamirano, Y. C. – Rincón, A. R., "El derecho al desarrollo y los derechos de la Naturaleza", *Revista Direitos Sociais e Políticas Públicas (UNIFAFIBE)* 8/2, 2020: 603-639.

Annino A., "Pratiche creole e liberalismo nella crisi dello spazio urbano coloniale. Il 29 novembre 1812 a Città del Messico", *Quaderni Storici*, vol. 23/69, 1988: 727–63.

Archer C. I., "Mexican War of Independence (1810–1821)", *The Encyclopedia of War* (2011).

Berlanga R. R., "La Reforma Urbana de México", *Pluralidad y Consenso* 7/33, 2017: 146-161.

Bojórquez-luque J., "Importancia de la tierra de propiedad social en la expansión de las ciudades en México", *Ra Ximhai* 7/2, 2011: 297-311.

Caballos E. M., "De esclavos a siervos: amerindios en españa tras las leyes nuevas de 1542", *Revista de Historia de América* 140, 2009: 95–109.

Calderazzi A. M., "Storia del Messico", *Il Milione*, Enciclopedia Geografica, Istituto Geografico De Agostini, 1963.

Carloni E., "La 'casa di vetro' e le riforme. Modelli e paradossi della trasparenza amministrativa", *Diritto pubblico* 15/3, 2009: 779-812.

Chalton K., *Sangue e coca: L'ascesa della narcocriminalità in Messico*, Fuoco Edizioni, 2014.

Connell B. R. et al., *What is universal design.*, NC: North Carolina State University, 1997.

Contreras Bustamante R., *La Ciudad de México como Distrito Federal y entidad federativa: historia y perspectiva*, Porrúa, México 2001.

Corral J. C., "Las 'Leyes Nuevas' del Emperador Carlos V: influencia de su espíritu proteccionista en el derecho laboral mexicano", *Revista Chilena de Historia del Derecho* 23, 2011: 129-169.

CRUICKSHANK GARCÍA G., "The Recovery of the Former Texcoco Lake Pro-Environment Engineering", *Voices of Mexico*, 2003.
CUNNINGHAM C. H., *The audiencia in the Spanish colonies as illustrated by the audiencia of Manila* (1583-1800), University of California Press, 1919.
DE LA TORRE VILLAR E., *La Constitución de Apatzingán y los creadores del Estado mexicano*, Universidad Nacional Autónoma de México, Instituto de Investigaciones Históricas, 1978.
DE ROJAS J. L., "Tenochtitlan", NICHOLS D. L. – RODRÍGUEZ-ALEGRÍA E. (ed.), *The Oxford Handbook Of The Aztecs*, 2017.
DE VITORIA F., *Relectio De Indis*, Edizione italiana e traduzione a cura di LAMACCHIA A., Levante Editori, Bari, 1996.
ESCUDERO A. G., "José María Morelos: El siervo de la nación mexicana", *Araucaria: Revista Iberoamericana de Filosofía, Política y Humanidades* 10/20, 2008: 235-247.
GARAVAGLIA J. C. – GROSSO J. C., "Criollos, mestizos e indios: etnias y clases sociales en México colonial a fines del siglo XVIII", *Secuencia* 29, 1994: 39.
GARAY-SALAMANCA, L. J. – SALCEDO-ALBARAN, E., *Criminalità e Stati. Come le reti illecite riconfigurano le istituzioni in Colombia, Messico e Guatemala*, Eurolink, 2012.
GARCÍA CORTÉS A., *La reforma urbana de México*, 1972.
GARCÍA P. V., *The Spanish Conquest of Mexico in 1521: After 500 Years*, presented at Scuola Sinderesi, Pontificia Università Gregoriana, Rome, 16 october 2021.
GARCÍA C. M., "La propiedad social en la actualización del modelo económico", *Revista Economía y Desarrollo (Impresa)* 147/1, 2012: 5-21.
GARNER P., *Porfirio Díaz*, Routledge, 2014.
GETINO L. A., "Influencia de los dominicos en las leyes nuevas", *Anuario de Estudios Americanos* 2, 1945: 265-360.
GRANADOS, L. F., *Cosmopolitan Indians and Mesoamerican barrios in Bourbon Mexico City: Tribute, community, family and work in 1800*. Georgetown University, 2008.
GRUZINSKI S., *La ciudad de México. Una historia*. Fondo de cultura económica, 2012.
HAAS L., *Saints and Citizens: Indigenous Histories of Colonial*

Missions and Mexican California, University of California Press, 2014.

HAENN N., "The changing and enduring ejido: a state and regional examination of Mexico's land tenure counter-reforms", *Land Use Policy* 23/2, 2006: 136-146.

HENDERSON T. J., *The Mexican Wars for Independence: A History*. Hill and Wang, 2009

HOLLER J., "Conquered Spaces, Colonial Skirmishes: Spatial Contestation in Sixteenth-Century Mexico City", *Radical History Review* 99, 2007: 107-120.

KANDELL J. – BIGNAMI A., *La capital: la historia de la ciudad de México*, Vergara, Buenos Aires, 1992.

KOURÍ E., "La invención del ejido", *Nexos* (México, DF) 37/445, 2015: 54-61.

KÜBLER D. – LEFÈVRE C., "Megacity governance and the state", *Urban Research & Practice* 11/4, 2018: 378-395.

LABBÉ D. – SORENSEN A., "Megacities, megacity-regions, and the endgame of urbanization", in *Handbook of Megacities and Megacity-regions*. Edward Elgar Publishing, 2020.

LI D. *et al.*, "Challenges and opportunities for the development of Megacities", *International Journal of Digital Earth* 12/12, 2019: 1382-1395.

LIRA A., *Comunidades indígenas frente a la ciudad de México. Tenochtitlan y Tlatelolco, sus pueblos y barrios,* El Colegio de México, 1995.

LOCKHART J., "Encomienda and Hacienda: The Evolution of the Great Estate in the Spanish Indies", *Hispanic American Historical Review* 49/3, 1969: 411–429.

MACUNE C.W., ZAPATA. J., *El Estado de México y la federación mexicana, 1823-1835*. 1978

MADRID L. ET AL., "La propiedad social forestal en México", *Investigación ambiental* 1/2, 2009: 179-196.

MAZZITELLI A., *Crimine organizzato e narcotraffico in Messico: cartelli e protomafie*, Rubettino, 2015.

MCCAA R., "The peopling of Mexico from origins to revolution", *A population history of North America*, 2000.

MORRIS, S. D., "The impact of drug-related violence on corruption in Mexico", *The Latin Americanist* 57/1, 2013: 43-64.

MORRIS, S. D., "Corruption, drug trafficking, and violence in Mexico", *The Brown Journal of World Affairs* 18/2, 2012: 29-43.

MUNDY B. E., *The Death of Aztec Tenochtitlan, the Life of Mexico City*, University of Texas Press, New York, 2021.

PASARA L. H., "Propiedad social: la utopía y el proyecto", *Derecho PUCP* 31, 1973: 211.

PÉREZ CASTAÑEDA J. C. – MACKINLAY H., "¿Existe aún la propiedad social agraria en México?", *Polis* 11/1, 2015: 45-82.

PÉREZ-VERDUZCO G., "Confianza en el Instituto Nacional Electoral mexicano: Una perspectiva comparada", *Reflexión política* 22/45, 2020: 103-115.

PERRAMOND, E. P., "The rise, fall, and reconfiguration of the Mexican ejido", *Geographical Review* 98/3, 2008: 356-371.

POLINA M. D. C. N., "El Constituyente de la Ciudad de México, el Congreso de la Ciudad de México y el parlamento abierto", *In El Poder Legislativo en la Ciudad de México*, Universidad Nacional Autónoma de México, 2020.

RIVAS E., "Violence, Coercion, and State-Making in Twentieth-Century Mexico: The Other Half of the Centaur", PANSTERS W. G. (ed.), *Canadian Journal of Latin American and Caribbean Studies* 37/73, 2012: 244-247.

RODRÍGUEZ KURI A., "Historia política de la ciudad de México (desde su fundación hasta el año 2000)", *Secuencia* 93, 2012: 70-71.

ROSE D., "Universal design for learning", *Journal of Special Education Technology* 15/3, 2000: 45-49.

RUSCITTI G. A. – PERINU P., "Quale ordinamento per Roma?", SANGALLI S. (ed.), *Roma: Quale futuro dopo l'ottavo saccheggio*, GBP Press, 2021.

SANDOVAL FORERO E. A., "Grupos etnolingüísticos en el México del siglo XXI", *Papeles de población* 8/34, 2002: 219-234.

SCHWALLER J. F. (ed.). *The church in colonial Latin America*. Rowman & Littlefield Publishers, 2000.

SIMPSON L. B., *The Encomienda in New Spain: The Beginning of Spanish Mexico*, Berkeley University of California Press, 1950.

STORY M. F., "Principles of universal design", *Universal Design Handbook*, 2001.

TORRES-ALVES, G. A. – MORALES-NÁPOLES O., "Reliability analysis of flood defenses: The case of the Nezahualcoyotl dike in the aztec city of Tenochtitlan", *Reliability Engineering & System Safety* 203, 2020.

VARGAS BECERRA P. N. – FLORES DÁVILA J. I., "Los indígenas en ciudades de México: el caso de los mazahuas, otomíes, triquis, zapotecos y mayas", *Papeles de población* 8/34, 2002: 235-257.

VÁZQUEZ CASTILLO, M T., *Land Privatization in Mexico. Urbanization, Formation of Regions, and Globalization* in Ejidos, Routledge 2004.

VÁZQUEZ J. L. P., "Mercado de tierras y propiedad social: una discusión actual", *Anales de Antropología* 47/2, 2013: 9-38.

VERA M. D., "Prevención de la corrupción en las Entidades de Fiscalización Superior. Buenas prácticas de la Auditoría Superior de la Ciudad de México", *Fiscalización, Transparencia y Rendición de Cuentas*, 2017: 87.

VILLELLA P. B., *Indigenous Elites and Creole Identity in Colonial Mexico, 1500–1800*, Cambridge University Press, 2016.

ZABLUDOVSKY A., *Historia oral de la ciudad de México. Testimonios de su arquitectura (1940-1966)*, Instituto Mora, 1995.

APPENDIX
Seven Original Sins of Mexico City

H.E. Prof. Alberto Medardo Barranco Chavarría – Ambassador of Mexico to the Holy See – Rome

I - Pollution

After the fall of Mexico City-Tenochtitlan, capital of the Aztec or Mexica Empire, the Spanish conquistadors decided to impose their stamp not only on beliefs and culture, but also on the infrastructure itself. If the new Christian temples were to be built on pagan vestiges, the layout of the new city, eventually called New Spain, was built in the style of medieval European cities.

With the design entrusted to the master builder Alonso García Bravo, the three dirt roads of the lake city, whose commerce and mobility were carried out in canoes, disappeared to give way to narrow streets.

If in the Ixtapalapam, Tlacopan and Tepeyacac roads, according to chroniclers, there was room for 25 men in a row with their arms intertwined, in the new roads there was barely enough room for horse-drawn carriages.

The new city opened with a grotesque episode that occurred when two of them ran head-on into each other in the alley of La Condesa, with the novelty that none of the elegant passengers wanted to retreat, using as reasons noble titles, prolonging the dispute for several days. Given that in this contest each one considered himself too much more worthy than the other to move in reverse, it had to be the viceroy who dictated a Solomonic solution: To back up the carriages at the same time under the rhythm of the sound of a small drum.

The scenario resulted in a bottleneck that made traffic slow and cumbersome in the heart of the city, what is now the Historic Center, with the consequent burden of air and noise pollution.

The need to open windows to prevent asphyxiation forced some wider avenues to be planned, which over the years destroyed the architectural harmony of the viceregal city, demolishing palaces and mansions of enormous value not only architecturally but historically.

II - Sinking

Once the canals of the Aztec city were drained to make room for the places where the natives were made to live, they had to build their houses not only over swamps and their stream of disease-transmitting insects, but also faced the risk of constant sinking of streets and houses whose greatest danger arose during the rainy season.
The softening of the soil caused the foundations of palaces and temples to be deeper and some stages had to be leveled to contain the possibility of sinking or at least cracking.
In this context, the instability of the soil caused the grotesque situation in which persistent rain caused the coffins of the graves in the Campo Florido cemetery, located south of Mexico City, to float in a sinister pattern.
The desiccated area clearly marks to this day the highest degree of danger in case of earthquakes in several areas of the city. The sketch points out with absolute certainty the danger of the sites in the specific case of the earthquakes of 1957, 1985 and 2017.
In 1956, when the tallest building, the 54-story Latin American tower, was built in the historic center, it had to be cemented under a system of control piles similar to the shock absorbers of vehicles to balance possible inclinations that could lead to collapse or sinking.
The mark of the scourge can be clearly seen in the two meters that the marble Palacio de Bellas Artes or Palace of Fine Arts, built during the first third of the 20th century, has sunk, and the 2.6 meters of the Independence Column, inaugurated in 1910, to which steps had to be added to prevent the loss of its perspective. Most of the temples built in the viceregal era show sinking. In some cases, such as the old Basilica of Guadalupe, this has not been repaired, placing the building in a dangerous incline.

III- Flooding

In an effort to increase lethality by placing a state of siege over Mexico City Tenochtitlan in 1521, the conquistador Hernán Cortés built a dike, known as albarradón, in the eastern zone to close the waters of Lake Texcoco and to place there brigantines transported piece by piece. The roar of the cannons instilled terror in the natives, and the shipment of provisions to the besieged city was canceled.

At the same time, the bridges over canals and irrigation ditches were destroyed on the same route to defeat the Aztec capital by starvation.

Over the years, the dike wall would be overflowed by the waters of Texcoco and the lakes of Zumpango and San Cristobal, whose lack of navigable canals through which to channel them caused them to flow over New Spain, whose drainage was supported by old mud pipes, insufficient to contain the torrent.

At the same time, as the Valley of Mexico was located in a basin bounded by mountain ranges, the scenario allowed the city to be left in the shape of a pan, with the possibility of floods with levels close to two meters.

The worst of these occurred in 1629, when after 48 days of endless rain the water completely flooded the heart of New Spain, prolonging the stagnation for five years with its consequent trail of epidemics and famines. The supply by canoe from the valley basin was sent to the rooftops. The priests carried the sacrament to the dying by the same waterway.

To mitigate the danger, colossal investments were made by both the Spanish crown and Independent Mexico, as tunnels had to be built to drain the main lakes. For example, the Huehuetoca or Nochistongo.

European engineers were called upon for the task, the most outstanding being the Dutch or German Henri Martin, known in Spanish as Enrico Martinez, who had to suffer prison sentences before being recognized for exceeding his technology in view of the magnitude of the problem.

The threat, centuries later, remains latent, even though new tunnels have been built, such as the Tequixquiac tunnel, which was completed at the dawn of the last century, in addition to the opening of a master drainage collector system in whose interior thickness three cargo trucks could circulate in a row.

IV - Overcrowding

With the layout of New Spain limited to a space barely similar to that occupied by the heart of Mexico-Tenochtitlan, it soon had to widen towards its flanks, displacing the indigenous neighborhoods to establish manufacturing centers as guild zones. Thus there were workers such as shoemakers, stonemasons, basket weavers or textile workers.
These in turn were displaced to the birth of new urban colonies, sometimes taking space from the orchards of the convents and even from cemeteries to be urbanized.
If the orchards of the convent of Propaganda Fide de San Fernando became the Guerrero neighborhood and the spaces of a ranch in San Rafael, the cemeteries of Santa Paula and San Andrés would be transformed into the Santa María la Redonda neighborhood, while the Campo Florido was transformed into the doctors' neighborhood.
Although the first Constitution of Independent Mexico, signed in 1824, had a federalist character, that is, it recognized the sovereignty of the federative entities, the tendency during the 19th century was centralist, that is, to place the nucleus of government from and towards the capital, which provoked the exodus of the inhabitants of the interior towards the opportunities of fortune, education and even survival offered by Mexico City.
Migration became suffocating during the first years of the 20th century, not only through efforts to flee the misery of agricultural areas, but also in search of security and order during the stages of the revolutionary movement.
The phenomenon extended the urban stain towards the eastern zone in a scenario of irregular settlements, lacking services, displacing even more the lake zone at the risk that the dried up lake beds would become a source of dust and, naturally, infectious diseases.

The setting accentuated the stark contrasts between the opulent spaces of what foreign visitors referred to as the City of Palaces, and the squalid spaces similar to the Brazilian favelas that were known as lost cities.

In various areas of the city, some convents became neighborhoods or warehouses for storing merchandise.

The demand for urbanization services caused a parenthesis in the modernization of the city when most of the public budget was allocated to meet the demand, taking advantage of the possibility of political patronage, which prolonged for decades the majority prevalence of an official party with a dictatorship profile.

Currently, the demand for housing is still a most sensitive issue, together with insecurity due to the lack of sufficient employment opportunities in the face of overpopulation, despite the fact that real social housing structures have been built within Mexico City and its suburban area, which now encompasses five states in the surrounding area.

V - Thirst

The Aztec city of Mexico Tenochtitlan was supplied with fresh water mainly from the springs in the wooded area of Chapultepec and channeled through irrigation ditches. At the time of the conquest, these would be canceled, giving priority to the transfer of liquid through an aqueduct that began in the area itself and ended in a fountain located in the southwest boundary of the layout.

The population was supplied right there, either directly or through muleteers who transported the liquid in clay barrels. The square where the animals settled was known as Tumbaburros.

When the aqueduct proved to be insufficient, another one had to be built towards the northeast of New Spain and with two fountains, one in the area known as Tlaxpana, and the other on the north side of the Central Alameda.

The aqueduct that ran from the Santa Fe area was located in the San Cosme neighborhood.

However, the springs of El Salto del Agua, Los Músicos, and La Mariscala, as they were called, were still far away for the inhabitants of several areas of the city, even those closest to the heart of the route.

When the situation became critical in 1803, Viceroy Félix Berenguer de Marquina decided to ingratiate himself with the population by building a fountain that would supply the area closest to the viceregal palace.

The problem was that there was no way to channel the water to the fountain, whose elegant structure became an ornament and an object of mockery of the authorities.

The need for the liquid provoked the feverish opening of wells that soon ran out, making the subsoil more unstable.

Further away, wealthy families opted to build summer mansions in the area known as Tacubaya, whose profusion of rivers allowed not only the domestic supply but also the possibility of guaranteeing extensive sowing and even taking advantage of the current as a driving force for wheat mills.

In fact, at the dawn of the 19th century, the possibility of relocating the capital to the area was analyzed.

The saturation of the habitable space, however, caused the water supply to the indigenous neighborhoods to diminish to the point of becoming a trickle. As the water was transported to the areas with the largest Spanish or Criollo population through hollow reeds, the natives drilled them with maguey tips in desperation.

In fact, in one area of Tacubaya, the scarce liquid recovered was baptized as 'El chorrito' (the little stream).

In this context, settlements multiplied on the banks of rivers that little by little would be absorbed by the urban sprawl. Moreover, some of them, such as La Piedad, Churubusco and La Magdalena, would be piped in order to build roads on their beds.

The Santa Anita Canal that connected the center of New Spain with Iztacalco, Mexicaltzingo and Chalco, which in the 19th century even allowed tourist transportation by steamboat, disappeared to make way for the Calzada de la Viga.

In turn, the National Canal that ran in the southern zone of the Valley of Mexico to connect the area of Xochimilco, would be fragmented, with only a symbolic fragment surviving.

And although agricultural and urban zones still coexist in the expansion of Mexico City, in the south and southeast of the city, farmland is gradually being displaced by urbanized spaces. This is the case in the Magdalena Contreras, Xochimilco, Milpa Alta and Iztacalco municipalities.

At the same time, the city's usual sources of water, whether groundwater or dams that store rainwater or water from rivers in the interior of the country, are gradually losing capacity.

The most notable example is the Cutzamala System, made up of 7 dams, 6 pumping plants and a drinking water treatment plant, which has an annual increase in water levels of only 0.6%.

Currently, at least 1,300,000 inhabitants of Mexico City do not receive drinking water in their homes and 1,500,000 do not receive it regularly.

The supply in several areas is provided by official or private pipes, with the novelty that the latter charge rates that are unaffordable for the majority.

From another angle, the city's subway water supply network, especially in the historic downtown area, is so aged that up to a third of the liquid is lost in leaks.

VI - Contrasts

Although the Aztec or Mexica education used different teaching programs, one for the children of nobles known as Telpochcalli and the other for the common people called Calmecac, finally the situation was open to all.

However, after the Spanish conquest, the natives would be excluded from any learning opportunity, with the notable exceptions of the teachings offered by religious congregations and the creation of the Santa Cruz de Tlatelolco school by the Franciscan Order to teach the Spanish language and various trades. Antonio Valeriano, translator from Nahuatl of the book called 'Nican Mopohua', which narrates the apparitions of the Virgin of Guadalupe in the Cerro del Tepeyac, graduated from this college.

Destined to serve the conquerors, either as laborers, as slaves in the encomiendas made up of large tracts of land, or as mining masons, porters or domestic staff, the indigenous people were marginalized to a sad struggle for their very survival.

The baptized attended liturgical acts in open chapels as they were prevented from entering the interior of the temples, and the most important garden in New Spain, La Alameda Central, had guards at its eight gates to prevent indigenous access.

Segregation reached not only mestizos and mulattos but sometimes the criollos themselves, who daily confronted those born in Spain, known as gachupines, with literary duels through the so-called pasquines, satirical gestures that appeared on sheets of paper attached to the walls or written on them.

Society was divided into castes in which the purity of blood was distinguished. Offensive denominations arose for the children resulting from unions of blacks and indigenous, Spaniards and mestizos, as well as other mixed unions.

Harassed by discrimination, sometimes stoned or falsely accused of crimes, the different racial groups were grouped in separate neighborhoods, which delimited emblematic zones of the capital of New Spain. The lower the purity of blood, the further away from the layout.

Naturally, the neighborhoods would be stigmatized as dens of lowlifes or spaces of degradation, promiscuity and insalubrity.

The division has prevailed over the centuries, in a contrast of areas of mansions and extensive gardens, versus others of dangerous overcrowding where public services are never sufficient.

And although housing units have been built whose size would resemble cities, such as the Miguel Alemán multi-family housing complex, the Nonoalco Tlatelolco urban complex or the Culhuacán and El Rosario housing units, the average living space per family is between 50 and 90 m2.

The need for domestic space has led to the occupation of high-risk areas with greater risk of flooding or landslides.

At the same time, there are civil organizations that promote the illegal occupation of abandoned houses or buildings.

Viceregal mansions, converted into neighborhoods, have become ruins.

The latest estimate speaks of 1.7 million inhabitants of Mexico City living in extreme poverty.

VII - Anarchy

The inexistence, from the moment Captain Hernán Cortés ordered the master builder Alonso García Bravo to design the layout of New Spain on the ruins of Mexico Tenochtitlan, of a minimum plan for the long or at least the medium term, opened the door to anarchy.

Although the viceregal government had a Cabildo, a governing council, its functions did not include urban planning. It would seem that the growth, ornamentation or development of the capital of New Spain depended on the discretion of the viceroys in turn... or on the needs of the crown.

Thus, viceroys such as Antonio María de Bucareli y Ursúa built the so-called Paseo Nuevo (New Promenade), which ran to the south of the city between sidewalks for carriages and horses, trees, benches and three magnificent fountains, while Luis de Velasco built the Alameda Central on marshy land where the San Hipólito market was located, making it the main place of relaxation in the metropolis.

In turn, Viceroy Miguel José de Azanza extended the Paseo Nuevo to the Piedad River, where the convent of the same name was located.

Other sites gave rise to the construction of convents, churches and mansions, and later the surrounding areas were urbanized to build new colonies.

For his part, Viceroy Gaspar de Zúñiga y Acevedo had the streets paved, while Juan Vicente de Güemes Pacheco dignified the city by combating the filth that infested almost the entire layout and turned the few surviving ditches into sewage canals, in addition to ordering the opening of sewers and drains in the city's main thoroughfares.

And although coexistence was gradually regulated, most of the governmental ordinances aimed more at a quick repair of problems than preventing them. Thus, the illumination of the streets was ordered just when the councils spoke of supernatural events, and the public use of weapons was regulated when the number of street duels had multiplied; the nocturnal transit of carriages was limited when the hooves of the horses hitting the cobblestones disturbed the tranquility of those who slept.

The response came when complaints accumulated.

By the nineteenth and twentieth centuries the city had practically eradicated haciendas and ranches from its interior. The great lung of the city was the Chapultepec forest, although even that had been stripped of half of the space marked by the decree of donation to the city by Emperor Charles V.

Erected as the main street of the city, the Paseo de la Reforma, designed by Emperor Maximilian for the transit of his carriage from Chapultepec Castle to the Imperial Palace, was transformed at the whim of the rulers in turn. Some widened its streets; others narrowed them. Some favored ornamentation, others sobriety.

And while some rulers preferred subway transportation, others opted to create or widen existing roads, whether peripheral viaducts, rings or road axes, while electric transportation service was reduced to a minimum.

Until three years ago, Mexico City generated 5% of the country's total greenhouse gas emissions, equivalent to 31 million tons of carbon.

From another angle, while some governors tried to stop the expansion of the Mexico City metropolitan area, others promoted it, which maintains a permanent deficit in the supply of public services, besides increasing major problems such as garbage collection and storage or the self-generation of clean energies.

The city of 500 years, heir to the greatness of the Aztec capital, demands a long-range planning horizon to maintain the route of Mexican greatness, the city of palaces and the most transparent region, La región más transparente.

Workshop n. 2

ECONOMICS
Sustainable Development in Mexico City:
A Look at the Eleventh UN Sustainable Development Goal in the Case of Mexico City

Darius Allen Lawrence LC

Under the Supervision
of Dr. Mylene Cano – Coparmex – Mexico City

Introduction

The future for most of humanity lies in the cities. Four billion people, over half the global population, live in cities that face worsening air pollution, inadequate infrastructure and services, and unplanned urban sprawl. Although cities occupy just 3% of the earth's land, they account for 60-80% of energy conception and 75% of carbon emissions.[1] A vision of a brighter future for humanity will therefore have to consider this ever-increasing trend of urbanization and the challenges that come with it.

This paper will look at sustainable development in the particular case of Mexico City. Mexico City is one of the ten largest megacities in the world, with a population of around 21.8 million people[2]. By studying the particular challenges the city faces, as well as the steps being taken to overcome them, we will hopefully be able to better understand the difficulties all megacities must face and gain insight into possible solutions. These challenges will include housing, basic service infrastructure, inequality, public transportation, urban planning, environmental impact, natural disaster prevention, green spaces, and public safety, among other topics. We will start by looking briefly at the history of Mexico City's economic development. After this, we shall look at the city's

---

[1] See: *Sustainable Cities: Why They Matter*, United Nations Sustainable Development Goals, United Nations, New York 2020, Site: https://www.un.org/sustainabledevelopment/wp-content/uploads/2019/07/11_Why-It-Matters-2020.pdf Accessed: February 5, 2022.
[2] *Data Mexico Valle de México Metro Area*, Secretaría de Economía, Gobierno de México, Site: https://datamexico.org/es/profile/geo/valle-de-mexico Accessed: March 5, 2022.

current development with respect to the eleventh goal of the UN Sustainable Development Goals concerning the sustainable development of cities.

1. Mexico City's Economic Development Over the Years

1.1 Tenochtitlan and the Spanish Conquista

Before the arrival of the Spanish *Conquistadores* in 1521, what is now known as Mexico City was the capital of the Aztec Empire and went by the name of Tenochtitlan. The economy of Tenochtitlan was primarily agrarian. Since the city was built on the Texcoco lake, the Aztecs had to build artificial islands called *chinampas* which contained arable land supported by planks. The planks held the earth in and separated it from the water canals that served as a thoroughfare for the Aztec boats. These *chinampas* can still be seen in modern-day Mexico City in Xochimilco, one of the city's 16 buroughs (*demarcaciones territoriales*). The presence of the *chinampas* led to Xochimilco becoming one of UNESCO's World Heritage sites in 1987, and it has become a center of much tourism.

The Aztec Empire was not made up of one homogenous ethnic group but was the result of an alliance between three Nahua city-states, Tenochtitlan, Texcoco and Tlacopan, which banded together in order to conquer the peoples around the Valley of Mexico. As a result, the economy of Tenochtitlan was also supported by the tributes paid by these conquered peoples.

In 1521 Hernán Cortés and his *Conquistadores* took the city of Tenochtitlan and it eventually became the capital of New Spain, changing its name from Tenochtitlan to Mexico City, or *Ciudad de México* in Spanish. The economy remained predominantly agricultural, although the importance of mining in the surrounding areas, particularly Hidalgo, began to grow. The Spanish continued the tradition of demanding tribute from the outlying peoples, and more and more gold and silver began to flow from the mines into the city on their way to Spain. A regular currency was set up. Gold was minted in sixteen, eight, four, and two pesos pieces, and silver was formed into pesos, half-pesos, quarter pesos, reales and half-reales. Nonetheless, as Guthrie points out, there was a "lamentable lack of small fractional coins with which to make minor purchases, and it was necessary to use such substitutes as cocoa beans" (Guthrie 1939: 103–134, 104).

1.2 The Porfirian Era and the Twentieth Century

Under the government of Porfirio Díaz, who was the president of México almost uninterruptedly from 1876 until 1911, Mexico City underwent extensive modernization. Porfirio sought to transform the city so that it would rival the great European capitals. He took Haussmannian Paris as a model, but he mixed this style with Amerindian and Hispanic elements, creating what came to be known as 'Porfirian' architecture. Many of the ornate European-style buildings in the city were built at this time and have since become the center of much tourist attention.

1936-1940 was a decisive moment for both Mexico City's history and economy. The second World War had disrupted international trade and this led to Mexico's adopting of an import-substituting industrialization program. The struggle to decrease Mexico's dependence on developed countries and to build an industry of its own was stimulated by indigenous capital as well as foreign investment. In the first few years of 1940, the national product grew by 13%, averaging a 6.7% growth for the whole decade and 5.8% during the 1950s. Much of this growth was in the new, expanding industrial sector, which was predominately localized in Mexico City. This was aided by state-intervention, which provided fiscal support and heavy investment in infrastructure that was attractive to industry. Already by 1965, 48% of the largest private national companies were located around Mexico City. This excessive centralization was in fact a concern to the government, which cut back on fiscal advantages in the city in 1955 (Ward 2013).

The newfound industry sector led to an increase in the need for labor. Combined with a declining productivity in agriculture in the surrounding areas, this need for labor led to a large migration of the population from the countryside to the city. It is estimate that 60% of migrants within Mexico at this time went to Mexico City. Between 1950 and 1960, the percent of the industrial output of Mexico City in relation to the rest of the nation increased massively from 27.2% to 42.7%, and within the city itself the industrial sector made up 39% of the total output. Nevertheless, by the 1960s, Mexico City began to make the transition to a service economy, with services reaching 66.6% of the city's output by the 1980s (Ward 2013).

1.3 The Current State of Mexico City's Economy

Mexico City in our own day continues to be one of the main centers of economic activity in Mexico, although it is rivalled by Monterrey in the north. The main sources of exports are the motor vehicle industry, petroleum and the mobile phone industry. Industrial production has almost tripled over the last fourteen years, growing by 195%. To put this in perspective, it would help to note that this is twice as much growth compared to the 84% growth of US production over the same time period[3]. The motor vehicle industry, which includes motor vehicles for the transport of goods as well as cars, made up 36.3 billion US dollars of the city's exports in 2020.[4] It is one of the most important industrial and manufacturing sectors in Mexico. In 2007 production grew from 1.6 million cars to 2.1 million, and in 2021 production was around 2.7 million,[5] making Mexico the world's sixth largest car producer overall.[6]

---

[3] *United States Exports by Country and Region 2019,* World Integrated Trade Solution, The World Bank, Site: https://wits.worldbank.org/CountryProfile/en/Country/USA/Year/2004/TradeFlow/Export Accessed: March 6, 2022.

[4] *Data Mexico Ciudad de México*, Secretaría de Economía, Gobierno de México, Site: https://datamexico.org/en/profile/geo/ciudad-de-mexico-cx Accessed: March 5, 2022.

[5] *Administrative record of the light vehicle automotive industry*, Instituto Nacional de Estadística y Geografía, 2022, Site: http://en.www.inegi.org.mx/datosprimarios/iavl/ Accessed: March 1, 2022.

[6] *Car Production by Country 2022*, World Population Review, Walnut 2022, Site: https://worldpopulationreview.com/country-rankings/car-production-by-country   Accessed: February 15, 2022.

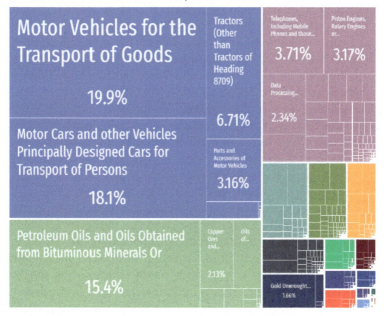

Figure 1. Mexico City's export products in 2020.[7]

Second to the motor vehicle industry is Mexico City's participation in the oil industry. The main petroleum company in Mexico is *Petróleos Mexicanos*, also known as Pemex. Pemex is state-owned and was formed in 1938 when President Lázaro Cárdenas del Río nationalized and expropriated all private oil companies in Mexico. In 2020 the petroleum industry accounted for 20.18 billion US dollars of Mexico City's exports. Nevertheless, Mexico City ended

---

[7] Graph from *Data Mexico Ciudad de México*, Secretaría de Economía, Gobierno de México, site: https://datamexico.org/en/profile/geo/ciudad-de-mexico-cx?foreignYearSelector1=2020#economia-ventas-internacionales Accessed: June 22,2022.

up still purchasing and importing 20.58 billion US dollars' worth of petroleum products in 2020, more it exported.[8] This is because of a curious situation in Mexico's petroleum industry. Due to a lack of refineries in the country, Mexico must sell its crude oil to the United States and then buy it back at a loss in refined form. It is for this reason that the president, Andrés Manuel López Obrador, plans to begin refining Mexican crude oil in facilities owned by Mexico by 2023. For this purpose, the Dos Bocas facility is currently being built in the state of Tabasco, and a facility is being bought near Houston (Stillman 2022).

Besides being a center for industry, Mexico City is also a center of services for the country. It is the financial center of the country and there is a growing tech sector as well. Due to its rich history, archeology, and architecture, Mexico City also has a booming tourist economy. These three make up a large part of the economic production within the city itself. Although the motor vehicle and petroleum industries account for much of the capital flowing into the city, this is more a result of the company headquarters being present there, not because oil is being extracted or cars are being produced within the city limits. It would seem that, in a certain sense, not much has changed since colonial times when money produced elsewhere used to flow into the city as a result of tributes. Mexico City's main trade partner is the United States, to whom goods and services worth 62.2 billion US dollars were exported and from whom 57.7 billion were imported in 2020. The next trade contender is China, who nevertheless has a much smaller share with only 3.22 billion worth of exports and 16.9 billion worth of imports in the same year.[9] In 2006 Mexico City had a trade deficit of 29.7 billion US dollars,[10] which meant that the city was importing almost twice as much as it was exporting. However, by 2020 this deficit had been decreased to only 10.7 billion, with

---

[8] *Data Mexico Ciudad de México*, Secretaría de Economía, Gobierno de México, Site: https://datamexico.org/en/profile/geo/ciudad-de-mexico-cx Accessed: March 5, 2022.
[9] *Data Mexico Ciudad de México*, Secretaría de Economía, Gobierno de México, Site: https://datamexico.org/en/profile/geo/ciudad-de-mexico-cx Accessed: March 5, 2022.
[10] Exports: 32.3 billion US dollars, imports: 62 billion US dollars.

the ratio of imports to exports being close to a balanced one to one.[11]

Unemployment had been hovering around 5% prior to the SARS-CoV-2 pandemic in 2020, at which point it rose to 7.26%[12]. Although a 5% unemployment rate would seem to be a fairly positive indicator of the city's economic health, the situation is unfortunately more complicated due to the fact that 48% of that employment is in informal labor.

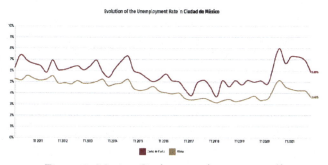

Figure 2. Mexico City's unemployment rate.[13]

2. Mexico City and Goal 11 of the UN Sustainable Development Goals

In 2015 the United Nations General Assembly ratified the 2030 Agenda for Sustainable Development. As part of this agenda, they approved the seventeen Sustainable Development Goals (SDGs), which seek to build on the previous Millennium Development Goals and complete what they did not achieve. According to the 2030 Agenda, there are three dimensions of sustainable devel-

---

[11] Exports: 95.3 billion US dollars, imports: 106 billion US dollars.
[12] *Data Mexico Ciudad de México*, Secretaría de Economía, Gobierno de México, Site: https://datamexico.org/en/profile/geo/ciudad-de-mexico-cx Accessed: March 5, 2022.
[13] Graph from *Data Mexico Ciudad de México*, Secretaría de Economía, Gobierno de México, site: https://datamexico.org/en/profile/geo/ciudad-de-mexico-cx#empleo-poblacion-economicamente-activa Accessed: June 22,2022.

opment: the economy, society, and environment.[14] All three are closely interrelated: an increase in social mobility and well-being leads to economic growth, the negative effects of climate change can lead to economic losses, and investment in society and the environment are aided by a strong economy.

We will be focusing on Mexico City's progress in relation to the eleventh of the seventeen SDGs: "make cities and human settlements inclusive, safe, resilient and sustainable".[15] This goal is further divided into the following seven subgoals: 1. By 2030, ensure access for all to adequate, safe and affordable housing and basic services and upgrade slums; 2. By 2030, provide access to safe, affordable, accessible and sustainable transport systems for all, improving road safety, notably by expanding public transport, with special attention to the needs of those in vulnerable situations, women, children, persons with disabilities and older persons; 3. By 2030, enhance inclusive and sustainable urbanization and capacity for participatory, integrated and sustainable human settlement planning and management in all countries; 4. Strengthen efforts to protect and safeguard the world's cultural and natural heritage; 5. By 2030, significantly reduce the number of deaths and the number of people affected and substantially decrease the direct economic losses relative to global gross domestic product caused by disasters, including water-related disasters, with a focus on protecting the poor and people in vulnerable situations; 6. By 2030, reduce the adverse per capita environmental impact of cities, including by paying special attention to air quality and municipal and other waste management; 7. By 2030, provide universal access to safe, inclusive and accessible, green and public spaces, in particular for women and children, older persons and persons with disabilities.[16]

---

[14] *2030 Agenda for Sustainable Development*, United Nations 70th General Assembly, New York 2015, Site: http://www.un.org/development/desa/jpo/wp-content/uploads/sites/55/2017/02/2030-Agenda-for-Sustainable-Development-KCSD-Primer-new.pdf Accessed: March 8, 2022.
[15] *Ibid.*, 14.
[16] *2030 Agenda for Sustainable Development*, United Nations 70th General Assembly, Ney

Each of these subgoals could be the subject of an article by itself, but we will seek to focus on some of the most important problems or signs of progress in Mexico City with regard to each.

2.1 Subgoal 1: By 2030, Ensure Access for All to Adequate, Safe and Affordable Housing and Basic Services and Upgrade Slums

One of the greatest difficulties in Mexico City is the incredible inequality of the standards of living between the wealthy and the poor. If one were to take the economy of the city alone, it would be the 46th richest country in the world, with a GDP larger than that of Finland or Portugal, and four times the size of that of Luxembourg.[17] Nevertheless, there are multiple slums in the city which lack access to even basic services such as water or sewage. 3% of people in the metropolitan area of Mexico City, around 650,000 people, do not have access to water.[18] Similarly, in 2011 over 3 million residents still lacked basic sewage and drainage infrastructure (Valenzuela-Aguilera 2011: 291–310, 300). The system for solid waste was overstretched and sewage treatment plants were inadequate for coping with the quantities produced. Even where water is accessible, there is an inequality in water use due to distribution – affluent districts consume 900 liters per person a day, whereas other parts have to cope with only 35 liters per person a day (Valenzuela-Aguilera 2011: 291–310, 300). Water was not scarce in Mexico until 35 years ago when the population reached over 6 million. Since then, water needs for consumption must often compete with the needs of industry, and the basin of Mexico is reaching its ecological and social limits to substitute or import the needed resources. 70% of the water is groundwater from underneath the city, which was built on a lakebed. A

York 2015, 22, site: http://www.un.org/development/desa/jpo/wp-content/uploads/sites/55/2017/02/2030-Agenda-for-Sustainable-Development-KCSD-Primer-new.pdf Accessed: March 8, 2022.

[17] *GDP Ranked by Country 2022*, World Population Review, Walnut 2022, Site: https://worldpopulationreview.com/countries/countries-by-gdp Accessed March 9, 2022.

[18] *Data Mexico Valle de México Metro Area*, Secretaría de Economía, Gobierno de México, Site: https://datamexico.org/es/profile/geo/valle-de-mexico Accessed: March 3, 2022.

study in 2011 showed that the main aquifer was being pumped at 55.5 m³/s but was only being replaced at 28 m³/s, causing the city to literally sink. The depletion of the lakebed's water volume and pressure causes the clay soils beneath the city to consolidate and the land on top to collapse. In order to deal with the water problem, the government set up in 1992 the *Comisión de Aguas del Distrito Federal* (Federal District Water Commission) with the goal of improving the management of potable water and drainage. In the past years there have been improvements: while 3% of the population still remains today without sufficient access to water services, this is much less than the 7% that was in this situation in 2010.[19]

Housing is one of the main themes of any city's politics, and Mexico City is no exception. The difficulty of providing low cost yet dignified housing for the poorest was only exacerbated by the destruction caused by the large earthquake that shook the city on September 19, 2017. In response the *Comisión Nacional de Vivienda* (National Housing Commission) set up the *Programa Nacional de Reconstrucción* (National Reconstruction Program, PNR), which provides subsidies for the partial or total reconstruction of affected communities. Another governmental initiative was the *Programa de Reactivación Económica y Producción de Vivienda Incluyente, Popular y de Trabajadores en la Ciudad de México* (Program of Economic Recovery and the Production of Inclusive, Popular Housing for Workers in Mexico City, PREVIT), which was launched in 2019. PREVIT published a program for urban regeneration and inclusive housing with the following goals: 1. Generate and implement a model of reconstruction for housing that was damaged in the 2017 earthquake; 2. Develop and invest resources in a model of attention to public and social housing that combats corruption and clientelism; 3. Develop new housing models with the concept of 'inclusive housing'; 4. Set up fiscal incentives in order to increase private investment in inclusive housing.

---

[19] *Data Mexico Valle de México Metro Area*, Secretaría de Economía, Gobierno de México, Site: https://datamexico.org/es/profile/geo/valle-de-mexico Accessed: March 3, 2022.

Despite the progress that has been made with these governmental programs, there is still the problem of a large presence of informal housing in Mexico City. Informal housing is defined by the OECD as "1. areas where groups of housing units have been constructed on land that the occupants have no legal claim to, or occupy illegally; 2. unplanned settlements and areas where housing is not in compliance with current planning and building regulations (unauthorized housing)".[20] To combat this situation various programs have been set up, such as the *Programa de Vivienda en Conjunto* (Overall Housing Project), which provides financing with zero interest for housing projects for people in a condition of vulnerability (low-income, indigenous, elderly, single mothers, disabled). This financing can be used to build a house, buy a house, or simply renovate a house with necessary services (water, sewage, electricity, etc.), ensuring that it is in accordance with the city's laws and regulations. Another recent project was the construction of *Tacubaya Sur, la Ciudad del Bienestar*, a housing project which provided apartments for 186 families (Zamarrón 2022). It was bult on the informal housing site of what had come to be known as the '*Ciudad Perdida*' ('Lost City') of Tacubaya.

The current government under the direction of the Head of Government of Mexico City, Claudia Sheinbaum, has taken steps to ameliorate the circumstances of the city's poorest neighborhoods. One such project is the planned construction of 300 *Puntos de Innovación, Libertad, Arte, Educación y Saberes* (Points of Innovation, Freedom, Art, Education and Knowledge), more commonly known as PILARES. These PILARES are centers in the poorest parts of the city that allow access to rights such as education, culture, sport, and work. The centers are free of charge and open to all, but they particularly wish to reach youth that have left school, in order to provide further education and capacitation for work. The PILARES offer cyberschools with computers and free Wi-Fi in order to learn programming, mobile app creation and comput-

---

[20] Glossary of Environment Statistics, Studies in Methods, Series F, No. 67, New York 1997, Site: https://stats.oecd.org/glossary/detail.asp?ID=1351 Accessed: March 1, 2022.

er skills, as well as to give access to online courses. Various other courses are offered for the sake of forming economic autonomy in subjects such as electricity, gastronomy, catering, plumbing, textile, fashion design, etc. A goal of the centers is to help those taking the courses to start cooperatives of micro-businesses, with help from the government for the providing of small capital sums. Besides these more economically oriented courses, there are also sport programs offering yoga, CrossFit, boxing, soccer, as well as courses in the various cultural arts, such as painting, dance, music, and theater, with the goal of organizing community festivals. To date 187 PILARES have been built, with work having begun on another 73, and the already existing PILARES have shown great success. 28,000 students were studying at the cyberschools by December 2019.[21] As a result of the program's success, the UNESCO International Center for the Promotion of Human Rights awarded the PILARES program the 2020 *Construir Iguadad* Prize.[22] Digitalization has also been at the forefront of public policy in the last few years. In a society that is spending an increasing amount of time online, access to internet has become more important than ever, particularly for economic growth and social mobility. In 2020, Mexico City won the prize for Digital Inclusion of the UN World Summit on the Information Society Forum (WSIS) for its free Wi-Fi program.[23] The city has built the second largest free Wi-Fi network in the world, setting up 13,694 points of connection in ten months.[24] The city was able to lower costs by

---

[21] "*PILARES, Puntos de Innovación, Libertad, Arte, Educación y Saberes*," El Universal, Dec. 16, 2019, 4, site: https://pilares.cdmx.gob.mx/assets/memoria-des/SUPLEMENTO_PILARES_FINAL.pdf, accessed March 4, 2019.

[22] *Ciudad de México y Goiás, las ganadoras del premio Construir Igualdad 2020*, UNESCO International Center for the Promotion of Human Rights, Buenos Aires 2021, Site: https://es.unesco.org/news/ciudad-mexico-y-goias-ganadoras-del-premio-construir-igualdad-2020 Accessed: February 26, 2022.

[23] *The best of the best in supporting SDGs with ICTs: Meet the 2020 WSIS Prizes winners*, UN International Telecommunication Union, Sep. 4, 2020, Site: https://www.itu.int/hub/2020/09/the-best-of-the-best-in-supporting-sdgs-with-icts-meet-the-2020-wsis-prizes-winners/ Accessed: March 3, 2022.

[24] *El Wifi gratuito de la Ciudad de México es galardonado como la mejor iniciativa de conec-*

using the already present security camera infrastructure, as well as 94 public spaces, 185 PILARES, and 56 digital libraries. Besides providing free Wi-Fi, as a result of the pandemic, the government of Mexico City set up in 2019 a digital app called "*Llave CDMX*" which allows citizens to enter all government sites with only one username and password. One is able to fill out forms and engage in procedures digitally, such as starting a business, renewing your driver's license, declaring taxes, soliciting documents such as birth certificates, etc. As of December 13, 2021, 2.7 million citizens had opened an account with *Llave CDMX*, and as total of 46,087 businesses had been started, partially as a result of the ease of this new digital means – one is able to open a business in 10 minutes with just a cellphone (Batres 2022). The ready availability of free internet in even the least developed areas of the city and the digitalization of bureaucratic processes will hopefully help to create opportunities for work, education, and social mobility for the city's poor.

After having become familiar with the various housing and social projects mentioned above, one would expect the city's spending to be exorbitant and the city's debt to be rapidly increasing. Fortunately, this has not been the case. In 2021 Mexico City's debt nominally increased only 4.5%, but actually had a real debt decrease of 2.6%.[25] The debt stands at 94.47 billion Mexican pesos, approximately 4.64 billion US dollars. To put this in perspective, it would help to note that Rome, a much smaller city with a population of only 2.87 million, has a debt of 12 billion euros, almost three times as much.[26] New York City with its 8.4 million

---

tividad a nivel mundial por la Unión Internacional de Telecomunicaciones, Agencia Digital de Innovación Pública, Gobierno de la Ciudad de México, September 9, 2020. Site: https://adip.cdmx.gob.mx/comunicacion/nota/el-wifi-gratuito-de-la-ciudad-de-mexico-es-galardonado-como-la-mejor-iniciativa-de-conectividad-nivel-mundial-por-la-union-internacional-de-telecomunicaciones Accessed: February 27, 2022.

[25] *Cuarto Informe Trimestral de la Situación de la Deuda Pública 2021,* Secretaría de Administración y Finanzas de la Ciudad de México, Gobierno de la Ciudad de México, October-December 2021, Site: https://servidoresx3.finanzas.cdmx.gob.mx/inv/DeudaPublica.html Accessed: February 10, 2022.

[26] *Debito, chiude gestione commissariale. Dal 2021 possibile riduzione Irpef e più risorse per*

inhabitants had a debt of 94.2 billion US dollars in 2021, a figure twenty times as large as that of Mexico City (Stringer 2022).

2.2 Subgoal 2: By 2030, provide access to safe, affordable, accessible and sustainable transport systems for all, improving road safety, notably by expanding public transport, with special attention to the needs of those in vulnerable situations, women, children, persons with disabilities and older persons

Public transport in Mexico City has always been a challenge due to the immense size and complexity of the city. Around 3.6 million people come into the city center to work every day, many of whom have incredibly long travel times (Valenzuela-Aguilera 2022). 1.7 million people have to travel more than an hour to get to their work and 473,000 have to travel more than two hours[27]. The city is famous for its horrific traffic and was ranked by TomTom as the "most traffic congested city in the world" in 2016.[28] In order to combat the traffic problem, more than half of the budget for transport the past years was used for road construction, particularly the double-decker elevated highway system. Some progress has been made, as the city dropped to the 28th place in the same TomTom index in 2021 with a 21% decrease in congestion.[29] The most innovative initiative for public transport was the Metrobus, based on the *Transmilenio* model of Bogota. The eighty Metrobuses replaced more than 260 mini-buses, have a dedicated lane, and cover 19 kilometers along the Insurgentes Avenue.

Mexico City's metro is the second largest metro system in North

---

la città, Comune di Roma, site: https://www.comune.roma.it/web/it/notizia/debito-chiu-de-gestione-commissariale-dal-2021-possibile-riduzione-irpef-e-piu-risorse-per-la-citta. page Accessed: March 8, 2022.

[27] *Data Mexico Valle de México Metro Area*, Secretaría de Economía, Gobierno de México, Site: https://datamexico.org/es/profile/geo/valle-de-mexico Accessed: March 3, 2022.

[28] *TomTom Traffic Index 2016*, TomTom, March 22, 2016, Site: https://corporate.tomtom.com/static-files/5289c5aa-310c-4965-a4c0-516760a8a6fd Accessed: March 4, 2022.

[29] TomTom Traffic Index Ranking 2021, TomTom, Site: https://www.tomtom.com/en_gb/traffic-index/ranking/ Accessed March 5, 2022.

America, after New York City. It is well used, but is unfortunately based mostly in what used to be the Federal District, leaving many of the inhabitants of the larger metropolitan area of Mexico City without direct access. In order to get an idea of the metro's use, in 2019 the metro transported 2.1 billion passengers, although in 2021 its use decreased dramatically to 794 million with the arrival of the SARS-CoV-2 pandemic.[30] Even with this decreased use, the metro still made up 66.8% of all trips using public transportation in December 2021, a fact which shows the central role it should play in political action concerning public transportation.[31]

Although the metro has such an important role in Mexico City, the service provided is still far from being sufficient. According to the *Instituto Nacional de Estadística y Geografía* (National Institute of Statistics and Geography, INEGI) and the 2017 *Encuesta Nacional de Calidad e Impacto Gubernamental* (National Survey of Governmental Quality and Impact), only 37,5% were satisfied with the service provided, a figure that is much lower than that of the metro in Nuevo León (69.2%) or Jalisco (86.2%).[32] One of the main problems is the lack of sufficient metro stations. As Murat, Delgado and Suárez point out, "subway users are willing to travel a distance of up to 800 meters in order to arrive to a train station" (Murata – Delgado Campos – Suárez Lastra 2017), making an 800-meter radius what can be considered the area of influence of the stations. In the case of Mexico City, this only covers 16.6% of the metropolitan surface area – one third of the density of stations in Tokyo, and nine times less than Paris. Coupled with this is the fact that the subway stations are positioned mostly around shopping and study areas and much less in residential areas. This means

---

[30] *Trasporte de pasajeros*, Economía y Sectores Productivos, Instituto Nacional de Estadística y Geografía (INEGI), Site:https://www.inegi.org.mx/temas/transporteurb/ Accessed: February 12, 2022.

[31] Calculated using data from *Trasporte de pasajeros*, Economía y Sectores Productivos, Instituto Nacional de Estadística y Geografía (INEGI), Site:https://www.inegi.org.mx/temas/transporteurb/ Accessed: February 12, 2022

[32] *Encuesta Nacional de Calidad e Impacto Gubernamental 2017*, Instituto Nacional de Estadística y Geografía (INEGI), Site: https://www.inegi.org.mx/contenidos/programas/encig/2017/doc/encig2017_principales_resultados.pdf Accessed: March 3, 2022.

that for most in cannot be the only means of transportation and must be coupled with a ride on a bus, car, or taxi. It would seem that the simplest solution is to build more metro stations, but this is complicated by the particular character of the soil underneath Mexico City. As we mentioned above, Mexico City is built upon a lakebed which continues to be a large aquifer.

Due to the difficulty of expanding the metro system of the city, the current government has introduced another form of public transportation that has so far seen much success. This new form of transportation is the *Sistema de Trasporte Público Cablebús* (Public Transportation Gondola System), a gondola system that is being built in the poorest sections of the city. These areas were often built with little planning and have very high population densities and incredibly narrow streets as a result, making them difficult to service with public means of transportation such as buses. Currently two of the four *Cablebús* lines have been built. In the case of the second line in Iztapalapa, there are seven stations and 10.6 kilometers with an average maximum of 5,000 users per hour.[33] The stations are connected at various points with the metro, trolly and the Mexico City Passenger Transportation Network (RTP). The gondola has managed to cut travel time in the area in half, doubling the residents' access to job opportunities as well as to places of commerce and recreation.[34] This increased mobility and connection to other means of transportation will help integrate these neighborhoods with the rest of the city and hopefully aid in raising them out of poverty.

A final mention must go to the current government's *Plan de Reducción de Emisiones*[35] (Emissions Reduction Plan), which seeks

---

[33] *Cablebús Línea 2 Constitución de 1917-Santa Maria*, Proyecto de Movilidad Integrada, Gobierno de la Ciudad de México, 2021, Site: https://semovi.cdmx.gob.mx/storage/app/media/jdg-cablebus-210808linea-2-constitucion-santa-marta.pdf Accessed: March 2, 2022.

[34] *Ibid.*

[35] *Plan de Reducción de Emisiones del Sector Movilidad en la Ciudad de México*, Proyecto de Movilidad Integrada, Gobierno de la Ciudad de México, 2019, Site: https://www.jefaturadegobierno.cdmx.gob.mx/storage/app/media/plan-reduccion-de-emisiones.pdf Accessed: February 22, 2022.

to improve public transportation infrastructure on several points. This plan hopes to construct 1,100 kilometers of dedicated lanes for public transportation, such as the Metrobus, as well as four *Cablebús* lines, as mentioned above. It is also seeking to expand the Metrobus network in six lines by 2024, as well as buying 30 new trains for the metro system and 500 new trolleys for the trolley system.

2.3 Subgoal 3: By 2030, enhance inclusive and sustainable urbanization and capacity for participatory, integrated and sustainable human settlement planning and management in all countries

Megacities are difficult to plan and administer. They are places of extreme complexity in governmental structures, as can be seen in the case of Mexico City. The metropolitan area is divided into three larger political units: Mexico City proper, as well as parts of the State of México and the State of Hidalgo. Mexico City is further divided into 16 boroughs, and has 59 municipalities in the State of México and 2 in the State of Hidalgo. There are coordination units between these entities, but they are not linked to political and financial authority, and thus have a limited influence (Hansjürgens – Heinrichs 2014: 16). Planned urbanization in Mexico City has been further complicated by its dramatic growth. Between 1940 and 1970 the city grew to six times its original size, going from 1.46 inhabitants to 8.7 million (Pacione 2013: 32). By 1980, Mexico City contained 20% of the national population. There are currently around 21.8 million living in the metropolitan area, and up until 2011 the city was still receiving 500,000 immigrants a year. As Valenzuela-Aguilera points out, "most of these new residents settle in makeshift, marginally illegal communities outside the traditional, formal realm of government regulation and service provision" (Valenzuela-Aguilera 2022). Often these irregular settlements are established on agricultural lands or on lands unsuited to urbanization. The largely uncontrolled development has led to a large urban sprawl and a huge fragmentation of the city's zoning. These problems must be overcome with an integrated urban development plan. The introduction of a new constitution for Mexico City in 2017, which gave the city more self-determination after having been under the control of the federal government, was certainly a step in the right direction.

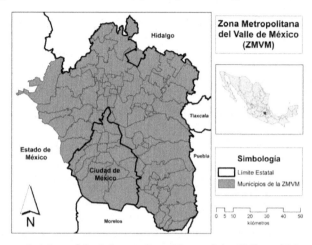

Figure 3. Map of the Metropolitan Zone of the Valley of Mexico.[36]

Controls on urban development are weak in Mexico. Articles 27 and 115 of the Political Constitution of Mexico and the General Act on Human Settlements in the 1900s led to a decentralization of control, putting more power in the hands of the municipalities. This decentralization has its positive aspects, leading to a more fluid land market, but it has also added to an uncoordinated and fragmented urbanization, with a reduced available land supply for the poor (Valenzuela-Aguilera 2022). The lack of systematic urban development has also exacerbated the problem of inadequate transportation infrastructure. The lower quality of transportation services in some parts of the city have only reinforced inequality in terms of access to employment and levels of investment.

The current government's efforts to improve transportation services in the poorer areas of the city were mentioned above.

---

[36] Source: Salinas-Arreortua 2017: 143–169.

Another positive initiative is the push for increased transparency. Transparency is a big part of participatory urban planning. The city government has set up a website called *Tu Ciudad Tu Dinero* (Your City Your Money) to explain the city's yearly budget, which was not available publicly in previous times.[37] Besides aiding in a more participatory city planning, this move to transparency has the other much-needed effect of combatting corruption in the city's finances. In fact, Claudia Sheinbaum claimed in 2019 to have freed 25 million Mexican pesos from corruption and to have dedicated them to public investment (Ordaz Díaz 2022).

2.4 Subgoal 4: Strengthen efforts to protect and safeguard the world's cultural and natural heritage

Mexico City has an immensely rich cultural and natural history. It is one of the oldest cities on the American continent, having been founded in 1325 by the Mexica people. The metropolitan area is home to four UNESCO World Heritage Sites.[38] In 1987 the historic center of Mexico City and Xochimilco, as well as the pre-Hispanic city of Teotihuacán were made UNESCO sites. They were followed many years later by the house and studio of the architect Luis Barragán in 2004, and the central university campus of the *Universidad Nacional Autónoma de México* in 2007. Besides these architectural sites, there is also a large presence of indigenous peoples in Mexico City, belonging in great part to the Nahuas, Otomíes, and Matlatzincas pre-Hispanic groups. These peoples and their towns are known as *Pueblos Originarios*. The city government has set up the *Secretaría de Pueblos y Barrios Originarios y Comunidades Indígenas Residentes* (Secretariat of the Original Peoples and Towns and Resident Indigenous Communities, SEPI), which has recognized 141 of these original towns. In 2021 the SEPI launched the program *Refloreciendo Pueblos y Comunidades* (Flourishing Peoples and Communities). This program

---

[37] https://tudinero.cdmx.gob.mx/
[38] *World Heritage List*, United Nations Educational Scientific and Cultural Organization (UNESCO), Site: https://whc.unesco.org/en/list/ Accessed February 27, 2022.

seeks to protect and promote the original indigenous languages by providing a yearly stipend to those who provide services of interpretation and translation, and by creating a network of official interpreters and translators of the SEPI.[39]

Following the 2017 earthquake the *Comisión para la Reconstrucción de la Ciudad de México* (Commission for the Reconstruction of Mexico City), in collaboration with the *Secretaría de Cultura de la Ciudad de México* (Secretariat of Culture of Mexico City) set up a mechanism for the reconstruction, restoration and rehabilitation of the historical patrimony of the *Pueblos Originarios* of Mexico City. At the center of focus were the churches that had been damaged. To date, 21 restorations are under way with the help of 15 companies, and a total of 126 million pesos are being invested.[40] In 2021 another program was set up to structurally renovate the *Ángel de la Independencia* in the downtown area, one of the main symbols of the city.[41] The new structural support using interior steel braces will strengthen it against future earthquakes.

2.5 Subgoal 5: By 2030, significantly reduce the number of deaths and the number of people affected and substantially decrease the direct economic losses relative to global gross domestic product caused by disasters, including water-related disasters, with a focus on protecting the poor and people in vulnerable situations

Mexico City is a risk area for various natural disasters. We have mentioned the September 19, 2017 earthquake, but a previous earthquake that occurred on the exact same day in 1985 had

---

[39] *Programa Social "Refloreciendo Pueblos y Comunidades" 2021*, Gobierno de la Ciudad de México, 2021, Site: https://www.sepi.cdmx.gob.mx/programas/programa/refloreciendo-pueblos-y-comunidades-2021 Accessed: March 2, 2022.

[40] *Reconstrucción del Patrimonio Cultural en Pueblos y Barrios Originarios con Recursos de la Comisión para la Reconstrucción de la Ciudad de México*, Comisión para la Reconstrucción, Gobierno de la Ciudad de México, 2021, Site: https://reconstruccion.cdmx.gob.mx/storage/app/media/Listado.pdf Accessed: March 2, 2022.

[41] *Columna de la Independencia Rehabilitación Estructural*, Gobierno de la Ciudad de México, 2020, Site: https://reconstruccion.cdmx.gob.mx/storage/app/media/Transparencia/Patrimonio%20Cultural/PP_Angel_Feb2020.pdf Accessed: March 9, 2022.

been just as destructive. The soil of the lakebed underneath the city unfortunately functions as an amplifier of seismic waves (Novelo-Casanova *et al* 2021). Following this earlier earthquake, the Mexican authorities started various initiatives to build a nation-wide civil protection system. It created the *Sistema Nacional de Protección Civil* (National Civil Protection System) and the *Centro Nacional de Prevención de Desastres* (National Center for Disaster Prevention) in 1986. Three years later the *Sistema de Alerta Sísmica* (Seismic Early Warning System) was developed, which gives approximately sixty seconds of warning before the arrival of damaging seismic waves.

Mexico City also lies in the Trans-Mexican Volcanic Belt. There are various volcanos on the south side of the city, making up the Younger Chichinautzin Monogenetic Field (YCMF). This volcanic structure is particularly notable because of its young age and thus its potential impact on the city. The Chichinautzin volcano last erupted in 1835, covering a large part of southern CDMX. Nevertheless, the YCMF has a recurrence rate of ~ 1700 years, which would lead one to hope that it will not prove to be an imminent threat (Novelo-Casanova *et al* 2021).

Some of the largest risks for the city have to do with water. Mexico City lies in an endorheic basin and was built on the soft clay sediments of an old lakebed. This lakebed is a major cause of subsidence. This problem has only been exacerbated by the rapid population increase in the city, which has led to water being extracted from the underlying aquifer much quicker than it is able to be replenished. As a result, some parts of Mexico City are known to sink at a rate of 40cm/year (Auvinet – Méndez – Juárez 2017: 3297). The mixture of Mexico City's location in a closed basin and the high rate of subsidence work together to create a permanent threat of flooding in several parts of the city. Some parts of the city do not have basic sewage draining, but even for the parts that do, the drainage system is often insufficient for the task and is in urgent need of upgrading.

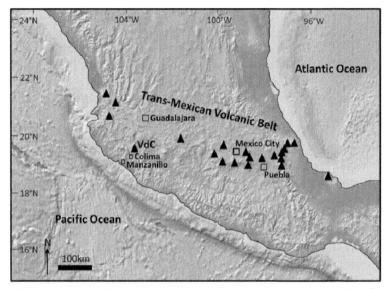

Figure 4. Map of Mexico showing the Trans-Mexican Volcanic Belt.[42]

A final risk for the city is the possibility of forest fires. The city, with its a subtropical highland climate, is home to many forests. One of the most famous of these grows on the Ajusco volcano in the south of the city. In order to deal with risk of forest fires, in 1999 the *Comisión Nacional Forestal* (National Forest Commission, CONAFOR) installed an early warning system. This system evaluates the hazard represented by fires based on measurements of temperature, humidity, precipitation and wind velocity. Nevertheless, since 2012 the budget of the CONAFOR has been reduced 43%, not leaving it with sufficient funds for its mission.[43]

---

[42] Source: Hutchison *et al* 2013: 203–228.
[43] *Recortes a Conafor alimentan el fuego*, Greenpeace México, March 2, 2020, Site: https://www.greenpeace.org/mexico/noticia/4169/recortes-a-conafor-alimentan-el-fuego/ Accessed: March 7, 2022.

2.6 Subgoal 6: By 2030, reduce the adverse per capita environmental impact of cities, including by paying special attention to air quality and municipal and other waste management

The location of Mexico City in a basin surrounded by mountains, together with frequent changes in temperature, means that it is especially liable to pollution problems (Pacione 2013: 45). The air in the city simply has nowhere to go. Levels of major air pollutants regularly exceed the maximum exposure limits of the World Health Organization (WHO). For example, the WHO warns that an 8-hour average ozone level exceeding 100 micrograms per cubic meter threatens human health.[44] In the period between 1986 and 2005 this was exceeded in Mexico City for 92% of days (Davis 2008: 38-81).

Vehicle emissions are the primary source of air pollution in Mexico City causing 99% of carbon monoxide, 81% of nitrogen oxides, and 46% of volatile organic compounds (Davis 2008: 38-81). In the 1990s the car industry boomed, leading to an additional 250,000 to 300,000 cars per year. In the same time period, population grew only 1.5%, which meant that the growth in the number of cars in the city was four times that of the growth of the population, leading to much more traffic and air contamination (Valenzuela-Aguilera 2022: 297). Record pollution levels in Mexico City has led to the introduction of various programs, and in fact, regulations concerning transport and air pollution have had a positive record of reaching metropolitan agreements. One such program is *Hoy No Circula* (No Circulation Today, HNC), which ban drivers from using their vehicle one day a week based on the last digit of the vehicle's license plate.

As we mentioned above, the current government has come up with a *Plan de Reducción de Emisiones*[45] (Emissions Reduction

---

[44] *Air Quality Guidelines Global Update 2005*, World Health Organization, Copenhagen 2005, Site: https://www.euro.who.int/__data/assets/pdf_file/0005/78638/E90038.pdf Accessed: March 11, 2022.

[45] *Plan de Reducción de Emisiones del Sector Movilidad en la Ciudad de México*, Proyecto de Movilidad Integrada, Gobierno de la Ciudad de México, 2019, Site: https://www.jefaturadegobierno.cdmx.gob.mx/storage/app/media/plan-reduccion-de-emisiones.pdf Accessed: February 22, 2022.

Plan) which has several action points. The government will seek to build 600 kilometers of cycling infrastructure as well as 16 massive or semi-massive bicycle parking spaces by 2024. It also plans to add 10,000 bicycles to the *Ecobici* bicycle sharing system that was launched in 2010. The government has decided as well to create a low-emission zone in the city-center, and already requires carpooling at some entrances to the city from 7:00 to 10:00 am. Other program points are the creation of a Metrobus line with zero or low emissions by 2024, the strengthening of the electric charging station network for private cars, and the transition to electric cars for the government car fleet.

2.7 Subgoal 7: By 2030, provide universal access to safe, inclusive and accessible, green and public spaces, in particular for women and children, older persons and persons with disabilities

Unfortunately, but perhaps not surprisingly, inequality in Mexico City also applies to the city's distribution of green public spaces (GPS). There is a direct correlation between the poverty of a section of the city and its diminished access to GPS (Fernández-ÁlvaREZ 2017: 399–428). Although the Federal District Environmental Law stated in 2002 that each borough in Mexico City was to be responsible for making a yearly report on the evolution of GPS in order to improve the situation, as of 2017 this duty had only been fulfilled in 2002 and not subsequently. A more recent project to increase green space in the city was the *Ecoductor*, a 1.6 kilometer linear park built over the Rio de la Piedad, a tubed river running under the park. The *Ecoductor* has 4,800 square meters of vegetation with 50,000 plants of fifty different species that reduce more than fifty tons of carbon dioxide.[46] Nevertheless, its location is once again in a more affluent area of the city.

---

[46] *Todo lo que necesitas saber del primer ecoducto en Río de la Piedad*, MXCity Guía Insider, Mexico City 2019, Site: https://mxcity.mx/2019/02/todo-lo-que-necesitas-saber-del-primer-ecoducto-en-rio-de-la-piedad/ Accessed: February 19, 2022.

Sustainable Development in Mexico City

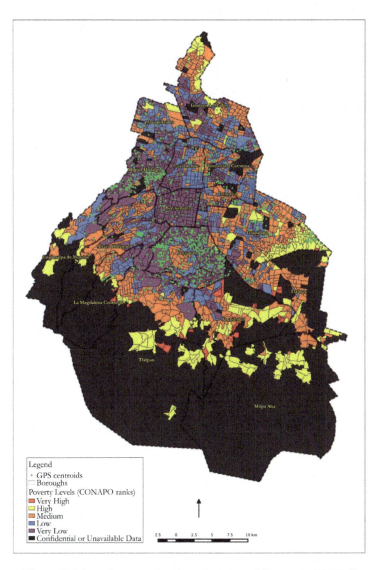

Figure 5. Map of poverty levels and green public spaces (GPS).[47]

---

[47] Source: Fernández-Álvarez 2017: 399-428.

There is a great need to increase safe public spaces for women and children in the city. The president of the *Instituto Nacional de las Mujeres* (National Women's Institute), Nadine Gasman Zylbermann, stated that 80% of women in México do not feel safe walking through the streets.[48] On a more positive note, the city recently won the Gold Award for the safe city category from the World Sustainable Cities Organization (WEGO).[49] The city was rewarded for it *Programa "Mi Ciudad Segura"* ("My Safe City" Program) which is made up of various initiatives. The first is *Sendero Seguro* (Safe Path). It includes the building of sidewalks, the provision of proper illumination, the setting up of safe pedestrian crosswalks, the installation of security cameras and panic buttons, the sowing of plants, and the setting up of artwork such as murals. As of January 2021, 260 kilometers of streets had been transformed into safe paths, with a total of 2,900 m^2 of mural paintings and 450,000 new plants.[50] A second part of the program is the installation of panic buttons with two cameras, a visual alert, speakers, and a connection to the local police. By September 2020 these buttons had been used a total of 59,832 times. Video surveillance of the city has also improved; since Claudia Sheinbaum became the Head of Government of Mexico City, the number of security cameras has gone from 15,088 to 63,191 (Batres 2022). The final aspects of the program are the installation of video-surveillance in public transportation and the installation of panic buttons in taxis and businesses.

---

[48] *Senderos Seguros: camina Libre, camina Segura, Gobierno de México*, Mexico City 2021, Site: https://www.gob.mx/inmujeres/articulos/senderos-seguros-camina-libre-camina-segura?idiom=es Accessed: March 3, 2022.
[49] *4th WeGo Awards*, World Smart Sustainable Cities Organization, Seoul 2020, Site: https://we-gov.org/wego-awards/4th-wego-awards/ Accessed: February 23, 2022.
[50] *CDMX ha habilitado 192 senderos seguros para mujeres con una inversión de 330 millones de pesos*, Infobae, January 19, 2021, Site: https://www.infobae.com/america/mexico/2021/01/20/cdmx-ha-habilitado-192-senderos-seguros-para-mujeres-con-una-inversion-de-330-millones-de-pesos/ Accessed: March 2, 2022.

3. Conclusion

In this paper we first looked briefly at the economic development of Mexico City throughout its history. We then looked at the city's progress with respect to each of the seven subgoals of the eleventh SDG concerning the development of cities, highlighting the city's most important strengths and opportunities for improvement. There is no lack of challenges for those responsible for the government of Mexico City. Inequality in income and access to green public spaces is rampant. Many still lack access to basic services such as water and sewage. The uncontrolled growth and complex political structure have made the city difficult to manage. Public transportation is inadequate, and the rate of informal employment and informal housing is very high. At the same time, considerable progress has been made in ameliorating the circumstances of its millions of inhabitants. It is easy to focus on that which is lacking in a city, and one must do so if one wishes to improve the situation. Nevertheless, there are many positive initiatives in Mexico City that are worth highlighting. The PILARES project is helping provide education and capacitation for thousands of the cities poorest. The *Cáblebus* transportation project is helping to integrate more marginalized areas with the rest of the city. The city has managed to digitalize its official procedures, while providing one of the world's largest free Wi-Fi networks. The *Mi Ciudad Segura* project is both improving security in the city as well as expanding public green spaces. We hope our general survey of Mexico City has helped to better understand the challenges megacities face throughout the world and provided insights into ways they can begin to be overcome.

References

Auvinet G. – Méndez E. – Juárez M., "Recent Information on Mexico City subsidence, in Proceedings of the 19th International Conference on Soil Mechanic and Geotechnical Engineering", *International Society for Soil Mechanics and Geotechincal Engineering*, Seoul 2017: 3297.

Batres M., "Las cifras del gobierno de la Ciudad de México", *El Financiero*, Bloomberg, Dec. 13, 2021, site: https://www.elfinanciero.com.mx/opinion/marti-batres/2021/12/13/las-cifras-del-gobierno-de-la-ciudad-de-mexico/ Accessed: March 2, 2022.

Comune Di Roma, *Debito, chiude gestione commissariale. Dal 2021 possibile riduzione Irpef e più risorse per la città*, April 4 2019, Site: https://www.comune.roma.it/web/it/notizia/debito-chiude-gestione-commissariale-dal-2021-possibile-riduzione-irpef-e-piu-risorse-per-la-citta.page Accessed: March 8, 2022.

Davis L. W., "The Effect of Driving Restrictions on Air Quality in Mexico City", *Journal of Political Economy* 116/1, 2008: 38–81.

El Universal, "PILARES, Puntos de Innovación, Libertad, Arte, Educación y Saberes," Dec. 16, 2019, Site: https://pilares.cdmx.gob.mx/assets/memoria-des/SUPLEMENTO_PILARES_FINAL.pdf, accessed March 4, 2019.

Fernández-Álvarez R., "Inequitable Distribution of Green Public Space in the Mexico City: An Environmental Injustice Case", *Economía Sociedad y Territorio*, 2017: 399–428.

Gobierno De La Ciudad De México, "El Wifi gratuito de la Ciudad de México es galardonado como la mejor iniciativa de conectividad a nivel mundial por la Unión Internacional de Telecomunicaciones", *Agencia Digital de Innovación Pública*, September 9, 2020. Site: https://adip.cdmx.gob.mx/comunicacion/nota/el-wifi-gratuito-de-la-ciudad-de-mexico-es-galardonado-como-la-mejor-iniciativa-de-conectividad-nivel-mundial-por-la-union-internacional-de-telecomunicaciones Accessed: February 27, 2022.

———, "Cuarto Informe Trimestral de la Situación de la Deuda Pública 2021", *Secretaría de Administración y Finanzas de la Ciudad de México*, October-December 2021, Site: https://servidoresx3.finanzas.cdmx.gob.mx/inv/DeudaPublica.html Accessed: February 10, 2022.

———, "Cablebús Línea 2 Constitución de 1917-Santa Maria", *Proyecto de Movilidad Integrada*, 2021, Site: https://semovi.cdmx.gob.mx/storage/app/media/jdg-cablebus-210808linea-2-constitucion-santa-marta.pdf Accessed: March 2, 2022.

———, "Plan de Reducción de Emisiones del Sector Movilidad en la Ciudad de México", *Proyecto de Movilidad Integrada*, 2019, Site: https://www.jefaturadegobierno.cdmx.gob.mx/storage/app/media/plan-reduccion-de-emisiones.pdf Accessed: February 22, 2022.

———, Programa Social "Refloreciendo Pueblos y Comunidades" 2021, Site: https://www.sepi.cdmx.gob.mx/programas/programa/refloreciendo-pueblos-y-comunidades-2021 Accessed: March 2, 2022.

———, "Reconstrucción del Patrimonio Cultural en Pueblos y Barrios Originarios con Recursos de la Comisión para la Reconstrucción de la Ciudad de México", *Comisión para la Reconstrucción*, 2021, Site: https://reconstruccion.cdmx.gob.mx/storage/app/media/Listado.pdf Accessed: March 2, 2022.

———, "Columna de la Independencia Rehabilitación Estructural", 2020, Site: https://reconstruccion.cdmx.gob.mx/storage/app/media/Transparencia/Patrimonio%20Cultural/PP_Angel_Feb2020.pdf Accessed: March 9, 2022.

Gobierno De México, "Data Mexico Valle de México Metro Area", *Secretaría de Economía*, Site: https://datamexico.org/es/profile/geo/valle-de-mexico Accessed: March 5, 2022.

———, "Data Mexico Ciudad de México", *Secretaría de Economía*, Site: https://datamexico.org/es/profile/geo/valle-de-mexico Accessed: March 5, 2022.

———, "Senderos Seguros: camina Libre, camina Segura", Mexico City 2021, Site: https://www.gob.mx/inmujeres/articulos/senderos-seguros-camina-libre-camina-segura?idiom=es Accessed: March 3, 2022.

Greenpeace México, "Recortes a Conafor alimentan el fuego", March 2, 2020, Site: https://www.greenpeace.org/mexico/noticia/4169/recortes-a-conafor-alimentan-el-fuego/ Accessed: March 7, 2022.

Guthrie C., «Colonial Economy: Trade, Industry, and Labor in the Seventeenth Centruy Mexico City», Revista de Historia de América No. 7 (1939), 103–134.

Hansjürgens B. – Heinrichs D., "Megacities and Climate Change: Early Adapters, Mainstream Adapters and Capacities", Kraas F. – Aggarwal S. K. – Coy M. – Mertins G. (eds.), *Megacities: Our Global Urban Future*, Springer, 2014.

Hutchison W. *et al.*, "Airborne thermal remote sensing of the Volcán de Colima (Mexico) lava dome from 2007 to 2010", *Geological Society*, Special Publications 380/1, 2013: 203–228.

Instituto Nacional De Estadística Y Geografía, "Administrative record of the light vehicle automotive industry", 2022, Site: http://en.www.inegi.org.mx/datosprimarios/iavl/ Accessed: March 1, 2022.

——, "Trasporte de pasajeros, Economía y Sectores Productivos", Site: https://www.inegi.org.mx/temas/transporteurb/ Accessed: February 12, 2022.

——, "Encuesta Nacional de Calidad e Impacto Gubernamental 2017", Site: https://www.inegi.org.mx/contenidos/programas/encig/2017/doc/encig2017_principales_resultados.pdf Accessed: March 3, 2022.

Malik Reyes B., Todo lo que necesitas saber del primer ecoducto en Río de la Piedad, MXCity Guía Insider, Mexico City 2019, Site: https://mxcity.mx/2019/02/todo-lo-que-necesitas-saber-del-primer-ecoducto-en-rio-de-la-piedad/ Accessed: February 19, 2022.

Murata M. – Delgado Campos J. – Suárez Lastra M., "¿Por qué la gente no usa el Metro? Efectos del transporte en la Zona Metropolitana de la Ciudad de México", *Investigaciones Geográficas*, 2017.

Novelo-Casanova D. A. – Suárez G. – Cabral-Cano E. – Fernández-Torres E. A. *et al.*, "The Risk Atlas of Mexico

City, Mexico: a tool for decision-making and disaster prevention", *Natural Hazards*, 2021.
Ordaz Díaz A., "Sheinbaum destaca combate a la corrupción en su primer informe, Forbes Mexico", Sep. 17, 2019, Site: https://www.forbes.com.mx/sheinbaum-destaca-combate-a-la-corrupcion-en-su-primer-informe/ Accessed: March 10, 2022.
Organisation For Economic Cooperation And Development, "Glossary of Environment Statistics", *Studies in Methods*, Series F, 67, New York 1997, Site: https://stats.oecd.org/glossary/detail.asp?ID=1351 Accessed: March 1, 2022.
Pacione M., *Problems and Planning in Third World Cities*, Routledge, 2013.
Salinas-Arreortua L. A., "Gestión metropolitana en la Zona Metropolitana del Valle de México: entre la legalidad y la voluntad política", *Papeles de Población* 23/91, 2017: 143–169.
Sheinbaum Pardo C., "Primer Informe de Gobierno Diciembre 2018-Septiembre 2019, Gobierno de la Ciudad de México", Site: https://informedegobierno.cdmx.gob.mx/wp-content/uploads/2020/08/2.-primer_informe.pdf Accessed: March 5, 2022.
Stillman A., "Mexico Shuns International Oil Markets to Produce More Gasoline at Home", Bloomberg, Dec. 28, 2021, Site: https://www.bloomberg.com/news/articles/2021-12-28/mexico-to-stop-exporting-oil-in-2023-in-self-sufficiency-quest Accessed: February 26, 2022.
Stringer S., "Fiscal Year 2022 Annual Report on Capital Debt and Obligations, New York City Comptroller", Bureau of Budget, site: https://comptroller.nyc.gov/reports/annual-report-on-capital-debt-and-obligations/ Accessed: February 20, 2022
TomTom, "TomTom Traffic Index 2016", March 22, 2016, Site: https://corporate.tomtom.com/static-files/5289c5aa-310c-4965-a4c0-516760a8a6fd Accessed: March 4, 2022.
——, "TomTom Traffic Index Ranking 2021", Site: https://www.tomtom.com/en_gb/traffic-index/ranking/ Accessed March 5, 2022.

The World Bank, "United States Exports by Country and Region 2019", World Integrated Trade Solution, Site: https://wits.worldbank.org/CountryProfile/en/Country/USA/Year/2004/TradeFlow/Export Accessed: March 6, 2022.

Unesco International Center For The Promotion Of Human Rights, "Ciudad de México y Goiás, las ganadoras del premio Construir Igualdad 2020", Buenos Aires 2021, Site: https://es.unesco.org/news/ciudad-mexico-y-goias-ganadoras-del-premio-construir-igualdad-2020 Accessed: February 26, 2022.

UN International Telecommunication Union, "The best of the best in supporting SDGs with ICTs: Meet the 2020 WSIS Prizes winners", Sep. 4, 2020, Site: https://www.itu.int/hub/2020/09/the-best-of-the-best-in-supporting-sdgs-with-icts-meet-the-2020-wsis-prizes-winners/ Accessed: March 3, 2022.

United Nations, "Sustainable Cities: Why They Matter, United Nations Sustainable Development Goals", United Nations, New York 2020, Site: https://www.un.org/sustainabledevelopment/wp-content/uploads/2019/07/11_Why-It-Matters-2020.pdf Accessed: February 5, 2022.

——, "2030 Agenda for Sustainable Development", United Nations 70th General Assembly, New York 2015, Site: http://www.un.org/development/desa/jpo/wp-content/uploads/sites/55/2017/02/2030-Agenda-for-Sustainable-Development-KCSD-Primer-new.pdf Accessed: March 8, 2022.

United Nations Educational Scientific And Cultural Organization, "World Heritage List", Site: https://whc.unesco.org/en/list/ Accessed February 27, 2022.

Valenzuela-Aguilera A., "Mexico City: Power, Equity, and Sustainable Development", Sorensen A. – Okata J. (eds.), *Megacities, X, cSUR-UT Series: Library for Sustainable Urban Regeneration*, Springer, 2011: 291–310.

Ward P. M., "Mexico City", *Problems and Planning in Third World Cities*, Routledge Revivals, Routledge, 2013.

World Health Organization, "Air Quality Guidelines Global Update 2005", Copenhagen 2005, Site: https://www.euro.

who.int/__data/assets/pdf_file/0005/78638/E90038.pdf Accessed: March 11, 2022.

WORLD POPULATION REVIEW, "Car Production by Country 2022", Walnut 2022, Site: https://worldpopulationreview.com/country-rankings/car-production-by-country Accessed: February 15, 2022.

——, "GDP Ranked by Country 2022", Walnut 2022, Site: https://worldpopulationreview.com/countries/countries-by-gdp Accessed March 9, 2022.

WORLD SMART SUSTAINABLE CITIES ORGANIZATION, *4th WeGo Awards,* Seoul 2020, Site: https://we-gov.org/wego-awards/4th-wego-awards/ Accessed: February 23, 2020.

ZAMARRÓN I., "'Ciudad perdida' de Tacubaya ahora podría ser 'ciudad del bienestar'", Forbes México, January 25, 2022, Site: https://www.forbes.com.mx/noticias-ciudad-perdida-de-tacubaya-ahora-podria-ser-ciudad-del-bienestar/ Accessed: March 11, 2022.

Workshop n. 3

SOCIETY
Santa Fe.
From a Garbage Dump to a Qualified City Neighborhood

Balam Quitzé Loza Ramos LC

Under the Supervision
of Dr. Rodrigo Iván Cortés Jimenez –
Red Familias – Mexico City

How did Santa Fe go from being a garbage dump to an exclusive financial enclave in Mexico City? This is the question that will be at the center of the research. In order to accomplish this purpose, this work will have three moments. The first one will be a historical journey to understand how the development of this area took place. In the second moment, we will see what were the causal factors that produced the change from a garbage dump to a financial district. The third moment will be a study of some of the consequences of this transformation. Finally, we will conclude with some existential reflections.

This topic is important because once we understand what happened in this area will help us to comprehend what was actually happening in Mexico, mainly between 1988 and 1994, period in which Carlos Salinas de Gortari governed the country. In his desire of getting out of the third world and reach the first world, the president of Mexico, Carlos Salinas, promoted several projects to achieve it. The one project that brings us to this study is one of the most important, as it sought to show externally a deeper change. Mexico City was intended to be a city with global influence. Santa Fe was intended to become the Mexican Manhattan (Moreno Carranco 2016: 83). What happened and how did it happen? This is what we will try to answer in the following lines. For this study we have mainly used the works of María Moreno Carranco, Cecilia Barraza, Nitzan Shoshan and Víctor Hugo Díaz de León. We have sought to make a comprehensive integration of the spatio-temporal situation and of how the development took place. Covering, mainly, the beginning of the 80s to the present, we also seek to go a step further. In view of the consequences, what can be expected? And what can the Church say in all this?

1. Historical Tour of the Area and Santa Fe's Current Constitution

1.1. From 1532 to 1980

What is known today as Santa Fe began to be inhabited in 1532. The Spanish lawyer Don Vasco de Quiroga arrived in 1531 as a judge ('oídor') of the Second Audiencia and maximum authority of the New Spain. It seems that when he sees the abuses committed by some of the protagonists of the conquest, he tries to remedy the situation. He acquired some land to the west of what is now Mexico City, in what was then known as the hills of Acatxóchitl. Months later, he began the foundation of a hospital under the name of Santa Fe. This place's purpose was to welcome the indigenous people in need of help. Different from the modern conception of hospital, in those times it was a place to welcome the needy where, in addition, they were given education and home (Arriaga 1966).

Indigenous families settle around the hospital and thus the town was founded. The ideal to which Quiroga's foundation looks to is the work *Utopia* (1516) by Thomas More. The Tata Vasco, as the indigenous people began to call him, wanted these towns to have a self-sustaining economy and to be governed by the Christian principles of giving out one's own resources at the service of the community and charity to the most disadvantaged. The main sectors in development were agriculture, shepherding and mining. And, undoubtedly, the proximity of the water source, from which water was distributed to the entire Valley of Mexico, was a great help. The place came to have approximately two hundred families in an area of 20 to 25 hectares. In 1565 Tata Vasco died, but not before obtaining for these populations a special fiscal regime, which consisted of a form of independent government with little interference from the Viceroy, which lasted until the XVIII century (Covarrubias Reyna 2015).

Towards the end of the 1700s and beginning of the 1800s, the area became a strategic and a military point of reference and it will be like this during the years of independence. From the 18th to the 20th century, the western part of the Valley of Mexico began to form part of the metropolis, due to its growth. This is evident

Santa Fe. From a Garbage Dump to a Qualified City Neighborhood

by the fact that it will appear on the maps of the city from that time on. There were two reasons for interest in the region during this period: on one side, there were sand mines, on the other, it was considered a recreational area for wealthy families. At the end of the 20th century, mineral exploitation intensified, leaving large gaps in the area. At the end of this period, it became the dump of the Federal District, which operated until 1980. It is from that year on that the City of Santa Fe's project began, which we will study in detail in the following part of this work. Some questions to consider are: how did Santa Fe go from being a garbage dump to a qualified neighborhood of the city? what were the causes? what were some of its consequences?

1.2. Santa Fe nowadays

Today, Santa Fe is the most important financial district in Mexico and one of the most important economic centers in Latin America. A business district (CBD)[1] (Moreno Carranco 2008) is a well-defined area of a city in which buildings, offices, stores and housing are concentrated for the purpose of doing business. In order to exemplify this global reality, we can look at Manhattan in New York, La Défense in Paris, the City of London in London or the Eur Zone in Rome. The main characteristic that defines these zones is that they are financial enclaves within cities and countries. They are usually the reference points for businessmen and the most important companies in the world. In addition to being united by this essential element, they are often very similar in terms of their physical appearance.

> The CBD characterizes all of its cities by the appearance of highly functional buildings, glass and concrete buildings covered with neon signs. Each building displays its name in lights. Sometimes, it has a helipad on top of it. Basements containing up to 6 or 7 floors of parking reserved for the various companies that have their own offices there. The density and height of the buildings plunges into

---

[1] Central Business District.

the gloom of the adjacent streets, and yet some towers are crowned with panoramic restaurants, or even swimming pools and solariums. The high hierarchy of companies occupies the upper floors, less subject to noise and with better panoramic views. The isolation of high-rise buildings is almost perfect: employees are working away from the hustle and bustle of the street. In some basements, it is the management teams that are connected to computer terminals that are connected to the network. The CBD is a kind of city within the city (Pérez Mejías 2012).

This financial district of the Mexican capital can be considered as such, since by 2008 it housed almost a third of the headquarters of the most important national and transnational companies present in the country, a 32% of the total. We talk about companies such as Banca Santander, Grupo Financiero Banamex, Harley Davidson, Ford Motor Company, Deutsche Post DHL, Coca cola-FEMSA, etc. It has approximately 70 thousand employees, 4311 residences, 4 universities among the best in Mexico and receives approximately 8 million visitors annually. These are some of the reasons why this area is undoubtedly one of the most important financial enclaves in Mexico City (Parnreiter 2011).

Santa Fe is located in the Álvaro Obregón and Cuajimalpa de Morelos districts. It covers an area of approximately 900 hectares and the buildings are mostly tall towers. There are approximately 1,700 people per square kilometer. The area is divided into ten neighborhoods: Cruz Manca, La Fe, La Loma, La Mexicana, Totolapa, Paseo de las Lomas, Peña Blanca, Bosques de Santa Fe and the school zone. It is bordered to the north by the neighborhoods Lomas de Memetla, El Yaqui, and Lomas de Vista Hermosa; to the west by the neighborhoods Lomas de San Pedro, Loma del Ocote, Contadero, and Pueblo San Mateo Tlaltenango; to the south by Ejido San Mateo, Pueblo Santa Lucía, Corpus Christi, Estado de Hidalgo, Garcimarrero and Ourense; and to the east by Pueblo Santa Fe, Bejero del Pueblo Santa Fe, Tlapechico, and Ampliación Jalalpa.[2]

---

2 MarketDataMéxico, Colonia Santa Fe, Álvaro Obregón, in Mexico City.

This mega-project is located in Mexico's most important financial corridor in the western part of the city. This corridor is made up of the Bosques, Lomas, Polanco and Reforma – Historical Center areas. The management offices of almost 100% of the national and transnational companies that operate in Mexico operate in this area. One of the factors that surely influences this phenomenon is that the Stock Exchange is located in Reforma. With these simple data it

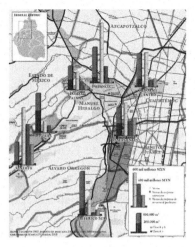

is possible to say that Santa Fe financial district has a relevant importance within Mexico. This is noteworthy for our study, since we are faced with an apparent paradox: how did Santa Fe go from being a garbage dump to one of the most exclusive 'neighborhoods' of the Mexican capital? This is the question we will try to resolve in the following lines.

2. From a Garbage Dump to a Financial District. Causes and Development of a Megaproject.

2.1. Causes. Search for a Global City and the Population Explosion.

Search for a Global City. The Santa Fe Financial Center must be contextualized in its global dimension, since it is only in this way that we can understand the identity and vocation of the project. That is why at the beginning of this section we will try to understand the remote causes, which will allow us to understand the proximate causes.

---

https://www.marketdatamexico.com/es/article/Colonia-Santa-Fe-Alvaro-Obregon-Ciudad-Mexico#:~:text=Seg%C3%BAn%20estimaciones%20de%20MarketData,370%20establecimientos%20que%20all%C3%AD%20operan.

At the end of the 19th century and the beginning of the 20th century, a city that stands out for its striking infrastructure appeared on the world scene: New York and, more specifically, the district of Manhattan. It was in this area that the great skyscrapers began to be built and where the financial, administrative and management center of the country was located. The flourishing of this area began, highlighting the Wall Street building with two towers with 110 floors that represented the center of world trading (World Trade Center). [3] This area of the city represents the American financial enclave that will become the canon for the rest of the world.

After this North American example, characterized by centralizing economic activities, at the end of the Second World War, many European cities in their reconstruction process and in the face of American influence began to consider this reality in their own planning. Some use the historical centers for this purpose. However, other European cities, in order to have greater freedom of action in terms of new construction, set aside areas of the suburbs for this specific purpose. The two outstanding European examples are La Défense, Paris (1960) and City of London (1970). Both were built *ad hoc*, with the purpose of being Financial Districts. In this context, Tokyo in Japan can also be highlighted (Pérez Mejías 2012), or Downtown Core in Singapore, a Third World city with a global projection.

The economy began to be globalized after the war and the undisputed leader of this phenomenon was the United States. So, those who wanted to enter this market had to apply its model and, in some way, follow in its footsteps. Financial centers are a means that is beginning to be applied in the most developed countries. It was only at a later stage that the underdeveloped countries began to adapt to these new realities. In 1991 Saskia Sassen described those cities with the greatest impact on the network of the global economy as **global cities,** [4] the three main ones being London,

---

[3] The WTC would be brought down by terrorists on September 11, 2001 and it is now known as Ground Zero.

[4] Characteristics of a global city are, in addition to its influence on the world economy,

Paris and New York. But other cities such as São Paolo, Buenos Aires or Mexico City can also be called as such, although to a lesser extent.

Mexico City entered this race to influence the global market at the end of the seventies and beginning of the eighties. There is a strong interest of the central government to turn the capital into a global metropolis, this is why it was urgent to provide it with the necessary means to fulfill the schemes of the neoliberal economies. One of the means used to achieve these goals was the elaboration of some megaprojects, among which the City of Santa Fe stood out. These are, as the name implies, large projects that are developed thanks to public and/or private investment that seek progress and the creation of infrastructure in a given area. They are usually characterized by their rapid construction and their strong impact on construction spaces.

The Santa Fe megaproject was planned with the purpose of attracting national and international investment and making this capital city a world financial center. Obviously, it was not an isolated project, but it was designed in conjunction with others such as the restructuring of the Historical Center, the Alameda, Polanco and Xochimilco. Thanks to this renovation of Mexico's infrastructure, the country's economy would open up to the global market and attract new investments (Moreno Carranco 2015: 280), by providing facilities to those who wanted to do so and concentrating the relevant financial factors. Indeed, the constitution of this reality has been one of the reasons why Mexico has been able to position itself in the market and become one of the most influential Latin American countries (Parnreiter 2011). We already have, then, the first cause that gave rise to the constitution of a project such as, Santa Fe, CDMX. It is time to see, now, what is the second cause of this reality.

---

a central location with a good airport system, good telecommunications infrastructure, being cosmopolitan, cultural environment, being the headquarters of international companies, etc. According to specific indicators, they are classified into three species, which are Alpha, Beta and Gamma.

Population growth. The population growth that Mexico City experienced between the 1950s and 1980s led the government to seek ways to remedy the lack of urban land for housing. London and Paris in 1750, New York in 1890 and Latin America in 1950 experienced an exponential development of their cities. The industrial revolution led to a demographic explosion, urban sprawl and ecological degradation (Zermeño 1991). These phenomena narrated by Charles Dickens in his novels, such as A Tale of Two Cities or Oliver Twist, in the mid 1800's, is what is replicated in the Mexican capital from 1950 onwards. A time of great industrial development coupled with a large population, accentuating the differences between the classes.[5]

The urban sprawl in Mexico City expands towards the south and west in the 1970s. The middle and upper middle classes settled in the west and the lower classes in the east. The reason why the western zone was inhabited by the wealthy classes of the city and also why it happened so late is due to the fact that this zone was a place with a very rugged geography. It should be remembered that this area had been a place of mineral exploitation and, therefore, traces of this activity had remained. It was, therefore, a difficult place to build new infrastructure and, therefore, greater care was required in the projection of such areas. This was something that only a few could afford.

We have, then, the two reasons why Mexico City had to reconfigure its urban physiognomy. On the one hand, it had to renew itself to become a center of attraction for new financial investments; to offer, so to speak, a comfortable place for investors. The second reason was the population growth experienced by the capital between the 50s and 80s, which demanded more living space. And

---

[5] To justify that the population increased in Mexico City during these years, it is enough to go to the INEGI statistics that prove it, saying that the population growth between 1950 and 1960 was from 3.1 million to 4.9 million; to 1970 6.9 million; to 1980 8.8 million. From the 1990s onwards, the population remained more or less stable. But those decades were of great growth to which the government had to find a solution.
https://www.inegi.org.mx/contenidos/saladeprensa/boletines/2021/EstSociodemo/ResultCenso2020_CdMx.pdf

although there are diverse causes, they have a common origin, the great development of the Mexican capital city, which made it become a focus of attention both nationally and internationally. At the center of the reflection, we place the Santa Fe megaproject as one of the causes of both problems. Let us now look at the moments that made this reality possible.

2.2. Construction of the Santa Fe Megaproject

Given the need to make Mexico a global economy, with its own headquartered in its capital, and in order to solve the problem of population growth, the Government had to enable new areas: "in mid-1984 the government of Mexico City issues a decree of expropriation of 426 hectares for the urban improvement of Santa Fe" (Barraza, 2018, p.4). For the planning of the expropriated area in 1987 a Controlled Development Spatial Zone (ZEDEC) is established, it meant public intervention in the specified area. This project was developed mainly during the six-year term of President Carlos Salinas de Gortari and, in addition to having the support of the state, it was also backed up by the business sector (Barraza 2018).

Originally, the distribution of the area was conceived as follows: 25% residential use, 12% offices, 3.5% commercial center, 2.6% urban services, 3.3% administration: health, education, and culture, 1.5% urban infrastructure, 1.5% urban sub-center, 0.77% sports and recreation, 23% protected ecological areas, 10.85% green areas and 14.89% circulation roads (Barraza 2018).

The area was still a garbage dump. Nearby, communities of families had been formed to sort and separate garbage, the so-called 'pepenadores'. To begin the project, the area had to be cleared by covering the dumps and displacing the inhabitants of the area. This process lasted until 1994, when the families were relocated to nearby neighborhoods such as Jalapa, Barranca de Río Becerra and Tlayacapa. In addition, the project included the construction of new housing units to accommodate the displaced in the Santa Lucía, Huizachito and San Mateo Tlatenanago neighborhoods (Barraza 2018). Approximately 300 families were relocated during this period (Díaz León 2009).

The Special Controlled Development Zones (ZEDEC) became Partial Urban Development Plans (PPDU) due to the approval of the Urban Development Law of Mexico City in 1996. The difference between the two realities was that the latter regulated the projects more accurately, thus avoiding discretion. In other words, the projects allowed less manipulation. However, the essential elements were maintained, that is to say, the search for the development of certain areas of the metropolis. The most relevant aspect of these plans, which the new law sought to emphasize, was that these projects had a strong dependence on government agencies and could not be modified by the rest of the agents involved in the project. Everything had to be approved by the government, even though many of the actions depended primarily on the private sector.

The development of the project went relatively smoothly until May 2012. Until then it seemed that everything was going smoothly, because the area was beginning to achieve its original objective. In other words, it was indeed becoming a financial focus. But there was something that was not quite working and this was evident because on that date the PPDU of Santa Fe was updated. It's motivating factor was published in the Official Gazette of the Federal District, alluding to the need of the new residents to establish clear rules regarding the creation of new commercial establishments. It seems that the neighbors are noticing that there is a lack of harmony, which in the future may affect their dignified living. This is due to the fact that new constructions no longer follow the original planning. In a way, it can be said that, in the face of the initial momentum of the zone, there is a process of accelerated real estate speculation. There are irregularities in the constructions and the way they are being used with respect to the original planning. This leads to problems at three levels. The first one is that which concerns urbanization, a modern development is seen but with a complicated roadway, first excess, the content exceeds the structural capacity to give flow. The second level is environmental, we see the need to focus on this reality to preserve the ecosystem. Finally, at the socio-economic level, the social fragmentation between what is known as City of Santa Fe and near by neighborhoods such as Jalapa and Carlos A. Madrazo, is observed.[6] The settlers' association recognizes the need to maintain objectivity among the settlers and to safeguard the environment; and thirdly, to take into account that a true development plan must ensure equality and pay attention to the most disadvantaged (Barraza 2018).

The question that arises is why did the original plan go off track? Why wasn't the project followed through? What was the lack of follow-up and oversight? What tends to happen with projects at the time of transitions is that when a new government arrives, the priorities of the previous government are pushed to the back burner. Manuel Camacho Solís was Mexico City's City Manager at the most critical moment of the project's elaboration and during Carlos Salinas de Gortari's presidency. He was one of the major promoters of the mega projects. In Camacho's mouth we find the following statement: "The new and large public and private investment projects will make it possible for Mexico City to once again become a center for tourist investment and for the development of services that will generate profits and make it more competitive".

It was during the Camacho Solís administration that the Santa Fe project took shape and was strengthened. However, in 1993, Camacho Solís resigned as governor of the then Federal District. The reason was that President Carlos Salinas de Gortari would not promote him to be his successor as President of the Mexican Republic. The project, it can be said, was Camacho's jewel. By stepping aside, the project does not fall into oblivion, but the supervision ceases to be attentive. The same people who were in charge of the development of the area affirmed that during his mandate "things were done with ease and the agreements were fulfilled" Years later (in 2005) he himself would recognize, in a colloquium held at the Universidad Iberoamericana, that during his government the process of construction of the area was careful (Barraza 2018: 87-100).

---

[6] An aerial photograph of the area shows this phenomenon. On the one hand, you can see what is commonly known as Santa Fe (the project) and on the other, the popular area, which is evidently poor. These are the three ruptures that the renovation of the Santa Fe PPDU seeks to solve.

I don't think there has ever been a more profitable public project than Santa Fe at its best. It was very impressive. However, we were trying to do things carefully. On no account could we allow a phenomenon of land speculation. The country and its cities are destroyed by land speculation. In order to avoid speculation, we made an agreement: whoever did not build on his plot of land would lose it. This was something never done before in Mexico. Failure to comply with the clauses of the purchase contract would result in the loss of the property and the return of the money invested. This measure obligated the owners of the property to build. In addition, the property tax for vacant lots was subject to a one hundred percent increase (Barraza 2018: 98-99).

It is in this way that we can understand, in some way, the administrative decline of the area. It is there that we find some of the remote causes of the lack of attention in the initial project.

Since the beginning of the construction of the project (approx. 1994), it can be affirmed that Santa Fe has been, effectively, a financial enclave of great importance for Mexico. It is a relevant factor for the application of neoliberal economic policies in the country, making it one of the most important global cities in Latin America and the globalized world. This is how this area went from being a garbage dump to one of the most exclusive neighborhoods in Mexico City. And it is here that we resolve one of the most important questions we were interested in solving. But, at the facto of being 'exclusive', there are still some questions that need to be solved. What were some of the consequences of the construction of this project. This is something that we will try to resolve in the third part of this work.

3. Consequences of the City Santa Fe Project. Exclusion and Exclusivity

The consequence of the creation of this project is exclusivity. At first glance, one might think that this is a good thing, but this may not be the case. First of all, let's take a look at what 'exclusive' means, and then we will study whether this concept is applicable to this neighborhood in Mexico City. After such an exposition, everyone will be able to draw conclusions.

Exclusive is a word derived from the Latin *exclusivus*. It is formed by the prefix ex -, meaning of or from, referring to a movement from the inside to the outside. The second constituent part of the term is *clusus*, which in turn derives from the verb *claudere*, meaning to close or enclose. As a whole, exclusive refers to a reality closed from the inside to any external interference. Antonym of exclusive is inclusive.[7] We wonder if the City of Santa Fe project has caused a process of closing itself, in some way, to external realities. We will study the process of exclusion with respect to external realities, but also how this has occurred within itself.

3.1. Exclusive with the External

From the beginning, the planning of the megaproject contemplated the eviction of families from a certain area, which we have already discussed. The area had to be cleared to begin construction *sicut tabula rasa*. Seen coldly, this is obvious. But a deeper analysis shows that it is not so simple. Starting in 1981 and during the ten years that followed, the topography was intensely modified, making a uniform plateau out of what was previously an uneven terrain. To make this possible, many of those who owned property in the area lost it completely, sometimes with little or no compensation. In fact, they were often offered relocation to new housing in areas further south, but what was offered was not equivalent to the loss. Not only on a material level, but also in terms of meaning and relative tranquility, since it was a more remote area and, therefore, out of the urban chaos (Shoshan 2015).

Nitzan Shoshan, making a deep analysis of the lived experience of the evictees, notes that they suffer a violent dispossession of their properties. He explains that it is not something that is lived with indifference and acceptance, but psychologically there is a process of struggle and rebellion against it. It occurs regardless of whether the act is more or less just. It is a spontaneous way of reacting. In his study he collects several testimonies that, due to the length

---

[7] Online Spanish Etymological Dictionary, *Etimología de exclusivo*, http://etimologias.dechile.net/?exclusivo.

of the work I cannot bring, but I mention it because it can be enriching to go and look for them. By way of synthesis I bring some textual words of the article that can help to see, in some way, how the process took place.

> The case of Santa Fe (...) forced evictions and dispossession form a traumatic past known and often lived as a personal experience. Even so, it is clear that such experience cannot be kept for certain in the past, for rather it persists and continues to raise a series of disturbing questions about a future understood as uncertain, and against which, it is not possible to speculate anything productive and meaningful (Shoshan 2015: 24).

There is a marked difference between the area covered by the project and the surrounding areas where the evicted people were relocated. Places with many needs and necessities of help, as Shoshan mentions. In the process, there are basically two moments; first, a large number of families are moved away; second, they are relocated to places with many needs, which brings, as an obvious consequence, more deprivation and inequality. As if that were not enough, Santa Fe's PPDU is being renewed in 2012 and the implementation of the road infrastructure is being considered. This puts the neighbors on alert, as it implies a new displacement.

The residential instability of the inhabitants of the surrounding areas generates in them a permanent state of alert, anxiety and skepticism towards any intervention of the local authorities. There is a rejection of government support for fear of repeating past histories of dispossession. Many of the government's social works are seen through the eyes of a traumatic past, and resentment against the State remains. So we have areas with many needs, but alienated from any governmental reality, as these are expelled by the local inhabitants, not out of malice but as a reflex act of the instinct of self-preservation.[8]

---

[8] My intention here is not to make a moral judgment, but simply to try to understand more deeply what the inhabitants of the surrounding areas of City Santa Fe, who are the same people who were once displaced, go through. In a few words, how these people

Santa Fe. From a Garbage Dump to a Qualified City Neighborhood

3.2. Exclusive with the Inmate

This process of exclusion does not only occur in this area with the surrounding area, but also within the residents of City Santa Fe. Victor Diaz Leon highlights in his study the lack of public space in this financial center. In the projection of this reality, the North American footprints are followed, giving importance to private transportation over public transportation, devising fast roads as the guiding axes of development. There is a process of 'entrenchment' limiting pedestrian and vehicular access.

> The purpose of this project is to be a financial enclave, so the primary motivator is the production of wealth, not coexistence or fun. Consequence of this are its structures.

> In Santa Fe the architecture and public space are defined by the absence of dialogue, the streets act as dividing spaces between the vehicular road and private property. Most of the buildings are walled around their perimeter and access to them is through controlled and guarded booths: access to private space is granted only if there is a reason to do so.

> Something that is striking in Santa Fe is the desolation of its streets, the lack of pedestrians and of places designed specifically for meetings, such as a backwater, park, square or public building for recreation or meeting (…) There was no will of any authority to turn the open, arid spaces, with almost no social life, into public space, of coexistence and congregation, but this is the result of putting the investor's interest in protecting and preserving the image and spatial form of the immediate surroundings of the buildings before a vision of the city.

---

have a trauma derived from the dispossession, sometimes violent, of their properties by the State and how once in their new establishments they reject a new intervention for fear of living the process again. The megaproject is still under construction and needs to be expanded, especially the access roads to the financial center. How can the access road infrastructure be expanded? The immediate answer is by taking land from somewhere, from whom? This is the dilemma and the reason for the fears of these people.

The activities seem to favor seclusion. (...) Santa Fe was designed to be traveled by car, the distances between the different spaces and buildings are impossible to traverse on foot, there are no roads that connect transversally or diagonally the project, so to move from one point to another you have to resort to the car or take long walks along elongated sidewalks. The exclusion of the corners gives the buildings an elongated profile, which makes it impossible for the street to dialogue with the construction and the exchange between neighbors. There is no way to enter Santa Fe without it being confusing to locate open places, due to the predominance of the great heights in almost all the development. (Diaz Leon 2009: 41-43).

It is true that on November 24, 2017 the La Mexicana park was inaugurated, in view of solving the absence of public places and conviviality; but that does not detract from the fact that the tendency of this project and this vision tends to give priority to the individual and isolate him from the community, in short, to isolate it from its own nature and its intrinsically political dimension.[9] Until then, one of the few realities that encouraged the meeting was the Santa Fe Center, a shopping mall with exclusive boutiques, movie theaters, corporate offices, stores and an event center. But as can be sensed, it is yet another demonstration of exclusion and exclusivity, as the doors are closed or opened according to individual possibilities (Díaz León 2009).
Surely there are many positive consequences. This is not presented with the purpose of being negative, but simply to evidence a reality that is rarely told. Santa Fe has been one of the megaprojects that have achieved the objectives envisioned at the

---

[9] This may be one of the great shortcomings of modern and contemporary economic models. Their limitation of seeing the individual as a member of a community. Many of the problems of modern societies derive from an incomplete vision of the human being. Perhaps it would be good to reread what the Greek and even medieval classics understood by society. And how cities were built on the basis of these conceptions. To give an example, one can look at the plans of Athens and read Plato's Republic or Aristotle's Politics, in whose thoughts the primacy of the common good of society and not of the individual was a primary concern. And this **good** was not understood as a materially quantifiable reality, but as a perfective one.

beginning of planning. They have positioned Mexico in an important place in the globalized world. But they have forgotten, perhaps, more existential realities of concrete individuals. Reality is complex, obviously, and the world cannot be divided into good and bad, but it is necessary to accept that not everything about globalization has brought positive consequences for the less developed countries.

4. Back to the Bases

At the beginning of this work, a historical review of the development of the area was made. By this time it may have been forgotten. But it was remembered how the area began to be populated thanks to a project of the lawyer Vasco de Quiroga to found a hospital to welcome the natives and help them in their needs. The affection of the people towards this personage was kept in history due to the nickname 'Tata Vasco'. Another fact that confirms the positivity of the Spaniard's project is that the people began to settle around the hospital, founding the town. It is said *bonum diffusivum sui*, the good radiates by itself and that does not need demonstration, because it is evident.

The solution to today's problems may not be obvious. But it may be light to return to those beginnings. Men who knew how to look each other in the eye, help each other, put aside their own interests and went out to meet those most in need without regard to race or social position. By way of conclusion it may help to reread the speech that Pope Francis delivered to the bishops on February 13, 2016 during his pastoral visit to Mexico. If the Catholic Church can contribute something in the construction of a civilization, the Pope's words can help to take steps in the right direction.

"On the other hand, do not be tired of reminding your people how powerful are the ancient roots that have made possible the living Christian synthesis of human, cultural and spiritual communion forged here. Remember that the wings of your People have already spread several times over many obstacles. Keep the memory of the long road travelled so far – be deuteronomic – and know how to raise the hope of new goals, because tomorrow it will be a land

'rich in fruit' even if it poses challenges that are not indifferent to us" (Num 13:27-28).
May your gaze, resting always and only on Christ, be capable of contributing to the unity of your People; of favoring the reconciliation of its differences and the integration of its diversities; of promoting the solution of its endogenous problems; of recalling the high measure, which Mexico can reach if it learns to belong to itself rather than to others; of helping to find shared and sustainable solutions to its miseries; of motivating the entire Nation not to be content with less than what is expected of the Mexican way of inhabiting the world." (Francis, 2016)
We can think of those displaced from their homes, who live with anxiety about the future. They do not need, primarily, a material help but a look that gives them peace and comfort. But we can also think of those who currently live in Santa Fe, who do not need material help either, but someone who will raise their eyes, make them come out of their self-absorption and discover that there is more than just purchasing power. The solutions are not simple. Many questions remain open. But it is undoubtedly important to give a deeper meaning to personal and community existence. Here the Church can contribute much.

Conclusion

Santa Fe goes from being a garbage dump to a financial district driven by two causes, the need to provide space for a city in continuous growth and the need to turn Mexico into a global state. This is the main conclusion of the work. However, in this process the objectives are achieved, but with exclusive and excluding consequences, which are not necessarily good. The costs and benefits of the project must be weighed in order to be able to say whether it has indeed been positive. Not only in terms of turning Mexico into a country with global influence, but also if it has helped concrete citizens. Some reflections were reached in the work, but they are still incipient. Therefore, the reflection must continue to develop.
The work has undoubtedly been fruitful. We have come to know, always partially, the situation of the place and its truthfulness.

Many questions remain unanswered. One that I think is of a vital importance is what has the Church contributed to avoid the exclusionary consequences of the project? And I say this because the first construction that was made in the megaproject was the Ibero-American University of the Society of Jesus, in 1985. Therefore, the Church has been the primary protagonist of the process. But as it has been mentioned, these are questions for future research.

References

Arriaga A., "Vasco de Quiroga, founder of towns", *Novohispanic History Studies* 1, 1, 1966). https://doi.org/10.22201/iih.24486922e.1966.001.3196

Barraza C., "Santa Fe City. Zoning, urban legal and social controversies", *Universidad Autónoma Metropolitana-Cuajimalpa, México*, 2018.

Covarrubias Reyna M., "Santa Fe. Utopian town absorbed by Mexico City", *Mexican Archeology* 134, 2015: 74-79. https://arqueologiamexicana.mx/mexico-antiguo/santa-fe-utopico-pueblo-absorbido-por-la-ciudad-de-mexico.

Díaz León V., "Architecture and public space. Representation, uses and meanings in a space of globalization: The case of Santa Fe", *Universidad Autónoma Metropolitana- Azcapotzalco, México*, 2009.

Online Spanish Etymological Dictionary, *Etimología de exclusivo*, http://etimologias.dechile.net/?exclusivo.

Gago García C. – Córdoba Ordóñez J. – Díez Pisonero R., "The lists of global cities. From research practice to their use as an argument in neoliberal urban planning", *International Journal of Sociology* 75, 1, 2017. https://doi.org/10.3989/ris.2017.75.1.15.11

MarketDataMéxico, Colonia Santa Fe, Álvaro Obregón, in Mexico City: https://www.marketdatamexico.com/es/article/Colonia-Santa-Fe-Alvaro-Obregon-Ciudad-Mexico#:~:text=Seg%C3%BAn%20estimaciones%20de%20MarketData,370%20establecimientos%20que%20all%C3%AD%20operan.

Moreno Carranco M., "The spatial production of the global: the public and the private in Santa Fe, Mexico City", *Alteridades* 18, 36, 2008: 75-86. Retrieved March 19, 2022, from http://www.scielo.org.mx/scielo.p

——, "Geographies under construction: the Santa Fe megaproject in Mexico City", *Universidad Metropolitana de Cuajimalma*, 2016.

Parnreiter C., Global city formation, real estate economy and transnationalization of urban spaces: The case of Mexico City.. *EURE (Santiago)* 37, 111, 2011: 5-24. https://dx.doi.org/10.4067/S0250-71612011000200001

Pérez Mejías C., "Characteristics of financial districts in urban space", *GeoGraphos. Digital Journal for Geography and Social Sciences Students* 3, 22, 2012. ISSN 2173-1276 [Date: 9-1-2012] http://web.ua.es/revista-geographos-giecryal

Shoshan N., "The temporalities of the crisis in Santa Fe, Mexico City", *Sociológica* 30, 84, 2015: 9-38. https://dialnet.unirioja.es/servlet/articulo?codigo=5334235

Zermeño S., "Disidentity and disorder: Mexico in the global economy and free trade", *Mexican Journal of Sociology* 53, 3, 1991: 15-64, https://doi.org/10.2307/3540623.

AFTERWORD

Mexico City to which this 2022 Sinderesi book edited by Msgr. Samuele Sangalli is dedicated, recalls the commitment of the Konrad-Adenauer-Stiftung at a global level. The book deals with many aspects: historical, social, political, economic, showing the complexity of Latin America through the example of the megalopolis of Mexico City. With this publication Sinderesi is making an important contribution to the debate about globalization and world equality.

The Konrad-Adenauer-Stiftung began its international engagement in 1962 in Venezuela and Chile. In the past sixty years the foundation has promoted Christian democratic politicians and strengthened the rule of law, social market economy and freedom of the media in Latin America, as well as organizing bilateral dialogue on current political developments.

In Rome, the Konrad-Adenauer-Stiftung has been working for more than ten years with Sinderesi. This international study project offers the opportunity of intellectual growth and the possibility of a critical exchanges of ideas with students and young professionals based on the principle of the Social Doctrine of the Church. That's why we have been operating in these areas since many years and it is the most important reason why I'm so proud to promote and to encourage the publication of this book, rich in contributions.

Msgr. Samuele Sangalli has guided the Sinderesi students with great knowledge and deep passion. We are grateful to him and to Dr. Antonella Piccinin for their strong cooperation. Thanks to the Gregorian University, the Alberto-Hurtado Center and its academic experts that are involved in the Sinderesi project.

Dr. Nino Galetti
*Director of the Konrad-Adenauer-Stiftung
in Italy and the Holy See*

Finito di stampare nel mese di novembre 2022 presso Printbee.it - Noventa Padovana PD